A Garland Series

THE ENGLISH BOOK TRADE
1660-1853

156 Titles relating to the early history of

English Publishing, Bookselling,

the Struggle for Copyright

and the Freedom of the Press

Reprinted in photo-facsimile in 42 volumes

edited, with bibliographical notes,
by
Stephen Parks
Curator, Osborn Collection
Beinecke Library, Yale University

Reminiscences of Literary London
from 1779 to 1853

Thomas Rees

—

The Rise and Progress
of the Gentleman's Magazine

John Nichols

Garland Publishing, Inc., New York & London

1974

Copyright © 1974

by Garland Publishing, Inc.

All Rights Reserved

Library of Congress Cataloging in Publication Data

Rees, Thomas, 1777-1864.
    Reminiscences of literary London from 1779 to 1853.

    (The English book trade, 1660-1853)
    Reprint of the 1896 ed. of T. Rees's Reminiscences
published by Harper, New York; and of the 1821 ed. of
J. Nichols' The rise and progress of the Gentleman's
magazine published by the author, London.
    1. Book industries and trade--London. 2. London
--Intellectual life. 3. The Gentleman's magazine
(London) I. Nichols, John, 1745-1826. The rise and
progress of the Gentleman's magazine. 1974. II. Title.
III. Series.
Z330.6.L6R43 1974   070.5'09421   74-11426
    ISBN 0-8240-0987-8

Printed in the United States of America

Contents

Preface

The 1853 edition of Thomas Rees's *Reminiscences*, described as "privately printed" in the preface to the later edition reprinted here, is an extremely rare book; I have not found a single copy. John Britton, however, and his friends and printers John Bowyer Nichols and John Gongh Nichols, were fond of issuing private pamphlets, in editions as small as a dozen copies; the 1853 *Reminiscences* may have been one of these.

The first publication of the Rees-Britton *Reminiscences* was, I suspect, in 1850, in the first volume of John Britton's long and rambling *Autobiography*. There, arranged rather differently, with long footnotes initialled T.R. and J.B., you will find the substance of these *Reminiscences* (pp. 198-256). There also, in a passage not present in the 1896 reprint, you may read Britton's tribute to his friend Thomas Rees, younger brother of Owen Rees, a partner in the publishing firm of Longmans (pp. 216-217). Thomas Rees, according to Britton, was connected with the firm from 1806 until about 1837; for some years he served as sub-editor of *The Athenaeum*. These anecdotes provide valuable sketches of personalities in the book trade, by two men who were long connected with the trade themselves.

Item B, *The Rise and Progress of the Gentleman's Magazine*, was written towards the end of his life by John Nichols, who had been concerned in its publication for many years. Nichols, apprentice then partner at William Bowyer the younger, joined David Henry in the management of the *Gentleman's Magazine* in 1778. He was solely responsible for the *Magazine* from 1792 until 1826. Nichol's son, John Bowyer Nichols, and his grandson, John Gongh Nichols, succeeded him in publishing the *Gentleman's Magazine* until 1856.

    A.   Brit. Mus. 012356.ee.27
    B.   Brit. Mus. 1421.h.1

April, 1974   *S.R.P.*

Reminiscences of Literary London.

Reminiscences

OF

Literary London

From 1779 to 1853.

With Interesting Anecdotes of Publishers,
Authors and Book Auctioneers
of that Period, &c., &c.

BY

Dr. THOMAS REES,

WITH EXTENSIVE ADDITIONS BY

JOHN BRITTON, F. S. A.

Edited by a Book Lover.

LONDON:
SUCKLING & GALLOWAY,
1896.

*T*HESE interesting "Literary Reminiscences," written about 1853, and privately issued, are known to but few persons, as but a limited number of copies were printed for presentation. The volume includes extensive recollections of Authors, Publishers, and Booksellers from 1779 to 1853. The authors were personally acquainted with all the prominent writers, artists, and makers of books, and many curious anecdotes, prices received by authors for their well-known works, editions sold, and personal peculiarities of literary and business men here given will be new to the reader. The work is now for the first time edited, with the hope that it may prove as enjoyable reading to the purchaser as it has been to the

New York, 1896.   *BOOK LOVER.*

PREFACE

By John Britton.

$\mathfrak{S}$T. PAUL'S Churchyard, Ave-Maria Lane and
Amen Corner were familiar names to the eye
and mind in my boy-days; but I had no more notion of the features and character of the places than
of the interior of a man-of-war, or of Robinson
Crusoe's island. After reading numerous magazines, and taking in several of the sixpenny numbers published by Harrison, Cooke, Parsons, etc.,
and thereby ascertaining something about authors, artists, printers, and booksellers, I became
curious and anxious to see such gifted personages, their homes, or haunts; and also where
the manufacturers of literature resided, what were
their peculiarities, and who and what sort of beings they were. I also coveted to see and read
more books than I could afford to purchase.
During the apprenticeship, I do not remember
to have had an opportunity of satisfying this curiosity, except early in a morning, before shops
were opened, or on Sundays, when they were all
closed, and "The Row," with its appendages, as

9

dull and silent as many village churchyards; but after being relieved from my apprentice-bondage, I found my way to the famed book-mart; traversed the narrow, dark street, miscalled Row; stopped to gaze at every shop window, and even stealthily looked in at every opened doorway, to see if a Harrison, a Cooke, a Hogg, or even one of their Grub-street workmen, or a rich author, could be descried. The names of Peter Pindar, Thomas Holcroft, Dr. Buchan, Wm. Godwin, Dr. A. Rees, Mr. Howard, Mr. Hall, Thos. Paine, the Misses Porter, Hannah More, Mrs. Radcliffe, and many others were familiar to me, and I longed to see such super-human beings, as I then regarded them. At length I ventured to enter some of the houses, and thus obtain a sight of labelled numbers, and volumes of new publications, and also the persons and faces of some of their proprietors. At that time most of the tradesmen attended in their respective shops, and dwelt in the upper parts of their houses; now, the heads of many of the large establishments visit their counting-houses only for a few hours in the day, and leave the working part to junior partners, clerks, and apprentices. Vast and numerous changes have taken place in the publishing and bookselling business since I first haunted Paternoster Row, and book-stalls; and many and important improvements have been introduced into all the essentials of book-making. Paper, type, ink, compositorship, and press-work, have advanced from almost the lowest to nearly the highest degree of perfection. The number and qualifications of authors have progressed in nearly an equal ratio. This assertion, I believe, will be fully verified, by referring to, and comparing, the books and periodicals which were published at the end of the last century with those of the year 1852. It would not be a difficult task to exemplify this by explaining the varieties and dissimilarities between the material and mental characteristics of literature of the two epochs; but I must limit myself to a brief account of Paternoster Row.

This far-famed thoroughfare is commonly said to derive its name from the stationers, or text-writers, who formerly dwelt there, and dealt mostly in religious books, horn-books, and others, which were marketable before .the Reformation. It more probably had its appellation from the rosary, or pater-noster makers, a more thriving trade than bookselling, before Henry the Eighth, of revolutionary memory, commanded the books of Luther to be burnt in the Churchyard.

Strype, in his edition of Stow's "Survey of London," 1720, says, "This street, before the fire of London (1666), was taken up by eminent mercers, silkmen, and lacemen; and their shops were so resorted to by the nobility and gentry, in their coaches, that oft-times the street was so stopped up that there was no room for foot passengers." Soon after that conflagration most of these moved to the vicinity of Covent Garden. Some of the mercers and silkmen renewed their residences in this spot in new houses; but near the east end there were "stationers and large warehouses for booksellers; well situated for learned and studious men's access thither, being more retired and private." St. Paul's Churchyard appears to have been the chief mart of the bookselling trade at the time of the great fire. Dugdale told Pepys that more than £150,000 worth of books were destroyed on that fatal occasion. Previous to this epoch, Little Britain, and Duke Street adjoining, seem to have been the most noted site for booksellers.

However sanguine my young imagination may have been, I did not dare to anticipate the possibility of ever writing or publishing a book; still less of being on friendly terms with the many partners of the largest publishing establishment in the world. Yet such has been my lot; and having in-

dulged the habit of continually visiting Paternoster Row, on the last day of every month for more
than forty years, it has become identified with
many and various associations and connexions
of deep and exciting interest; and I have often
meditated on writing an account of this literary
emporium. But I have thought it advisable to
solicit my old and esteemed friend, Dr. Thomas
Rees, to indulge me with his opinions and recollections on this subject. With his usual kindness
and courtesy he promptly favoured me with the
following letter, to which I have subjoined a few
memoranda of my own.

My Dear Britton,

You ask me to furnish some reminiscences of
Paternoster Row, in the earlier period of my acquaintance with it, towards the conclusion of the
last, and the commencement of the present, century. Our long and intimate connection, our
kindred pursuits, and our joint labours on some
occasions, in the same field of literary research,
render it difficult for me to meet your wishes with
a denial; at the same time I feel very sensibly that
in recurring to a period so long past, between
which and the present, half a century has inter-
vened, important matters relating both to events
and persons may have escaped my recollec-

tion, or may be recalled too indistinctly and im-
perfectly to be of real value for a practical object.
I will, however, endeavour to revive the image of
this locality, as it appeared to my view at the
period alluded to; and to awaken the memory of
such facts and incidents relating to the character
and enterprises of its inhabitants, as may be likely
to afford some interest or amusement to your
readers.

DR. THOMAS REES.

Contents.

PART I.

PART II.

PART III.

Part I.

—

PATERNOSTER ROW

AND ITS VICINITY.

Part I.

PATERNOSTER ROW

AND ITS VICINITY.

NEAR the close of the eighteenth century,
"The Row," as it is now popularly called,
contained two or more printing establishments,
one of which was conducted by the late "George
Woodfall," who had succeeded his father, Henry
Sampson Woodfall, well known as the printer and
publisher of the "Public Advertiser," in which ap-

peared the far-famed "Letters of Junius." The latter was still living, and I had the pleasure of seeing him in the enjoyment of a "green old age,"
when I first visited London. Those daring epis-
tles, with the newspaper in which they were published, excited intense curiosity during the course
of their publication. There were also two houses
of wholesale stationers; one belonging to the family of Key, and the other to Peter Wynn. The
University of Oxford had, under the management
of Mr. Gardner, a depot to supply the London
trade with their editions of Bibles and Prayer-
books. But with these, and a few other excep-
tions, the majority of the houses were tenanted by
persons who were strictly, in the ordinary sense,
Booksellers. The varieties of these may be classed
under three divisions. The first comprehends
publishers only, whose sale of books was confined
to their own property. The second might be designated book-merchants, who were chiefly wholesale dealers, and carried on an extensive and important trade with country booksellers; they were
also publishers upon a large scale, both of periodicals, under the designation of magazines, and
reviews; and likewise works on general literature
and science, of the larger and more important and
costly descriptions. The third were chiefly retail

traders, mostly in old books, but in some instances were publishers of pamphlets, and books of comparatively small expense.

In the first class, at the time under consideration, three persons were conspicuous, viz.: Harrison, Cooke, and Hogg. The first, on many accounts, is entitled to pre-eminence, as he took the lead in a class of publications which deserve great praise for valuable improvements in their editorial qualities, and particularly in pictorial illustrations.

It is not easy to pronounce decidedly the exact time when books of magnitude were first divided into small portions and issued periodically in numbers; but Harrison may be said to be one of the first persons who embarked, with much spirit and upon an extensive scale, in such a mode of publication. His first speculation of the sort was "The Novelist's Magazine," which embraced several of the larger standard and popular English novels then known. They were printed in octavo, in double columns, stitched up in small numbers, and published weekly, at sixpence each. The most striking feature of this publication, and one of its chief attractions, consisted of engraved embellishments. Harrison had the judgment to select artists of acknowledged merit, who afterwards rose to distinguished eminence; including Stot-

hard, R. Corbould, Smirke, and Burney; whilst
the engravings bear the names of Heath, Sharpe,
Grignion, Smith, Milton, Neagle, etc. The "Novelist's Magazine," commenced by him in 1779, extended to twenty-three good-sized volumes. Its
popularity may be estimated by the fact that, at
one time 12,000 copies of each number were sold,
weekly. The success of this work encouraged
Harrison to publish, on the same plan, with embellishments by the same eminent artists, "The
New Novelist's Magazine," a series of short tales;
which was followed by "The British Classics,"
embracing the Spectator, Tatler, Guardian, Con-
noisseur, etc., of which a very large edition was
sold. These publications still maintain their
credit; and clean copies, with good impressions
of the plates, are puchased at fair prices. He also
produced a corresponding work, entitled "The
Sacred Classics."

The same publisher embarked in another literary speculation, somewhat singular in its plan;
a "General Geography," upon a large scale, extending to forty numbers, in quarto, closely printed. He engaged to supply its purchasers, without
additional charge, with a pair of twelve-inch
globes. Harrison published "The British Magazine," in 3 vols., with beautiful engravings of por-

traits, views, and prints of historical and fancy subjects. These included also a large portion of Biographical, Historical, and Critical Essays, with Poetry. His next publication was "The Musical Magazine," which, in an octavo size, gave a selection of the works of the most eminent and popular composers, arranged for the piano-forte. The purchaser of the entire work was entitled to receive a square piano-forte. Dr. Busby, at that time a popular musical professor, was employed as editor, and the instruments were examined and attested by him. This gentleman was much employed by Sir Richard Phillips, in writing for the "Monthly Magazine," etc., and later in life made himself very conspicuous, and amenable to severe public criticism, by translating "Lucretius," and "giving living recitations of the translation, with tea and bread and butter," at his house in Queen Anne Street, to select parties of friends, who were invited to endure the one and relish the other. I was among the number, and must own that the display of poetry, oratory, and coxcombry was lamentably ludicrous. Never did I behold a young man more vain, impudent, and heartless, than the juvenile Busby, and rarely, perhaps, has the diploma of "Mus. Doc." appeared more ridiculous and degraded than by the conduct and appearances of the musical professor with his finical son. These gentlemen made a finishing exhibition of themselves on the re-opening of the famed Drury Lane Theatre, after its memorable rebuilding. It is very generally known that an Address was sought for amongst the authors of the age, and that in the mass presented was one from Lord Byron, accepted, and another from Dr. Busby rejected. The mortified and vain Doctor fancied that he could bring the committee to shame, if not repentance, by publishing his own poetry and prose, in a truly novel manner. Accordingly, he and his accomplished son were seen in the stage box of the theatre soon after its opening. At the end of the play the young gentleman leaped upon the stage, with his father's rejected address in one hand, and an opera hat in the other, and repeated the following lines:

" When energizing objects men pursue,
What are the miracles they cannot do?"

Here, however, the juvenile spouter was stopped by Mr. Raymond, the stage manager, and a constable, who handed the young gentleman off the stage. The "Rejected Addresses," by James and Horace Smith, contain a good burlesque imitation of the Busby address.

Amongst the periodicals of Harrison was "The Wit's Magazine," edited by Thos. Holcroft, and containing a variety of amusing articles both in prose and verse, written by the editor, by Mr. Harrison, and by other authors of talent. It was embellished with large prints, folded. His "Biographical Magazine,'" an 8vo. volume, contains small engraved portraits, with short notices of each subject, well executed.

Harrison issued two periodicals of smaller size, the "Pocket Magazine" and the "Lady's Pocket Magazine," which were published monthly, and embellished with portraits and a séries of small engraved views of places, from drawings by the late J. M. W. Turner, R.A., who eventually became the most eminent landscape painter in the world. These works contained writings of several young authors, some of whom afterwards attained eminence; amongst them were my esteemed friends, the Misses Porter, and their brother, the poet, artist, and traveler. A frequent writer in these magazines was R. A. Davenport, who sometimes officiated as editor. Both Charles and Thomas Dibdin contributed many well-written and amusing papers; as did also Peter Courtier.

Contemporary with, and a near neighbour to

Harrison, was John Cooke, who for many years carried on a large and successful business as publisher of periodical works. He was probably one of the earliest of the Paternoster Row booksellers who applied himself to this branch of trade, upon a large scale. The subjects and form of his books and their illustrations were, however, very different from those of Harrison. Cooke confined himself, for some time, to religious publications, the principal and most popular of which was Southwell's "Commentary of the Bible;" it had a large sale, and produced a profit of many thousand pounds. After the appearance, in numbers, of Chambers' "Cyclopædia," under the editorial care of Dr. Abraham Rees, Cooke published an imitation, with the name of Hall, as editor, of some merit, but inferior to its predecessor. All Cooke's publications were in folio, divided into small portions, and issued weekly, at sixpence each number; they were "adorned with cuts," which were of the old school, both as to drawings and engravings.

At an advanced age Mr. Cooke retired to the country, with a handsome fortune, and died, in 1810, at the age of 79. His son, Charles, continued for some time his father's principal publications; but he soon commenced a new course, which was attended with great success. The copyright of Hume's "History of England," belonging to Cadell and Longman, having expired, Cooke availed himself of the circumstance to publish an edition, with Smollett's Continuation, in weekly numbers, at sixpence each. It was neatly printed, and embellished with portraits and vignettes tolerably executed. Contemporaneously with this, he also published a series of the older popular English Novels, with attractive embellishments. The original drawings and paintings, from which the prints were taken, were exhibited in a picture gallery, at the rear of his shop. At a later time Cooke published an edition of Bell's "British Theatre," under the editorship of Richard Cumberland. Besides inheriting a handsome fortune from his father, he acquired a considerable increase by his own speculations. He built a new house in Epping Forest, where he lived a short time, and died, in the prime of life, after a painful operation performed by Sir Astley Cooper. Although my (Britton) finances would not allow me to purchase the whole of Harrison's and Cooke's publications, I bought some of them, at what is technically called "trade price," and must own tha* they not only afforded me much amusement and instruction, on repeated perusal and examination, but, I believe, created that love of literature and art which progressively rose to a confirmed passion. The periodicals, by the publishers above noticed, were sought for and hailed with intense curiosity as they made their appearance; and I may safely aver that the embellished works, which I have since produced, sprang from the seeds which the Cookes and Harrisons sowed, at the end of the last century. The very beautiful and effective drawings and engravings by Stothard and Heath were eminently calculated to fascinate the young eye, as they gratified also that of the learned professor of art. Harrison's "British Magazine," of which three volumes were published in 1782, 3 and 4, contained several very highly-finished plates by Heath, from Stothard's designs. A short time before his decease I spent a day with Charles Cooke, at his rural villa, which had attained the cognomen of Cooke's Folly. Though expensively fitted up and furnished, it was wholly devoid of the elegancies of high life, and exhibited more ostentatious finery and show than classical or simple beauty. Its walls were, however, amply covered with paintings, drawings, and prints.

Alexander Hogg, who lived next door to Cooke, formed his literary schemes on the model of his neighbour. His publications were chiefly religious, and issued in weekly sixpenny numbers. The principal were, a "Bible with Annotations," by the Rev. Timothy Priestly, the brother of the eminent philosopher of that name. Like Cooke, Hogg brought out an "Encyclopædia," with the name of Howard, as editor. All his publications were in folio; with a profusion of most wretched prints. Miserable as these works were, both as to literary and artistic execution, their proprietor contrived to derive from them a handsome fortune. Amongst the books published by Hogg, was a large folio volume, called "Antiquities of England and Wales," with the name of Henry Boswell, as author, or editor. It has a great number of prints wofully executed, both as to drawing and engraving, and copied from any and every source that was accessible. For pirating one or more from Grose's "Antiquities," the publisher was sued, and sentenced to pay damages, with costs. The letter-press was quite in harmony with the prints, and equally valueless, being taken from any book or books that could be obtained, without acknowledgment. The editor is said to have been a servant of Hogg's, who was paid by the week for his services, in cutting up books for the printer, and reading the proofs.

That there was not much congeniality of sentiment, or friendly feeling between Harrison and
Hogg, may be inferred by an epigram which the
former wrote for and inserted in the "Lady's
Pocket Magazine," July, 1795.

ON A STUPID BOOKSELLER.

By Peter Pindar Esq. (James Harrison.)

> Thou Beast! amid the sons of Wisdom plac'd,
> Who, times of old, as well as modern, grac'd,
> Couldst thou not catch a portion of their fire?
> Rolls not thine eye upon their works each day,
> And canst thou, from them, nothing bear away,
> To lift thy HOG-like soul above the mire?

At the period under consideration, Hogg's publishing business was conducted by a young man,
familiarly known in the trade by the name of
"Thomas," who was much liked by the booksellers' collectors. He served his master many
years, and was with him when the latter died. He
declined to serve in the same capacity under the
son, who had previously been a stranger to the
business; and therefore, after some demur, was admitted by the latter into partnership. The union
did not last long. Hogg retired, and the business
devolved on "Thomas," who introduced important

changes into it, by which he raised the character of the house and improved his own fortune. He rose gradually in the esteem of his neighbours, and the shopman of Mr. Hogg is now deservedly respected as Mr. Alderman Thomas Kelly.

My next class comprises the greater wholesale booksellers and publishers, inhabitants of the Row. The first of these, at the sign of the "Bible and Crown," were the Rivingtons. Almost all the booksellers' houses of London, as well as those of other trades, were formerly contra-distinguished from each other by Signs, either over the doors, or projecting into the streets. The latter becoming a nuisance were prohibited by Act of Parliament; but the former are still continued, in many places. The following are some of those Signs: Bible and Ball; Anchor; Black Swan; Black Boy; Golden Anchor; Cicero's Head; Shakspere's Head; Red Lion; Ship and Black Swan; Raven; Sun; Bible and Crown; the Dunciad; and the Star.

The Rivingtons constitute an old and highly-respectable firm, with premises extending from the front to St. Paul's Churchyard. The earliest of this family whom I have been able to trace was Charles, whose name appears in the beginning of the eighteenth century. It is certain he

carried on business here as early as 1710. In
1730 his name is joined with that of Thomas
Longman and some others, as publishers of Thu-
anus's great historical work. He died in 1742,
and was succeeded by his son, John. This family
has always been distinguished for its zealous attachment to the Church of England, and has consequently enjoyed an intimate connexion with the
established clergy. It is related of John Rivington, that he was a very assiduous attendant on the
services in St. Paul's Church, and was seldom
absent from the early morning prayers, at six or
seven o'clock. If surprised by the bell before he
had quitted his bed, he has been known to put on
his clothes hastily, and finish dressing in the
church, during the service. He died in 1792, at
the age of 73, and was succeeded by his two sons,
Francis and Charles, who constituted the firm
when I first became acquainted with the Metropolis. The first died in 1822, and the second some
time in 1831. The Rivingtons engaged largely in
the publishing trade, but chiefly in books relating
to the Established Church. In 1791, during the
political and religious excitement produced by
the French Revolution, they commenced the
"British Critic," a monthly review of literature,
professedly intended to uphold the tenets of the

Established Church, and the Tory politics of the
ruling government. The principal and most influential periodical of this class was the "Monthly
Review," which was ably conducted by Dr. Griffiths, who had the assistance of several eminent
writers. The first number was published in May,
1749, when he carried on the trade of a bookseller at the "Dunciad," in Ludgate Street. In
1754 he removed to a new shop in Paternoster
Row, afterwards occupied by H. D. Symonds, and
in 1759 to the Strand, where he continued his original sign of the Dunciad. On relinquishing business in 1764, he committed the publication of the
Review to Mr. Becket. Dr. Griffiths died at Turn-
ham Green, in 1803. After his death the Review
was conducted by his son, Colonel Griffiths. At
his decease the copyright was sold, but the publication was not long continued. At the time of
which I am writing, there were two other reviews, published monthly—the "Critical" and
"Analytical"—both of which, as well as the
"Monthly," were the property of the liberal dissenters. Under these circumstances it was thought
desirable to bring out another Review, which
should counteract and neutralize their principles
as much as possible; and, at the same time, de-
velop and sustain the religious and political opin-

ions of the party who were attached to the Established Church. Hence originated the "British Critic," as an antagonistic publication. It was projected and conducted by two learned and able clergymen, the Rev. Richard Nares, and the Rev. Wm. Beloe, the translator of Herodotus, who were aided and supported in the undertaking by Dr. Parr and other eminent writers. It may well be supposed the articles contributed by such men were distinguished by erudition and general literary merits; and yet the Review was never, I believe, a popular or profitable work. Of late years it has been changed from a monthly to a quarterly publication. In association with Mr. Nares, was my old and much-respected friend, the Rev. John Whitaker, author of a Life of Mary, Queen of Scots, and of many other learned and "party-coloured" works. He was very severe in his criticisms on those authors whose religious and political opinions differed from his own prejudices.

Another periodical, published by the Rivingtons, was the Annual Register, originally brought out by Dodsley, with the literary aid of Edmund Burke. The Rivingtons purchased the copyright, and continued the work on its original Tory principles. It was for some years edited by Mr. R. A. Davenport. The principal books of the orna-

mental class published by the Rivingtons were
those written by the late Mr. Donovan, on several
subjects of natural history. He was an excellent
naturalist, and an accurate and skillful draughts-
man.

On the south side of the Row, near the premises described, was located Robert Baldwin, at the
time of which I am writing. He was greatly esteemed as an upright and honourable tradesman.
For many years he published the "London Magazine," which commenced almost as early as the
"Gentleman's," the first number bearing the date
of 1732. This was for many years a very popular periodical. Mr. Baldwin died in 1810. His
nephew and successor commenced a new magazine in 1820, with the same title, under the avowed
editorship of John Scott, a young author of excellent character and considerable literary talents.
The work was proceeding very satisfactorily, and
rising into popularity, when the editor was un-
happily involved in a quarrel, which ended in a
duel. The meeting was conducted by young men
wholly unaccustomed to such affairs of "honour,"
and the fatal result of the rashness and inexperi-
ence of his second was the cause of the death of
Mr. Scott. In traversing Lincolnshire for the
Beauties of England, in the year 1810, I met Mr.

Scott, at Stamford, where he was engaged by Mr. Drakard, to edit a new weekly newspaper, which the latter had started. The high tone of politics and powerful writing of Mr. Scott soon attracted popularity, and the writer was invited to contribute articles to some of the London periodicals. These also excited both the admiration and envy of many readers and authors. A controversy arose in the London Magazine and in Blackwood's Edinburgh, which became sarcastic, vindictive, and personal, and ended as above stated, in a manner which created a mingled sensation of sorrow and horror in many minds. The magazines and newspapers of the time were much occupied, afterwards, with a succession of papers on the ceremonies, folly, and unhallowed practices of duelling. At the time of penning this note (June, 1852) "an affair of honour," as a duel is misnamed, has occurred between two "honourable gentlemen" of the House of Commons, which has fortunately turned the event into ridicule, and will be likely to produce good moral effects.

Charles Baldwin, brother of Robert, had an extensive printing business in Bridge Street, Blackfriars, and realized much profit by printing the "St. James's Chronicle," a newspaper which at one time attained great popularity. It is still conduct-

ed by his son, Charles, who is also its printer, and
it is said he is joint proprietor of the "Morning
Herald," and the "Standard." He is a gentleman
of the highest respectability, and of extensive
knowledge.

The Robinsons, at the end of the eighteenth
and beginning of the nineteenth centuries, when
I first became acquainted with the firm, carried on
the largest business of any house in London, as
general publishers, and also as wholesale and retail booksellers. George, the head and founder
of the house, had been an assistant to John Rivington, and about 1763 embarked in business in
partnership with John Robinson, at whose death,
in 1776, he was left alone in the concern. His
rising reputation for personal integrity and steady
habits of business recommended him to the friendly notice of Thomas Longman, the second publisher of that name, who, well knowing the difficulties which young tradesmen had to encounter
with a deficient capital, voluntarily offered to give
him any credit he might require for books of his
publication. By unremitting attention, and the
judicious application of strong natural talents,
his business steadily and rapidly increased, so that
by the year 1780 his wholesale trade had become
the largest in London. About that time, the ne-

cessity for assistants in the management of the concern led him to take into partnership his son, George, also the two brothers, John and James, the firm being then designated that of G., G., J. and J. Robinson. They published largely books of considerable size and of great value. The head of the firm was considered to have an excellent judgment in the difficult and often critical undertaking of the superintendence and management of the literary concerns of a publishing establishment. He greatly respected meritorious authors, and acted with singular liberality in his pecuniary dealings with them. Besides the works of which they were the sole proprietors, they were engaged jointly with several of the principal houses in numerous works of great extent, such as Kippis's "Biographia Britannica."

In 1780 they commenced the "Annual Register," following the plan of Dodsley's, but advocating a different system of politics. They engaged in the preparation and conducting of this work gentlemen of high character and established literary reputation, by which it soon acquired great popularity. The current sale of each volume, for many years, exceeded 7000 copies. They were also the publishers of the "Town and Country Magazine," of which there were sold about 14,000 copies, monthly; and of the "Ladies' Magazine," a publication for a long period of equal popularity and emolument. For many years the confidential friend and literary adviser of the house was the late Alexander Chalmers, who possessed many qualifications for that delicate and difficult office. He is said to have contributed largely to their several periodicals, and had a prominent share in the editorial direction of the "Biographical Dictionary," which extended to 32 volumes 8vo., and was in progress of publication from 1812 to 1817. Having often had occasion to refer to this work, in the expectation of finding full and accurate information, with discriminating comments on the writings and merits of the authors, whose memoirs it professes to narrate, I have too often been disappointed and mortified. A good Biographia Britannica is a literary desideratum. I cannot conscientiously praise the execution of this Dictionary, yet I feel sincere respect for the man, and admiration of many of his literary works. He was a truly estimable professional literary character, and it is said that "no man conducted so many works for the booksellers of London; and his attention to accuracy of collation; his depth and research as to facts, and his discrimination as to the character of the authors under his review,

cannot be too highly praised." Such is the remark
of Mr. Timperley, in his "Dictionary of Printing
and Printers," 1839. Besides writing for several
periodical works, Mr. Chalmers edited "The British Essayists," in 48 vols. 18mo. 1803; an edition of
Steevens's Shakspeare, with Life and Notes, 9
vols. 8vo. 1803—1805; A History of the Colleges,
&c., of Oxford, 2 vols. 8vo. 1810; an edition of
"The English Poets, from Chaucer to Cowper,"
21 vols. royal 18mo. 1810. He was also author
of an original work, in 3 vols. second edition, 1815,
which had previously appeared in the Gentleman's
Magazine, intituleᴅ "The Projector," a periodical
paper, originally published between January 1802
and November 1809. Of this work Mr. Timperley
fairly writes that "it successfully seized on the follies and vices of the day; and has displayed in their
exposure a large fund of wit, humour, and delicate
irony." Mr. Chalmers was a pleasant, convivial
companion, which, with his conversational talents,
and intimacy with the principal London publishers, secured him a seat at the Hall Dinners of the
Stationers' Company at all their public meetings.
I met Mr. Chalmers frequently, and ever found
him cheerful, communicative, and friendly. He
died Dec. 10, 1834, aged 75.

Though George Robinson had succeeded in creating and sustaining the largest bookselling and publishing trade of his time, he failed to provide for his successors that mental organization and machinery which were indispensable for continuing it: conscious that the concern was of his own creating, he seems to have thought that he could not keep the management too exclusively to himself. His son and his brothers he admitted, indeed, into partnership, and assigned to each his place and duties; but they were treated by him rather as agents than principals. He was king and autocrat; and whilst he conceded to them, nominally, the position of equals, in rank, he carefully retained the supreme and ruling power. The consequence became painfully manifest, immediately after his death, in 1801. The surviving partners found themselves engaged in a large and intricate business, of which neither of them knew much beyond the particular department to which his attention had been almost exclusively devoted. Ignorant of the pecuniary position of the house, of the money capital at their disposal for sustaining it, and equally so of the means and method of its proper application, they saw no hope of relief but by a friendly commission of bankruptcy. The affairs were wound up, the property sold, and, to their surprise, it was found that there was enough to satisfy every creditor, in full, with a surplus of £20,000. The surviving partners arose from this painful investigation with their personal credit and honour untarnished, but their commercial importance had departed.

It remains that I now give some account of the Longmans—the first of whom was Thomas, at the sign of "the Ship and Black Swan," whose name appeared to books in 1726, joined with Thomas and John Osborne. He appears to have realized a good fortune, and, dying in 1755, left the property to his widow. She, with the nephew of her first husband, Thomas Longman, conducted the business for some time. They possessed valuable copyrights, in Greek and Latin school-books of the higher class, which, at that time, had a large sale. This nephew was esteemed a tradesman of correct judgment, of great integrity in his dealings, and of kindly disposition. I had opportunities of seeing him occasionally towards the close of his life. He retired from business about 1793, retaining only so much of it as was connected with the sale of the stock belonging to his copyrights, and died at his house at Hampstead in 1797, at the age of 60, greatly esteemed by all who knew him. His eldest son, Thomas Norton Longman, succeeded to the father's business as wholesale and

retail bookseller and publisher, on the same plan
and scale, his principal assistant being Christopher
Brown, the father of my excellent friend, Thomas
Brown, who served his apprenticeship to Mr.
Longman, and now deservedly occupies the honourable post of a principal partner in the house.
In 1797, my eldest brother, Owen Rees, who had
been thoroughly trained to business in one of the
principal bookselling houses in Bristol, joined Mr.
Longman, when the firm was briefly designated,
"Longman & Rees." Finding his health declining,
in 1837, he determined to close his connexion with
the house, and arrangements were made with this
view. Before they were concluded, he went to
Wales for the removal of what was deemed a temporary indisposition, and on the 5th of September,
died, in the 67th year of his age, upon the estate
(then his own property) on which he had been
born, and where he had hoped to pass some years
in tranquil retirement, after the anxieties and fa-
tigues of a long life of arduous and unremitting
application to business.

Of this once-amiable and estimable person, I
(Britton) avail myself of the present opportunity
to put on record an expression of my own warm
feelings of attachment and sincere friendship. Intimately acquainted with him for nearly forty

years, and often associated in the counting-house, on committees, at the social board, and in other pursuits, I knew him well, and not only respected him for generosity of conduct and sentiment, but for that friendly and kindly disposition he manifested on all occasions. Never was there a man who more fully and truly acted the character of "Harmony" on the great stage of the world, than Owen Rees. In an extensive intercourse with authors and artists, with booksellers and other tradesmen, indeed, with all classes of society, he was bland, courteous, candid, and sincere. In the numerous meetings of the partners in the "Beauties of England," when I was but little known to or by Mr. Rees, and when there were often angry contentions between the booksellers and the authors, I always found him eager and anxious to reconcile differences, to sooth irritated feelings, and endeavour to urge the authors to industry and perseverance, and his colleagues to forbearance and generosity. Such conduct and such manners could not fail to create a friendly feeling in my heart, and, from a more intimate connexion with him afterwards, in consequence of the firm having a share in the "Beauties of Wiltshire," the "Architectural," and the "Cathedral Antiquities," and in others of my literary works, I invariably found a sin-

cere friend in Mr. Rees. Many happy hours have I
spent in his company, in Paternoster Row and at
my own humble home, and never saw him with a
frown on his benignant countenance, nor heard a
harsh, ungenerous sentiment from his lips—I
loved him, whilst living, and have often lamented
his loss, since death has parted us.

In 1804, Thomas Hurst and Cosmo Orme were
added to the firm. The story of Thomas Hurst
may afford a lesson and warning to speculators,
and also to generous-hearted persons, who are
susceptible of being imposed on by the seductions
of the cunning and crafty. I knew him some years
before he joined the firm of Longman and Co.,
and found him then, as I did in his days of prosperity, kind, friendly, and generous. At first he
conducted a business nearly opposite Longman's,
and supplied several country booksellers with the
London publications. By diligence, devotion to
his customers, and obliging manners, he soon augmented his property and profits, and was doing
well when he joined the new firm. In this he man-
aged the country department, and was highly es-
teemd by all who knew him. He was living in an
elegant, but unostentatious style, with a carriage
and good establishment, on the brow of High-
gate Hill, where I have spent many joyful hours in

the company of cordial friends. In an evil moment he became connected with an artful and unprincipled man, who was engaged in a good bookselling business in Yorkshire, and who afterwards embarked in a large and daring undertaking in London. John, the elder brother of Thomas Hurst, who was a man of retiring disposition, of unassuming manners, and of punctilious honesty of principle, was partner with the person alluded to, but wholly unfitted for the hazardous game in which he became involved. He was quiescent, whilst his partner was artful and ostentatious. Their capital was soon sunk, and credit was then obtained to a vast extent; for the partner, not satisfied with a large business in books and prints, embarked in building houses, and speculated in hops. The elder Mr. Hurst saw and felt the imminent danger in which he was embarked, and prevailed on his brother to sign accommodation bills to a great amount. He had not courage to refuse, but drew in the name of the firm, of the Row, as he had been accustomed to do in the regular routine of business. Some of these bills were duly paid, but they became so numerous and to such large amounts, that Longman and Co. required an explanation, dissolved the partnership, and bound Mr. T. Hurst to be personally responsible for all further outstanding bills. They also paid to their retiring partner more than forty thousand pounds, his valued share in the house. But even this sum was not enough to meet all the liabilities: whence he became a ruined man. He made two or three efforts to regain credit and business; but these were not to be obtained. The elder brother, John, died broken-hearted; and Thomas was reduced to the mortifying state of seeking an asylum for old age, as an inmate to, and dependant on the charity of the Charter House, in which he died in the year 1850. In consequence of some subsequent changes occasioned by the death of my brother, and later by that of T. N. Longman, the retirement of Hurst and Orme, and the introduction of other persons, to take their places, the firm has assumed its present form of "Longman, Brown, Green, and Longmans." After the introduction of these new partners, of excellent business habits, various new schemes for the enlargement and extension of the trade were carried into execution. Hence, within a short period, the house rose to an importance and reputation which had never before been attained by any similar establishment in the world. To the retail branch they devoted a distinct department, to which was joined a choice and extensive library of old books. This was a novelty in a publishing house, and I believe that it originated in obtaining a large collection of scarce and curious books, on old Poetry and the Drama, which the partners had purchased, for a very large sum, from Thomas Hill. The event was at a time when Bibliomania was raging in London,—when certain noblemen and gentlemen were in the habit of attending sales, and competing for large and tall-paper books, and for rare copies, many of which had become so from their worthlessness. A remarkable Catalogue, called "Bibliotheca Anglo-Poetica," of the Hill library, was prepared in 1816 by——Griffiths, a clerk in Longman's house, and secured much praise from the book-buyers, and the learned in black-letter lore, for the knowledge and tact it manifested. Thence forward, for many years, the house continued to purchase largely at sales, and from individuals, either libraries or collections of books, and occasionally issued catalogues. After the death of Mr. Griffiths, his place was supplied by Mr. Reader; but within the last few years the whole collection was sold by public auction. I am not a little surprised and mortified to look over the pages, and meagre Index, of the Rev. Dr. Dibdin's "Reminiscences," in vain, for some notice of T. Hill, and Mr. Griffith's "Bibliotheca." The general wholesale trade, for the supply of country booksellers in the British Isles, and for the foreign markets, surpassed that of all preceding establishments; whilst the publishing business, if it cannot be said to have gone beyond that of any other British house, was unquestionably inferior to none.

In adverting to the publications of this firm, it is curious to observe one name of some eminence in literature and science, which has been in association with Longman and Co. for more than 120 years. This is Ephraim Chambers, the author, or editor, of the original "Cyclopædia," which work was first published by subscription in 1728, in two volumes, folio. It soon acquired great popularity, and attained a second edition in 1738. The author, finding his health impaired by literary labours, went to France, in hopes of recruiting his mental and bodily strength, and at the same time collecting materials for his projected book. I have in my possession some interesting letters written by him during this tour, addressed to his publisher. The "Cyclopædia" was reprinted under his superintendence in 1739, and was his last literary effort. His constitution gave way, and he died in May, 1740. The work was again reprinted in 1741, and also in 1746, when it was thought desirable to add a Supplement, to embrace the more modern discoveries in science and in the arts. This Supplement, prepared by Dr. Hill, and Mr. G. L. Scott, was published in 1753, in two folio volumes. After an interval of some years, the work still maintaining a high reputation, the proprietors projected a new edition, incorporating the Supplement, together with new matter of importance. Some difficulty was experienced in finding a suitable editor. At last Dr. Abraham Rees was chosen, who was then mathematical tutor at a dissenting college in London, and had acquired considerable reputation for his scientific knowledge and literary talents. The first number, in folio, was published in 1778, and the work was continued weekly till completed, in 418 numbers, forming four large volumes, with numerous prints. The current sale for many years amounted to 5000 numbers weekly, and there was a large demand for the work, in this form, for a long time after its completion. At length it was found expedient to publish another edition, or rather an entirely new work, under the same title, and under the same learned and laborious editor, who called to his aid a number of writers holding high rank in the several important departments of science. The work received the designation of the "New Cyclopædia." It was published periodically, in parts, or half volumes, and appeared regularly till completed in 40 volumes. The publication, which commenced in 1802, occupied about sixteen years; but the labour of the indefatigable editor, including the period of preparation, extended over twenty years, measured, as he said, not by fragments of time, but by whole days, of twelve and fourteen hours each. In the general preface, the editor has given the names of his principal coadjutors, and I find your name recorded in the list, in connexion with the subjects of antiquities, topography, &c., upon which you furnished many valuable articles.

I had the gratification of introducing the following gentlemen to the firm, to write articles on subjects connected with their professional studies: E. W. Brayley, who wrote on Enamelling; T. Phillips, R.A., on Painting; and Sharon Turner, on English History. The last gentleman became intimate with the partners, was employed by them for many years afterwards, and attained great popularity and handsome remuneration for his historical works, through the medium of such publishers.

Reminiscences respecting this once important work, and its phalanx of contributors, in art, literature, and science—of their frequent intercourse at the Soirées which the publishers established at their great book manufactory and mart, No. 39,

&c., Paternoster Row—are impressed on my memory and feelings with intense pleasure, mixed with some painful emotions of having for ever lost the converse and excitement which emanated from the friendly and intellectual collision, then and there produced. The respectable firm of Longman and Co. not only invited and assembled nearly all the contributors to the "Cyclopædia," periodically for several successive winters, but were in the habit of calling many of them together around the social and splendid dining table, where the acknowledged professors of literature and art met, on equal and friendly terms, eminent amateurs of both. Such unions were novelties in England, and I believe, in Europe; and were eminently calculated to foster good feelings, and promote harmony and intimacy between persons in different gradations of trade, literature, art, and science. Hence friendships were made; new discoveries were proclaimed; opinions, public measures, and the conduct of public men, canvassed; courtesies and civilities were exchanged between persons whose studies and pursuits were often in rivalry, and human amenities were cultivated. In such company, and under such influences, I own that I not only felt elated and proud, but substantially benefited, both mentally and morally. The amiable and benignant editor of the "Cyclopædia," who often formed one of these parties, seemed, to my fancy, something above humanity: for never was there a man more deservedly beloved and respected than the Rev. Dr. Abraham Rees.

Besides giving to the editor the assistance and co-operation of eminent writers in literature and science, the proprietors spared no expense to provide artists of the first talents for its illustrations. Among those who furnished drawings, were Howard, Landseer, Donovan, Russell, Opie, Ottley, Phillips, and Farey; while among the engravers, were Milton, Lowry, and Scott. The "New Cyclopædia" was in all respects a great and important undertaking. It embodied writings by some of the most distinguished scientific men of the age, on subjects of primary consequence, and it involved an expense almost unexampled in the history of literature: the pecuniary outlay could not have been less than 300,000 pounds sterling.

Another literary speculation of considerable importance, undertaken in 1803, was the "Annual Review," intended to comprise, in one large volume, an account of the entire English literature of each year. The editorship was committed to Arthur Aikin, whose scientific and literary attainments eminently fitted him for such an office. He

was ably assisted by the distinguished members
of his own family, and by many persons of note in
the literary world: among whom may be mentioned, in theology, the Rev. Chas. Wellbeloved,
of York; in natural history, the late Rev.
Wm. Wood, of Leeds; and in general literature,
Robert Southey, and William Taylor, of Norwich.
The numerous letters by Taylor and Southey, in
"A Memoir of the Life and Writings" of the former, 2 vols. 8vo., by J. W. Robberds, are truly interesting, as calculated to unfold some of the
mysteries and fascinations of authorship and re-
viewing, as well as characterising two writers,
whose works produced many and great effects in
the world of literature, between the years 1793
and 1836. Though not much known to the reading community, Mr. Taylor was an extraordinary
writer; and from the number and variety of his
criticisms and essays, in the "Monthly Magazine,"
the "Monthly Review," the "Annual Review," the
"Athenæum," in magazines, and other periodicals, he must have produced strong and important
results on the readers of his works. The work
was conducted by Mr. Aikin for six years, when,
in consequence of new arrangements in the management of the literary concern of the house, I undertook to prepare the seventh volume. In this

arduous task I was materially aided by most of the gentlemen who had lent their service to my esteemed predecessor, and I had the gratification of receiving a valuable contribution from Walter Scott, on a subject, for the treatment of which he was perhaps the fittest writer of the age;—"Ancient Romance." With the seventh volume the work ceased.

In the year 1807, Longman and Co. entered on the publication of a new periodical, called "The Athenæum," under the editorship of Dr. Aikin, in competition with the "Monthly Magazine," which had been commenced a few years before by Mr. R. Phillips, of St. Paul's Churchyard. This publication consisted of monthly numbers, at one shilling each, was continued to the close of the seventh half-yearly volume, and, under the able editorship of Dr. Aikin, assisted by the contributions of various members of his own family, with Dr. Enfield, and other persons of distinction in literature, had acquired great popularity. The projector was at the time regarded as a sufferer from his political principles; and Dr. Aikin, with other friends to liberal opinions in politics, readily espoused his cause, and lent their talents to assist him. No sooner, however, had the magazine obtained an extensive circulation, than Phillips took the entire management, and dispensed with the services of his first friend. The magazine, however, if it lost from this cause much of the literary excellence and refinement which had characterized the earlier numbers, retained, by his judicious selection of miscellaneous matters of general interest, its hold of the popular mind, and commanded a very extensive sale. It occurred to Longmans that a magazine, which should be devoted to topics of a higher literary character, might be successful; and under this conviction they projected the periodical above-mentioned, under the title of "The Athenæum." The work included contributions by Dr. Falconer, of Bath, and Mr. Dewhurst, of London; Robert Southey,—Bland, Elton, and many others. On this periodical I had the pleasure of acting as sub-editor, and furnished for it most of the larger articles of obituary. But the sale did not yield an adequate return to compensate the publishers, and the work was on that account relinquished.

Not long after the discontinuance of the "Athenæum," the house embarked in an undertaking of great magnitude and expense, entitled "The British Gallery of Pictures," which was intended to consist of fine engravings from the best works of the old masters, in the private collections of Eng-

lish noblemen, &c., some of the prints being coloured in imitation of the originals. In the plan of
this work two objects were embraced:—firstly,
small prints, including all the pictures in certain
celebrated collections; and, secondly, copies of a
selected number only of the more important and
admired works. The latter prints were on a larger
scale than the former, some being of the actual size
of the original pictures. Each series was accompanied by appropriate letter-press, and the prints
in both cases were coloured. Eminent artists were
employed to copy the pictures for engraving, as
well as to colour the prints. Among the engravers were Cardon, Schiavonetti, and other able
artists; and, whilst the artistic arrangements were
entrusted to Tomkins, the literary department was
confided to Henry Tresham, R.A., and W. Y. Ottley; both gentlemen being well qualified for their
respective duties. An immense outlay was incurred upon this work, which was carried on for
some years with great spirit; but it proved to be a
very profitable speculation, and was brought to a
premature close, when the only portion really finished was the Cleveland-house collection, in one
volume, folio. The water-colour drawings from
the original pictures had been exhibited to the
public in a gallery specially appropriated to them

in Bond Street; and, on the termination of the work, the proprietors obtained an Act of Parliament to dispose of the pictures, with the engravings, by lottery.

But whilst the house thus employed a large capital, in the production of what may be termed periodical works, it was liberal in the appropriation of other portions to standard books, on important literary subjects, by authors of the most distinguished reputation. Amongst these were the Aikins, Scott, Moore, and Southey. Complaints have often been made of the sordid spirit of booksellers, and their inadequate remuneration of authors. No doubt writers are often very badly paid for works upon which they have bestowed much time, labour, and talent; and the cause of literature has, it may be believed, suffered on this account. But I am quite sure the evil has not always originated with publishers, who, like other tradesmen, give for the material the amount which they deem it to be worth in respect to the profit it is likely to yield. Generally, I believe—and I speak from a long experience—the booksellers act with commendable liberality. A reference to a list of prices given by Lintot to authors, early in the last century—a curious document, printed by Nichols, and now in my possession—shows that authors, at that time, were handsomely paid. In well-known instances, booksellers of a later date,—the Robinsons, the Dillys, the Johnsons, the Cadells, the Murrays, and lastly the Longmans,—have dealt most liberally by authors, and on some occasions have given sums of large, not to say exorbitant amount, for manuscripts, on the bare supposition that the returns might justify the expenditure, and yield a fair trading profit. In my personal knowledge, I can say that the firm, now alluded to, always acted in such transactions with great and generous spirit.

At a later period, Oct. 1802, Longman and Co. became part-proprietors and London publishers of the "Edinburgh Review." This produced them an important accession of literary friends of eminent abilities, among whom were Walter Scott, Rev. Sidney Smith, Francis Jeffrey, Henry Brougham, Francis Horner, James Mill, and others.

About this time they became connected also with John Pinkerton, the author of "General Geography," which appeared first in three, and afterwards in two quarto volumes. It was a work of great labour, being written and compiled from the best authorities in the European languages, and illustrated by numerous maps, engraved by Lowry. Pinkerton also prepared a large "General Atlas," a well-executed folio volume; and, more especially, a "Collection of Voyages and Travels," in sixteen quarto volumes, with prints by the Cookes and others. These large and costly works were the joint property of Longman and Co. and Cadell and Davies. Pinkerton was a singular and degraded man. I (Britton) was made too well acquainted with him for my own reputation and for my own domestic comforts. He rented, and occupied, for a short time, a house, No. 9, Tavistock Place, next door to my own. His home was frequently a place of popular disturbance, by females whom he had married, or lived with, and deserted. When in want of money, or over-excited by drink, they knocked at his door, broke the windows, and otherwise behave riotously. He was a disreputable character; and though he had been most liberally paid by Longman's house, he went to Paris in the latter part of his life, and died in poverty in 1826. He was an author of several works, in poetry, history, geography, criticism; all of which, says the writer in "The Penny Cyclopædia," "with all their faults, not only overflow with curious learning and research, but bear upon them the impression of a vigorous, an ingenious, and even an original mind. His violence and dogmatism, his arrogance and self-conceit, his pugnacity and contempt for all who dissented from his views, but above all, his shallow and petulant attacks upon the common creed in religion and morals, have raised a general prejudice against Pinkerton, which has prevented justice being done to his acquirements and talents." Mr. Dawson Turner possesses a large collection of his correspondence, from which two octavo volumes have been published, but not much to the credit of the Scotchman. A later speculation, on a large scale, published by Longman's house, was "Lardner's Cabinet Cyclopædia," in small 12mo., extending to 133 volumes; for which many distinguished writers were engaged, and heavy expenses were incurred.

For several years it was the custom of the firm to give Dinners at certain intervals, when the partners assembled around their hospitable board a number of authors and artists of high reputation; and, besides these more limited réunions, they opened the house in Paternoster Row, one evening in the week, during several seasons, for a Soirée, which was rendered easily accessible to persons of literary tastes, and from all countries.

I come now to the third Class of booksellers who chiefly dealt in retail; whose traffic was mostly with their brother tradesmen, whom they supplied with a single copy, or several copies of

books, at what was called the trade price, which
produced them only a small profit. Paternoster
Row contained, at that time, several respectable
booksellers of this class. Mr. Bladon's shop was
the well-known depository of old plays. You may
remember to have seen, some years ago, in Leadenhall Street, a large hardware warehouse, which
attracted the notice of all passengers by its filthy
appearance, both on the outside and the inside.
The proprietor was scarcely less notorious on account of his dingy aspect, which obtained for him
the designation of "Dirty Dick." Bladon was
greatly respected as a tradesman, but his shop
might have rivalled the Leadenhall Street repository for its affluence in dust and soot. The next
to be noticed is Symonds, who carried on a large
business in the sale of periodicals, which he purchased in quantities, as they were published, and
sold singly, or in small numbers to booksellers'
collectors, at the wholesale prices. By this plan
the trade was greatly accommodated, and his own
interest promoted. He pursued the same course
with respect to the more popular pamphlets of the
day. In times of great political agitation, such as
those in which he lived, this practice of publishing
for authors was not without danger, as Symonds
had the misfortune to experience. One tract, to

which he had permitted his name to be attached,
who pronounced a libel; and he had to endure the
penalty by an imprisonment of some months in
Newgate, where I once visited him. He died in
middle life, greatly respected. The business of this
house was afterwards conducted on the same scale
and plan, by Mr. Sherwood, who had been Mr. Symonds' active and valuable assistant. Contiguous
to this shop was that of Parsons, who sold books
and pamphlets upon the same plan, but on a less
extensive scale. He was occasionally a publisher,
on his own account. His chief speculation was an
edition of Hume and Smollett's "History of England," in 18mo., which, like that by Cooke, was
embellished with prints and portraits.

Thomas Evans, though advanced in age, ranked
among the retail booksellers of the Row. He was
originally a porter to Johnson, a bookseller of
Ludgate Street, and succeeded to the business of
Howes, Clarke, and Colfins, by which he obtained
respectability and a good fortune. The bulk of
his property he bequeathed to Charles, father of
the present T. Brown, already noticed. In his will,
he directs that his funeral expenses do not exceed
forty shillings. In early life he acted as the publisher of the "Morning Chronicle," which first appeared in 1770, and in that capacity had the mis-

fortune to offend Oliver Goldsmith, who went to
the office and unceremoniously assailed Evans
with a stick. The sturdy Welshman, however,
soon recovered from his surprise, and with one
blow laid the poet prostrate on the floor. Another
of the retail booksellers of this period was John
Walker, who for some time officiated as (what was
called) the "Trade Auctioneer." He was greatly
respected by his neighbours. In the latter part of
his life his name was familiar to the public as publisher of Dr. Wolcot's, alias Peter Pindar's, works.
It is a common adage that there are "secrets in all
trades;" and it is well known that every craft and
calling has its peculiar customs, privileges, and
technicalities of language. A few of the large
wholesale publishers of London are in the habit
of making up, either annually or occasionally,
what are called "trade sales;" when they prepare a
catalogue of their large stock books, and distribute
it to a select number of retail dealers, who are invited to meet the publisher and his auctioneer at a
certain tavern, where, after partaking of an early
dinner, the "trade auctioneer" proceeds to dispose
of the works named in the catalogue, to the parties present. The various lots comprise many
copies of recently-published works, and are offered
and sold at rather less than the usual trade prices;

the purchasers being, moreover, allowed to give bills, at three, at four, eight, twelve, and sixteen months, according to the amount they buy, or take a moderate discount for cash. Hence have originated two great evils in the bookselling business; namely, the encouragement to print large editions of books, from the facility of disposing of them at reduced prices, and the depreciation of those works in the public market, by copies being offered at such sales much below their original prices. Mr. Walker, I believe, was amongst the first trade auctioneers, and was followed by Mr. Saunders, a prompt, off-hand man, whose language and peculiarity of manners are humorously burlesqued in "Chalcographiomania." The celebrated William Hone was for a short time auctioneer to the trade, but was irregular in his accounts, whence arose many embarrassments in after life. Two large stock-holders of books have since become their own salesmen, on these occasions: both eminently qualified, from promptitude of thought and action, and extensive knowledge of business. The late Thomas Tegg of the "Poultry," when I first knew him, kept a small shop in St. John's Street, for pamphlets, songs, &c. Thence he removed to Cheapside, where he accumulated a large stock of books, and established an evening auction. He afterwards took the old Mansion-house in the Poultry, and progressively published numerous books. Having settled one of his sons in Australia, he thereby obtained a channel for the sale of large editions of cheap books, and deemed it expedient to adopt the practice of some of the great publishing firms, by making up an annual sale, and acting as auctioneer. My friend, Mr. H. G. Bohn, has followed the same track, and has astonished the Metropolitan traders in literature by the stock brought forward, the rapidity of dispatch, and the novelties he has introduced into this branch of London business. Mr. Hodgson, of Fleet Street, is at present the confidential and respected agent of the London publishers. The poems of Peter Pindar, this once noted and powerful satirist, were extensively read at the end of the last century. They were, however, very dear to the purchaser, being printed in thin quarto pamphlets at 2s. 6d. each, and containing only a very small portion of letter-press. His first attacks, in 1782, were the Royal Academicians, some of whom he assailed with bitter satire, sarcasm, and irony. King George the Third was next vituperated, in a poem called "The Lousiad," descriptive of the circumstances of an animal, unnamable to "ears polite," being seen on the plate of the monarch at a royal dinner. For some years the author continued to publish his philippes against artists, royal and noble personages, and also on some authors; one of whom, Wm. Gifford, who had written the "Baviad and Mæviad," a poem, in which many of the authors of the time were severely castigated, also wielded his galled pen against the morals and poetry of Dr. Wolcot. This castigation was so stringent and caustic that the Doctor was provoked to seek his lampooner in the shop of Mr. Wright, a political publisher, of Piccadilly. Thither Peter repaired, with a stout cudgel in hand, determined to inflict a summary and severe chastisement on his literary opponent. Gifford was a small and weak person; Wolcot was large, and strengthened by passion, but he was a coward, and after a short personal struggle was turned into the street by two or three persons, then in the shop. Gifford afterwards wrote and printed an "Epistle to Peter Pindar," with an "Introduction and Postscript," 1800, in which he dealt out a most virulent and unqualified tirade against the Doctor. It acquired great popularity, and in a few weeks attained a third edition. The pamphlet has not any publisher's name. This was the second victory which Gifford had achieved over literary opponents; a former being Anthony Pasquin, alias John Williams, a man notoriously acrimonious and severe in his poetical and prose criticisms on actors, actresses, and authors. Gifford was amongst the number, who smarted from his lashes, and who retaliated by lines more caustic and personal. For these Williams brought an action for libel, but was driven out of the Court of King's Bench by the unanimous reprobation of judge, jury, and the auditors assembled. I was present at that memorable trial; and can never forget the severity of sarcasm and irony exerted by Garrow, counsel for the defendant, against the notorious libeller, who had the effrontery and impudence to ask for damages, in a court of law, for what he called injury to private and public character. Notorious, and despised for his long career of literary vituperation and scandal, the Judge interrupted Mr. Garrow, and asked the Jury if they thought it desirable to proceed further with the trial, or non-suit the plaintiff. The latter was pronounced instanter. In the wide and diversified annals of literature, the reader will seek in vain for three more notorious and unprincipled satirists than the triumvirate here alluded to.

Wolcot's connection with Paternoster Row and John Walker arose from the latter becoming the publisher of some of the former's writings, and ultimately proprietor of the whole. I have heard Peter boast, he was the only author that ever outwitted, or "took in" a publisher. His works had attained great popularity, and produced for the writer a large annual income; and many of them were often out of print. Walker was disposed to purchase the copyrights, and print a collected edition. He first made the author a handsome offer in cash, and then an annuity. The poet drove a hard bargain for the latter, and said that "as he was very old and in a dangerous state of health, with a d—d asthma, and stone in the bladder, he could not last long." The bookseller offered £200 a year, the poet required £400; and every time the Doctor visited the Row he coughed, breathed apparently in much pain, and acted the incurable and dangerous invalid so effectively, that the publisher at last agreed to pay him £250 annually for life. A fine edition of his works was published in three volumes, 8vo., 1794, with a portrait and engraved title-pages; other editions have since appeared. Another portrait of him was published, as a separate print, which did not sell to any extent; but its proprietor derived a great profit by taking out the name of Peter Pindar and substituting that of "Renwick Williams, the Monster," who was notorious for stabbing ladies in the streets. This event was related to me by the Poet. A good account of his life is given in the "Penny Cyclopædia." Mr. Cyrus Redding, who had been familiar with Wolcot for many years, gave some interesting anecdotes of him in the "New Monthly Magazine," vols. 17 and 19; and has recently written further notice in "The Athenæum" for May and June 1852, to correct certain mis-statements in Jerdan's "Auto-Biography." Wolcot died in Somers-Town, Jan. 13, 1807, in the 81st year of his age, and was buried at St. Paul's, Covent Garden.

Mr. Bent was a bookseller of long standing in the Row, but he was chiefly known as the publisher of that very useful work, the "London Catalogue of Books," first printed in 1799, which is still continued monthly by Mr. T. Hodgson. This gentleman is also editor of "The London Catalogue of Books, published in Great Britain, with their Sizes, Prices, and Publishers' Names, from 1814 to 1846," 8vo. 1846; and "Bibliotheca Londinensis: a Classified Index to the Literature of Great Britain during Thirty Years," 8vo. 1848. Bent also published "The Universal Magazine," a periodical which at one time had an extensive sale.

I may conclude my list of retail booksellers with the names of the Wilkies, brothers, who were long respected inhabitants of the Row. With their retail business they carried on a wholesale trade of some extent in supplying country booksellers. One of the brothers, Thomas Wilkie, trafficked also in the public securities, and kept an office for the sale of lottery tickets. He removed to Salisbury, where I became acquainted with him, 1798, and found him obliging and kindly disposed. Amongst other things, he told me that on the first performance of Sheridan's play of "The Rivals," which the Wilkies published, the author was so scantily supplied with wardrobe, that he borrowed a shirt of Mr. W.'s father to witness the first acting of his own play, but forgot to return the said shirt; as he did also a few guineas, which he had borrowed of the same party.

In Ave Maria Lane, the firm of Scatcherd and Letterman carried on a large wholesale country business. Amongst other works they published, was "London and its Environs, or the General Ambulator." The 12th edition, 1820, greatly enlarged and improved by Mr. Brayley, is now before me, and is a very useful work, though supplanted by the justly-popular publications by Charles Knight: "Pictorial London," 6 vols. 1841. In the same lane, the house of Law was chiefly noted for school-books. An apprentice, and afterwards managing clerk, in that business, was Peter

Courtier, whose partiality for poetry induced him to write and publish a volume of "Verses," some of which had appeared in periodicals. He was the first mover, in and an active supporter of "the School of Eloquence."

The Laws were succeeded by the Whittakers, whose active exertions and skill in business speedily increased it to a great extent. Amongst many of their publications, was one in five volumes, by Miss Mitford, called "Our Village," which has passed through several editions, and is justly admired for the vivid fancy, the pathos, and amiable sympathy which pervade its pages. This work is now brought into two volumes by Mr. H. G. Bohn, and issued in his popular series of books. She first appeared as a poet in 1810. The reader will find some pleasing, and justly complimentary, remarks on Miss Mitford's writings, in a recently published and interesting volume, "A Journal of Summer-time in the Country," by the Rev. R. A. Willmott. Second edition, 1832.

William Pinnock was author of a long list of books, which, though little known in the literary world, have been of great value in the advancement of education and knowledge. All his writings have been adapted and addressed to the juvenile age, and have been peculiarly calculated to "teach the young idea how to shoot," and tempt it to pursue the path of learning with pleasantry and even fascination. By "The London Catalogue from 1814 to 1846," I see that Pinnock has produced twelve volumes of Catechisms, eight of Histories, and twenty-two others on Grammar, Languages, Arithmetic, Geography, Poetry, &c. These books have all been very popular and profitable to the publishers, though the author has, like too many other improvident ones, known the galling pressure of indigence.

Near Mr. Law's house, was the printing and publishing establishment of J. Wilkes, who became well known by the "Encyclopædia Londinensis," with numerous engravings, a work which extended to twenty-six volumes, at £63, and had a considerable sale. The names of Wilkes, Ave-Maria Lane, and Encyclopædia Londinensis, are indelibly impressed on my (Britton's) memory. On my first visit to Salisbury, in 1798, I assumed the title, or rather it was forced upon me, of Artist; and Mr. Easton, a bookseller and printer of the city, asked me to make a drawing of Salisbury Cathedral, to be engraved for, and published in, the great "national work" above-named. My ambition was aroused, but I was terrified; for I knew not how or where to begin, nor how or in what manner I was to proceed, even if I dared undertake such a herculean task. I was impelled to try; had pencils, rulers, and a table placed opposite the middle of the North chief transept. With the print from Price's "Survey," from the same point, before me, I sketched, and scratched, and rubbed out; and continued thus occupied for three successive days, with several persons looking on, and wondering at my temerity and incompetency. Often have I reflected on this scene and event; and more than once have I heard friends, who were there, remark on the exhibition, and their astonishment at seeing afterwards a tolerably-executed engraving from the sketch then made.

In Stationers' Court was the warehouse of B. Crosby, one of the original partners in the "Beauties of England and Wales," who had a very extensive country business, which has for some years been conducted by Simpkin and Marshall. Though not distinguished as publishers, this firm carries on the largest business in the book-trade of any house in Europe, and is only rivalled perhaps by the Harpers, of New York. The only daughter of the late Mr. Simpkin is the wife of the most enterprising and energetic publisher and bookseller of this metropolis, Henry G. Bohn, whose Catalogue of Books of 1841 is unprecedented for the number, value, and variety of its articles. It extends to no less than 1948 octavo pages.

This paved Court is associated with my own personal and topographical reminiscences too memorably to be passed unnoticed. In this central part of London, resided John, Duke of Bretagne and Earl of Richmond, during the reigns of Edwards II. and III., in a large mansion which was afterwards occupied by an Earl of Pembroke, and called Pembroke's Inn. It was afterwards possessed by the Company of Stationers, who rebuilt it of wood. That was burnt in the great fire of London, after which the present plain, tasteless Hall was erected. According to Clarendon, the stationers' property then destroyed was valued at £200,000. Here the Company of Stationers hold their courts, transact their business, register and deposit books, and assemble frequently at the festive board. At two of the Master's feasts I have been a guest, and enjoyed the company, conversation, and civic repasts with much zest. The Portraits preserved here remind us of names and literary works which have excited our curiosity and gratified our feelings in early reading days. These are of Richardson, Prior, Steele, Hoadly, Nelson, Dryden, Alderman Boydell, and others.

The first was one of the Masters of the Company, and had his wife painted for the place, to keep him company. Leigh Hunt, speaking of these portraits says, that representing the author of Clarissa Harlowe represents him as a "sensitive, enduring man—a heap of bad nerves." He further remarks, that Hoadly, "looks at once jovial and decided, like a good-natured controversialist." Concerts, as well as dinners, were frequently performed in this hall. Odes and other pieces were written for such occasions. Amongst these, Dryden's "Song for Saint Cecilia's Day," was produced in 1687; and, ten years afterwards, "Alexander's Feast" was written, composed, and performed: the composer being Jeremiah Clarke, who shot himself "for love." Though the Hall and Company of Stationers are associated with pleasant memories, persons, and events, there are others which tend to lower both in my own estimation. From the commencement of my (Britton's) literary career to the present time, I have been obliged (by Act of Parliament) to present one copy of every book which I have written and published to this company. This is the only London Company whose members are restricted to their own craft. It is called, "The Mystery or Art of the Stationers." For many years the said Stationers assumed the exclusive privilege of publishing all the almanacs of the country, and produced many which were frivolous and illiterate in style and matter. To counteract these, Charles Knight projected and published, for "The Society for the Diffusion of Useful Knowledge," in 1828, "The British Almanac," which has become eminently and justly popular, and has also superseded most of the almanacs which disseminated astrological nonsense and literary absurdity. The reader will find a very interesting paper on the history and characteristics of almanacs in "The Companion to the British Almanac," for 1829; also in "The London Magazine," for December, 1828.

Proceeding to the northwest corner of St. Paul's Churchyard, we recognize a name associated with the earliest recollections of youthful readers,— that of Newberry, who, after Carnan, furnished the largest and most interesting contributions to the juvenile libraries of the country. On the death of Newberry, his widow continued the business aided by John Harris, who afterwards became her successor. He was in turn succeeded by his son, who soon transferred the business to the present firm of Grant and Griffiths.

Francis Newberry, a member of the above-mentioned family, had a house on the east side of the Churchyard, near Cheapside, where he sold Dr.

James's celebrated fever powder, as a patent medicine. He was also proprietor of Paterson's "Road
Book," which, by judicious management and pro-
gressive improvement, he rendered a very lucrative property. The editing and publication of that
volume was a favourite occupation of Francis
Newberry, and he pursued it to the end of his life.
The stock and copyright were afterwards possessed by Mr. Mogg, who made further improvements. The volume is now extinct: railways have
superseded stage coaches, and steam power that
of horses.

Joseph Johnson long occupied a prominent station in St. Paul's Churchyard. He held the same
position amongst the liberal Protestant dissenters
that the Rivingtons did with the members of the
Church of England. He was truly generous in
dealing with authors, by frequently adding to the
price originally agreed on for a successful manuscript; and in this manner he is said to have paid
as much as £10,000 for Hayley's "Life of Cowper." Johnson issued the works of Price, Priestley, Belsham, and many others; together with
"The Analytical Review." Having published a
libellous pamphlet, by Gilbert Wakefield, reflect-
ing on Dr. Watson, Bishop of Llandaff, the author
was imprisoned for two years, and Johnson, as the

publisher, for six months. This incarceration appears to have produced beneficial effects to the warm-hearted publisher. Instead of enjoying the converse and social company of his talented authors, he studied his ledger, which had been neglected; and by sending notices of its unsettled contents to different debtors, he realized a large amount of income on being released from prison. At stated periods his house was open to literary men; and his parties derived great interest from the presence of such persons as Doctors Price, Priestley, Geddes, and Aikin; Bonnycastle, Fuseli, Gilbert Wakefield, Mary Wolstoncraft, and many others.

Sir Richard, then Mr., Phillips, commenced business in St. Paul's Churchyard, by publishing "The Monthly Magazine," in 1796. He had previously been settled at Leicester, first as a schoolmaster, and afterwards as a bookseller; but political causes obliged him to quit that town. His case met with much sympathy in London, as he had incurred heavy losses by his removal. He was a mon of strong mind and varied attainments, and, with a view to repair his injured fortunes, he projected the magazine above-mentioned. Dr. Aikin, who was much interested in Phillips's success, edited this periodical, and was aided by his

sister, Mrs. Barbauld, by his friend, Dr. Wm. Enfield, also by Godwin, Holcroft, and many other
writers. Johnson at first published this periodical, as agent for Phillips; and his extensive connexion enabled him to promote its success. The
speculative proprietor was, however, soon induced
to open a small shop for himself, and about the
same time he also undertook the task of editing
his magazine; thus dispensing with the services
of two of his best friends. The "Monthly" rapidly
increased in popularity and profit, and for many
years continued to be a valuable property. Phillips published numerous other works, chiefly edu-
cational, many of which were written by himself,
but appeared under the names of popular authors;
who probably revised the proofs, and allowed
their names to be attached, for a pecuniary consideration. Like his competitors, Phillips published an
"Encyclopædia," professedly under the editorship
of Dr. Gregory; but which was in fact mostly written by Jeremiah Joyce, whose varied scientific attainments were most inadequately appreciated. In
the year 1807, this enterprising publisher served as
one of the Sheriffs of London, and discharged the
duties of that important office with zeal, energy,
and great credit. During this period he was
knighted, on presenting an address on behalf of

the ministers. In the latter part of his career he suffered severely by the panic, and was obliged to surrender his business to his creditors. Besides numerous original papers in "The Monthly Magazine," Sir Richard was also author of the following literary works: "A Letter to the Livery of London, on the Office of Sheriff," 8vo. 1808; "On the Powers and Duties of Juries, and on the Criminal Laws of England," 8vo. 1811; "A Morning's Walk from London to Kew," 8vo. 1817; "Golden Rules of Social Philosophy, or a New System of Practical Ethics," 8vo. 1826; "A Personal Tour Through the United Kingdom," 8vo. 1828. It is also stated that he originated and published numerous treatises on "The Interrogatory System," in school education, which has proved eminently successful. He was likewise author of "Twelve Essays on the Proximate Causes of the Universe," being a reformed system of natural philosophy; substituting matter and motion for what he called "the silly superstitions and fancies" of attraction, repulsion, &c. These works abound with originality of thought, expressed in terse and pungent language. Though the "Walk to Kew" and the "Personal Tour" do not contain much topographical and antiquarian information, they tempt the reader to accompany and sympathize with the

LITERARY LONDON.

writer, by the fund of anecdote, vivid description,
and shrewdness of commentary, which pervade
every page. In reading these works, the young
student cannot fail to regard the author amongst
the philosophers and moralists of his age and
country. Sir Richard was a native of London,
where he was born in 1767, and died at Brighton,
April 1st, 1840. He thus writes to me from Brighton in April 1838, two years before his decease:
"Your friendly letter was a ray of sunshine on a
very dull day. You struck out for yourself a path
of literary renown, and I am quite sure you have
reached the summit. For my own part, my pursuits have been so diversified for the last twenty
years, that I had almost forgotten one of my
youngest literary children—'The Walk to Kew.'
Your approbation I value, because on such a subject you are a first-rate judge. You must have
read fifty such works: I never read one; and therefore, in my mind, there is no element of comparison. I had no design of the book when I took the
walk; and my notes were very scanty. Had it
been republished with a dozen good engravings,
it might have become popular. Another volume
might have been devoted to Hampton Court, and
a third to Windsor."

The name and house of Carrington Bowles, on

the north side of St. Paul's Churchyard, were noted
for the number and variety of popular Prints which
were distributed thence all over the country at the
end of the last and beginning of the present century.
"Death and the Lady," a figure half skeleton, half
female—"Keep within compass," a beau with
cocked hat, scarlet coat, &c., standing between
the two legs of a pair of compasses, and other
showy, admonitory pictures, were to be seen in
the farm-houses and cottages in Wiltshire, in my
youth-days, whence the names of publisher and
place were impressed on the young mind. The
late Mr. C. Bowles, on retiring from business with
a handsome fortune, built a large villa or mansion
at Enfield, on the bank of the New River, and
called it Myddleton House, in compliment to the
adventurous speculator in that important undertaking. Mr. Bowles's ancestor possessed shares in
the New River Company, which were bequeathed
to the son, who for many years was an active member of that company. He was a Fellow of the
Society of Antiquaries and took great interest in
its weekly meetings.

Charles Dilly, of the Poultry, was the survivor
of two brothers, who published largely, and accumulated handsome fortunes. On relinquishing
business, he was succeeded by Joseph Mawman,

of York, who afterwards removed to Ludgate Street, where he was succeeded by Mr. Fellows. Mr. Mawman published "An Excursion to the Highlands of Scotland," &c., 8vo. 1805, which contains two prints from drawings by Turner.

The firm of Vernor and Hood had removed the business from Birchin Lane to the Poultry, where they published many literary works, and with whom I (Britton) commenced my literary career as a Topographer. My business and personal connections with that House involve reminiscences of persons, books, and events, which would afford matter for a moderately-sized volume. From the year 1799 to 1810, I was in almost constant communication with Mr. Hood, who was the managing partner, and who was an active, persevering, punctilious man of business. The House attained considerable distinction in the literary world by the publication of Bloomfeld's "Farmer's Boy," and other volumes of poems by the rustic, self-educated author—by the exuberant praises of Capel Lofft—by the publication of "The Monthly Mirror," under the editorship of Edward Dubois and Thomas Hill—by "The Poetical Magazine," edited by David Carey, who had published "The Pleasures of Nature," with other poetry, novels, &c. Among many works which issued from this firm was "The Beauties of Wiltshire" and "The Beauties of England and Wales," with the accompanying "British Atlas." In 1808 the House acquired much notoriety by a trial in the Court of King's Bench, when Sir John Carr brought an action-at-law against these publishers for a libel on himself and his literary works. This author had obtained much reputation for his Tours in France, in the North, in Holland, in Ireland, &c., and has been rewarded by different publishers with nearly two thousand pounds for copyrights. His "Tour in Holland," one volume 4to, 1807, which was purchased and published by Sir Richard Phillips, was turned into ridicule by Edward Dubois, in a sportive, ironical, and satirical small volume, entitled "My Pocket Book," written in a fluent, anecdotical, gossipping style. The "Tours" were much read and abundantly commented on by the regular reviews and by daily journals. The author obtained fame and fortune, when the witty and caustic satire alluded to provoked him and the publisher to prosecute the writer of "My Pocket Book." A verdict was given, in behalf of the liberty of the press, against the plaintiff, who was non-suited, and driven from the court in disgrace. A full account of the trial was published, with several letters from the Earl of Mountnorris, Sir Richard Phillips, and the author of "My Pocket Book"—Edward Dubois. See account of this publication and of the "Pocket Book" in "The Annual Review," vol. vii. 1808.

C. Forster, of 91, Poultry, published, amongst other works, "The Literary Magazine and British Review," which extended from 1788 to 1794. It is distinguished for a series of well-engraved portraits, mostly by T. Holloway, accompanied by original memoirs; also other prints and essays on literary and scientific subjects.

Under the Royal Exchange, John Richardson, who was a highly respected tradesman, carried on an extensive trade amongst the city merchants. He was one of the original proprietors of "The Beauties of England," and was assisted by a nephew of the same name.

In the same street, Mr. J. Sewell, a worthy but eccentric man, published the "European Magazine;" the biographical articles in which, especially those connected with the drama, were written by Isaac Reed, who edited the work for many years, and was succeeded by Stephen Jones. Mr. Moser was a prolific writer in this popular periodical, which contained many well-engraved portraits. Amongst them was one of Dr. Joseph Priestley, in profile, drawn by myself, from life, when the reverend philosopher was reading a farewell discourse to a crowded congregation in Hackney Church, in March, 1794.

At the northeast corner of Bishopsgate Street, Messrs. Arch, two Quaker brothers, enjoyed an excellent retail trade. They had shares in "The Beauties of England," and were the publishers of Turner and Cooke's "Southern Coast," which contains many fine specimens of the skill of the respective artists. This work, somewhat like "The Beauties," was the cause of repeated disputes between the publishers and the artists and authors. The late amiable William Alexander, then one of the curators of the British Museum, wrote an urgent and kindly-expressed letter to Messrs. Arch, advising them to pay more liberal prices to the engravers. I have a copy of that letter, from the original in possession of Dawson Turner, Esq.

The "Minerva Press," by Wm. Lane, in Leadenhall Street, must not be omitted in this short retrospect of the older metropolitan publishers. It was noted for the number and variety of books, called novels, which were continually produced and distributed to all the circulating libraries in the country. From ten to twenty pounds were the sums usually paid to authors for those novels of three volumes. The Colburns and Bentleys drove this trash out of the market.

Part II.

——

FLEET STREET, RED LION PASSAGE, CHANCERY LANE, HIGH HOLBORN.

Part II.

FLEET STREET, RED LION PASSAGE, CHANCERY LANE, AND HIGH HOLBORN.

Fleet Street and its Immediate Vicinity—McCreery—Nightingale Rylance—John Major—Walton and Cotton's Angler—Walpole Anecdotes—Rev. T. F. Dibdin—Kearsley—Quarterly Review—John Murray—George Cruikshank—W. Hone and his Trials—Wm. Cobbett—E. Williams—The John Bull—London Magazine and its Contributors—J. Taylor—J. H. Wiffin—Duke of Bedford—T. Bensley—Red Lion Passage—John Nichols and his Literary Anecdotes—A. J. Valpy—Wm. Pickering—The Bridgewater Treatises—High Holborn—The Architectural Antiquities of Great Britain—John Britton's Partners—O. Rees—Josiah Taylor.

FLEET Street and its immediate vicinage are noted in the annals of Literature for the number and estimation of authors, printers, and publishers who have been located here, in addition to those already named. Amongst these may be specified John McCreery, an eminent printer, who had distinguished himself at Liverpool by writing and publishing a poem, called "The Press." This was reprinted and a second part added, on his settling in the metropolis. He was strongly recommended to the London publishers by Mr. Roscoe. In his employ were Ralph Rylance and John Nightingale, two young men, who were afterwards engaged in writing and editing several literary works for London publishers. Three volumes on "London," part of "The Beauties of England," were compiled by the latter, in a very heedless manner. He was author of two octavo volumes, "Portraitures of Methodism" and of "Catholicism." His friend and associate, Rylance, was a learned, diligent, and trustworthy author, and was much employed by the house of Longman and Co. in translations, preparing the manuscripts of inexperienced authors for the press and on miscellaneous literature. He was a most worthy and honourable man. He became deranged in intellect and died in the prime of life, respected by all who knew him.

Benjamin Martin, an optician and author already referred to, had a shop and lived many years in this street. The long list of his publications— more than sixty volumes, all of which were eminently useful, and many of them popular, specified in Watts's "Bibliotheca Britannica"—show that he must have been industrious and scientific; but also prove how fleeting and evanescent is literary fame.

John Major lived on the south side of Fleet Street, for some years, having removed from No. 71, Great Russell Street, Bloomsbury. He was much respected by a numerous circle of book-lovers and book-buyers, and particularly by the followers and disciples of Isaac Walton: by artists, poets, and the friends of the three. A poet, himself, and fond of books, not only as articles to impart good counsel, and the most disinterested and wholesome advice, he was constantly in their company. His shop was well stocked with some of the choicest, and he successively published, with useful and discriminating notation and fine embellishments, "Walton and Cotton on Angling;" the "Physiognomical Portraits," 100 heads beautifully engraved with Biographical Sketches, 2 vols. large 8vo., and large 4to. 1824; "Robinson Crusoe," designs by Stothard; "Hogarth Moralized," by the Rev. Dr. Mavor; Walpole's "Anecdotes of Painting," in 5 vols. imp. 8vo., 1835; "The Cabinet Gallery of Pictures," with Critical Dissertations by Allan Cunningham, 2 vols. imp. 8vo., 1833. This interesting publication contains 72 prints, and a series of essays on the respective subjects and their authors, by one of the most honest and discriminating writers on such matters.

Walpole's "Anecdotes," from the manuscript collections of Virtue, was a work in much estimation by readers in the fine arts, for some time after its publication; but thence to the time Major produced his new edition, there were various sources opened, and further information easily obtainable, for correcting and greatly enlarging the book. Had Major engaged Allan Cunningham instead of the Rev. James Dallaway, he would have benefited himself and have satisfied his critical customers. But, alas! this was not the case: an unsatisfactory and erroneous book was produced, though lavishly embellished with 150 prints of portraits, &c., also good paper and printing. Some of the portraits were skillfully engraved by Robinson, Scriven, Worthington, and Finden. From printing too many copies, a large remainder was sold off after the bankruptcy of its publisher, and Mr. Bohn disposed of them at the reduced prices of £4 for the small, and five guineas the large paper, with India proofs; instead of ten guineas for the former, and fifteen for the latter.

Some of these publications obtained the unqualified encomiums of the Rev. Dr. T. F. Dibdin, in his "Reminiscences of a Literary Life," 1836; but it was unfortunate for the honest bookseller to be too familiar and confiding in the unprincipled parson. The former accepted bills to a large amount drawn by the latter, who failed to honour them, and the consequence was bankruptcy and total ruin. Major sunk never to rise again: for his mind became deranged, and he was placed under restraint. Recovering, in some measure, he was released from the asylum, and found a retreat and comparative comfort in the Charter-house, London, where three other respectable booksellers were then sheltered and maintained in old age.

Mr. Kearsley, of the same street, published the "English Review;" also the "English Encyclopædia," in several quarto volumes: the last publication possessed considerable merit. He also produced many other works, which became exceedingly popular and profitable—the "Beauties" of different authors. Those of Sterne, Johnson, Shakspeare; of the Spectator, Tatler, and Rambler, and other periodicals, were selling for many years, and reprinted in several editions. These, with Adams's "Flowers of Ancient and Modern History," "Flowers of Modern Travels," "English Parnassus," "Curious Thoughts on the History of Man," constituted a large portion of my early library. I have now before me "the eleventh edition" of Sterne's "Beauties," 1790.

In Fleet Street originated "The Quarterly Review," which was commenced in February, 1809, by John Murray. This gentleman, in a respectable line of business, evidently possessed strong religious and political opinions, and was annoyed at the popularity and signal effects which the "Edinburgh Review" was producing in the republic of literature. To oppose, and endeavour to counteract its "virus," as called by Mr. Canning, he addressed a letter to that gentleman,—then Chancellor of the Exchequer,—suggesting and urging the necessity of printing a periodical, the joint production of some of the most eminent Tories of the time, in opposition to the famed "Northern Review." He tells Mr. Canning that "he is no adventurer, but a man of some property, inheriting a business that has been established for nearly a century." This led to a correspondence, and to communications with William Gifford, Walter Scott, George Ellis, Hookham Frere, George Rose, Robert Southey, and some others of name and note, and very speedily to the publication of the first number. The high and rancorous spirit of Tory party, which then prevailed, thus obtained a dauntless champion, who has combated vigorously and intrepidly four times in the year up to the present age of peace, and a comparative truce

in the war-fields of politics. Both reviews have
produced decided and important effects on the literature and politics of the country; and it cannot
fail to interest and instruct the lover of books to
look over and compare the early writings in these
periodicals with the "Monthly," the "Critical," the
"Anti-jacobin," and other "Reviews" which had
long occupied the critical market. Mr. Murray
removed from Fleet Street to Albemarle Street
in 1812, to premises that had been occupied by
William Miller, who had published some fine and
expensive books. Amongst these were Forster's
"British Gallery of Engravings," folio; Blome-
field's "History, &c., of Norfolk," 10 vols. 4to. and
imp. 8vo.; "The Itinerary of Archbishop Baldwin
through Wales," 2 vols. 4to. 1806. The last work
is peculiarly impressed on my mind, by a circumstance which gave me much annoyance at the
time of its publication. Mr. Miller, knowing that
I was acquainted with many book collectors and
antiquaries tempted me to subscribe for six
copies, by allowing a discount of thirty per cent.
under the publishing price, and payment by bill
at three months after delivery. This induced me
to speculate: I gave the bill, and was prepared to
pay on the day it became due. The banker's clerk,
however, failed to present it, and on the next day

I had a notice that the bill was at a banker's, and there was 3s. 6d. due for noting the same. Unacquainted with bill transactions, but sensitive to everything that might impeach my credit, I hastened to Albemarle Street and paid the money, explaining that I had remained at home all the preceding day. The clerk's excuse was that Burton Street was too far out of town, and he had not time.

Mr. Murray became popular, successful, and much respected, not only by some of the most talented and eminent authors of his time, but by many of the nobility. His liberality to the literati, his tact in business and general information, were frequently exhibited in his correspondence with the parties above named, and many other distinguished writers. At the social and friendly board, both at home and abroad, he manifested engaging conversational powers; and it has been my good fortune to have been repeatedly amused and informed by him, in company with some of the bright literary planets which have appeared in, but have left, our hemisphere. In my library I often refer to some of those beautiful and valuable books which he has published, and honoured me with as presents.

At No. 55, Fleet Street, William Hone had a

small shop, in 1815, where he published "The Traveller," a newspaper; also "The Life of Elizabeth Fenning," who was hung for attempting to poison an idiot, though Hone's account of her life shows she was guiltless of the act. At this house appeared the first of his famed political pamphlets, which was graphically and effectively illustrated by his young and talented friend, the now eminent literary artist, George Cruikshank. Of this most witty, poignant, morally satiric and talented artist, an interesting biographical essay has been preserved in "The London Journal," November 20th, 1847, from the fluent and discriminating pen of Dr. R. Shelton Mackenzie, with a clever woodcut portrait. This paper not only shows the reader the peculiar graphic merits of the highly-gifted artist, but gives a vivid review of the political and moral character of the age in which he lived and worked, and points out the merits and demerits of some of the most prominent actors on the stage. Hone and Cruikshank continued in association for many years, and had the bookseller fully profited by the counsels of the artist, he might have escaped State prosecutions, become a respectable and successful tradesman, and have lived to witness his friend's pre-eminence. Though they often differed in opinions on religious and even political subjects, they remained in friendly attachment during the chequered life of Hone. I have often wished that the artist had given to the world a graphic and literary review of his own career and connections, and still hope he may be incited to execute it; for his pen and pencil are competent to produce one or two volumes of surpassing and unparalleled interest.

Hone very soon moved from Fleet Street to the Old Bailey, where, in conjunction with Cruikshank, he produced successively and successfully "The Political House that Jack Built," "A Slap at Slop," and three "Parodies on the Book of Common Prayer." The first of these publications became so popular, that more than fifty editions were published, as appears by a volume now before me, entitled "Hone's Popular Political Tracts: containing The House that Jack Built; Queen's Matrimonial Ladder; Right Divine of Kings to Govern Wrong; Political Showman; Man in the Moon; The Queen's Form of Prayer; A Slap at Slop," 8vo. with numerous cuts, for William Hone, 1820. The last pamphlet was a smart and smarting attack on Dr. Stoddart, and his daily paper, called "The New Times." But Hone's Parodies were the most noted, and the most successful in their results, though productive of cruel and vindictive persecution and prosecution to the author. For printing and publishing these, three several indictments for libels were tried against him, in the Court of King's Bench, on the 19th, 20th, and 21st of December, 1817. Justice Abbott presided on the first, and Lord Ellenborough on the second and third days. The strong political prejudices of the latter judge were well known, and became apparent on the trials; but Hone conducted his own defence, with a firmness, fortitude, and talent which astonished both his friends and foes. His addresses to the jury, as stated in a note in the printed report of the trials, lasted, "on the first day, six hours, on the second, seven, and on the third, upwards of eight hours;" yet he was in a bad state of health, oppressed and depressed, and manifested much physical exhaustion. Still he was clear, close, resolute, and self-confident, and was listened to with intense interest by the court, but with evident signs of mortification by the judge. The result was an acquittal upon each indictment. Rarely have there been criminal trials which excited more popular sympathy and curiosity during their progress, or more general rejoicing in their termination. The accused returned to his home in triumph, and a large public subscription was raised on his behalf. He had removed from his small shop in the Old Bailey to a large and expensive house on Ludgate Hill. Here he was followed, caressed, and praised by a succession of visitors—real, or affected friends,—amongst whom were some of the most popular members of opposition in the two Houses. A sum of nearly £4,000 was raised for him by voluntary subscription. With such a vast fortune, to him, and living and faring sumptuously every day, he had neither time nor incentive to write, or attend to shop business. The consequence was natural. The down-hill road from affluence to poverty is often travelled with special-train velocity, and terminates in the "slough of despond." Such was the case with our once-fortunate, but many times unfortunate, political and poetical hero; for a short time his affairs were involved in the labyrinth of bank-ruptcy; and ruin, irretrieveable ruin, ensued, from which he never became released. In February, 1834, he appealed to the Literary Fund for aid, when he intreated my intercession in his behalf, in a letter, wherein he says: "I am too much en-feebled to move about, and my family is in great distress, and I am worried out by little claims upon me, and have not a shilling." The Commit-tee of that noble institution inquired into his case and character, and finding the first to be urgent, and the second to be more "sinned against than sinning," awarded him a handsome grant. I knew him well, and respected him for warmth of heart, kindness of disposition, and strength of head; but he was most improvident and indiscreet in the management of money affairs. Had these been placed in the charge of an honest, good accountant, William Hone might have lived to be a rich man, and died a happy one. His later publications were useful and valuable, as calculated to combine amusing with good historical, topographical, and antiquarian information. They were "The Every-Day Book," "The Year Book," "The Table Book," and "Ancient Mysteries." Never, perhaps, was political and personal satire, irony, ridicule, burlesque, caricature, sarcasm, and unflinching temerity of language and graphic representation carried to such a pitch as in his once-popular pamphlets, which, with the exalted and illustrious personages represented and ridiculed, are now scarcely to be descried in the haze of distance. Had there not been gross delinquency and bad conduct in the parties satirized, and also palpable originality and talent in the author and the artist, these publications would not have attained their surprising and unprecedented popularity.

The Poets' Gallery, 192, Fleet Street, was a place of much distinction at the end of the last century and beginning of the present. Thomas Macklin, its proprietor, was a publisher and print-seller, and besides using the Gallery for temporary exhibitions, continued to keep on view a succession of works of art; amongst which was the popular picture of "The Woodman," by Thomas Barker, of Bath. Many of these were painted by the most eminent English artists for the splendid "Bible," which he published. This was produced in rivalry of Boydell's magnificent "Shakspeare" and Bowyer's "England." These contemporary publications surpassed all literary works either of this or any other country; as comprising and displaying the finest examples of paper and typography, with the highest specimens of the fine arts of England. Herein Bowyer, Boydell, and Macklin did more to benefit art, and the sciences connected with printing, than had ever before been done, or perhaps will be effected, by any triumvirate of tradesmen. Macklin died at the early age of 43, in Oct. 1800. The Gallery has since been occupied as an auction-room.

The old-established bookselling firm of Benjamin and John White, at No. 63, Fleet Street, was amongst the most respectable of the class in Lon-

don fifty years ago. Its stock was large and of
the best books. They published some fine works
in Natural History; amongst which were those of
Pennant, Latham, and White, of Selborne. The
last was a relation to the booksellers, as acknowledged by John, who edited the collected edition
of his works in 2 vols. 8vo. 1802, in which is a very
brief notice of that most amusing and amiable author. The last of the Whites of Fleet Street joined
in partnership with J. G. Cochrane.

The once-noted and eminently-notorious William Cobbett issued many of his remarkable
"Weekly Registers" from an office in this street,
and, for several years afterwards, from his printing establishment in Bolt Court, where most of his
voluminous publications on history, politics, travels, grammar, &c., were produced. In the annals
of the human race, and particularly amongst its
remarkable men, Cobbett appears conspicuous, if
not pre-eminent. Emerging from the humblest of
peasant society, without education, and struggling
against many difficulties and privations, he advanced himself to high political and national distinction, obtaining a seat in the British Parliament,
and writing several volumes, which secured great
celebrity for some years, and which will be read
with surprise and gratification in future ages. His

works are numerous, very voluminous, and on various subjects. Amongst them is a copious, and apparently very candid Auto-Biography, which details a pretty faithful account of his public career and writings. But I would more particularly direct the young reader to "The Life of William Cobbett," a small thick volume in 18mo., of which the third edition appeared in 1835, extending to 422 pages. This is dedicated "To the Sons of William Cobbett," and contains apparently a fair, discriminating account of the man, the author, and the politician. It also reprints the opinions and criticisms of Wm. Hazlitt, Gifford in the "Standard," and others from the "Morning Chronicle," the "Times," and the "Atlas." Charles Knight has recorded his opinions and remarks on Cobbett, in the "History of England during the Thirty Years' Peace," vol. i. p. 48.

At 186, Fleet Street, was the shop of the Eton School Books, for many years conducted by Edward Williams, grandson of Joseph Pote, the historian of Windsor. He was one of the Court Assistants of the Stationers' Company for the last five or six years of his life, and proved himself an active and zealous member of that famed corporation. He was also active in the committee of the Literary Fund, and there, as well as in public and private life, manifested general benevolence, suavity of manners, true philanthropy, and those social, amiable traits of disposition, which conciliate all associates. Hence his company was generally courted. To a natural cheerfulness of temper he added the happy qualification of writing and singing songs, appropriate to times, persons, and places. In Jan. 1838, as he was walking in one of the streets of London, near the Haymarket, he fell on an ice slide, and received such serious injury as occasioned his speedy death. His eldest son, Edward Pote Williams, has succeeded him both in London and at Eton.

"The John Bull," weekly newspaper, has been printed and published at No. 40 Fleet Street, ever since its commencement in Dec. 1820. If not projected and edited at first by the celebrated Theodore Hook, it is generally known that he was intimately connected with it for many years, and that he wrote many of its highly poignant articles. Conservative and of high church principles, it has continued an unflinching course of advocating these two branches of the government, and to censure and ridicule all classes of society, and all departments of politicians of opposite opinions. The eminently witty, and as eminently reckless, editor soon rendered it popular and profitable to the proprietors, and to himself, by the severity of its political articles, and by the poignant wit and satire of its personal and literary essays. It is said that he derived at least £2000 a year from writings in this journal; at the same time he was in receipt of nearly as much more for novels, farces, &c.: yet he was often in debt and embarrassment. Never, perhaps, was there a man of such precocious and versatile talents. "As a wit, confessed without rival to shine," his company was courted, and he was incessantly flattered by princes, nobles, and the most noted in the world of fashion and of fame. As a writer of novels, farces, songs, and particularly in improvisation, he was, perhaps, unrivalled in the world of genius. Having been several times in his fascinating company, I can bear witness to these qualifications: when in contact and competition with the famed authors of "The Rejected Addresses," he seemed to shine with additional brilliancy. Yet this man, this accomplished wit and novelist, was imprisoned and degraded for disreputable neglect of his duties in a public government office, in which he was misplaced by political friends. His story and his leading characteristics are well described in the last volume of Knight's "Penny Cyclopædia."

"The Dispatch," of 139, Fleet Street, a weekly

newspaper diametrically opposed to the "John Bull," has continued to have a popular and prosperous career from 1818 to the present time. Besides a copious amount of political matter and general news, this journal has long been noted for its smart reviews of literary works, the fine arts, the drama, and the theatres. For some years my respected friend, Edward Dubois, contributed numerous witty articles on those subjects.

At No. 93 in this street, "The London Magazine" was published, by Taylor and Hessey, from Midsummer 1821 to the same month in 1825. It was edited by Mr. Taylor, who made the work highly popular, with the aid of such men as Henry Southern (now our Ambassador at Brazil), J. H. Reynolds, Thos. Hood, Chas. Lamb, the Rev. H. F. Cary, Allan Cunningham, Barry Cornwall, Charles Phillips, Horace Smith, Charles A. Elton, Thomas De Quincy, Wm. Hazlitt, Bernard Barton, J. Clare, the Rev. G. Croly, Hartley Coleridge, Dr. Bowring, Thomas Carlyle, and other similar writers. With such a phalanx of wits and literati (now nearly all dead), it is not surprising that this periodical was very popular. In 1827, these publishers sold the magazine to a new editor and proprietor. They published some works of older and eminent authors, under careful editorial superintendence, and embellished from clever designs by Hilton, who was then coming into notice, and who attained just honours as an artist of the higher class. Taylor and Hessey brought out several successful books by the amiable moral writers, Mrs. and Miss Jane Taylor, of Ongar (no relatives of the publisher), and also other works. They afterwards removed to Waterloo Place, and on the establishment of the London University, Mr. Taylor was appointed its bookseller, which induced him to settle in Upper Gower Street, where he has continued in co-operation with Mr. Walton to the present time. He is author of a well-written volume on the controverted and never-ending dispute as to the authorship of Junius's Letters, in which he endeavours to prove that Sir Philip Francis was the writer; but of which evidence I cannot admit the validity. In a learned volume, "The Emphatic New Testament," and other works on scriptural criticism, and in several pamphlets on currency, Mr. Taylor displays much erudition and acute logical argument.

Arthur Collins, called by Watt ("Bib. Brit.") "the laborious antiquary and heraldic writer," who was editor and publisher, if not author, of the first edition of the English Peerage, in 1700, then lived at the Black Boy, in Fleet Street. Edward Curll

published several books "at the Dial and Bible, St.
Dunstan's Church." Bernard Lintot was living
here at the beginning of the last century; and the
amiable Izaak Walton was a denizen of this dis-
trict. The first edition of his "Angler" was published in 1653, in St. Dunstan's Churchyard, price
1s. 6d.—(A copy sold at Haworth's sale for thir-
teen guineas.)

Michael Drayton, the poet, died in a house
near Saint Dunstan's Church, according to Aubrey
The same authority tells us that Cowley, the more
voluminous author, was the son of a grocer in this
street. T. Snelling, who drew, engraved, and
published numerous plates on English Coins, had
a shop in this street, where he dealt in those, in
medals, &c.

Branching off from Fleet Street, to the south, is
Bouverie Street, at the bottom of which my once
much-esteemed and confidential friend, James
Moyes, built large premises for a printing establishment, after the destruction, by fire, of his former offices in Greville Street. Here he produced
numerous literary works for different publishers,
also some for private friends, and was in an extended and respectable way of business, when the
severe commercial panic of 1826 involved him,
with several of his friends, in bankruptcy. The

shock was much more severe to his susceptible nerves, and high sense of honor, than the former calamity. His mental and corporeal faculties seemed paralyzed for some weeks, and his friends were alarmed; but rallying, and aided by a few gentlemen who knew his integrity of principle and moral worth, he took new premises in Castle Street, Leicester Square, where he progressively obtained a large amount of business, and was prosperous and happy, until death arrested his career in 1838, at the age of 59. He was interred in a vault in the cemetery of Kensal Green, where a marble slab is placed to his memory. Intimately acquainted with this honourable tradesman for a quarter of a century, I can conscientiously assert that he fully deserved the encomium Pope applies to "the noblest work of God"—an honest man. I never knew a person more widely and uniformly esteemed. In business, he actively and zealously endeavoured to secure the confidence and good opinion of every employer; and, I believe, was always successful. As a man, he was well informed, upright, kind-hearted ,and generous both in word and deed, and as completely exempt from the infirmities of poor human nature as any of his species. With such qualities, and a thorough knowledge of business, he must have attained a good fortune in a few years.

He printed different literary works for me, entirely to my satisfaction and to his own credit. Besides being employed by many respectable publishers, he printed "The Literary Gazette" and "Fraser's Magazine" for many years; also several successive volumes of "The Gems of Beauty," "Friendship's Offering," and other works, under the editorship of Lady Blessington. He also worked for the "Admiralty" and for other public offices; and produced two handsome and beautifully printed books for J. H. Wiffin, of "Jerusalem Delivered," and "Historical Memoirs of the House of Russell," in two vols. royal octavo. This led to a connection with John, Duke of Bedford, for whom Mr. Moyes printed different works, on the pictures, statues, grasses, ferns, &c., at Woburn Abbey. I have now before me letters from this truly generous nobleman, also from Lady Blessington, Mr. Wiffin, and others, expressing approbation of his works, and thanking him for skill and kind attentions. Though I have been acquainted with several Quakers, I never met with one who was more sincere, candid, warm-hearted, and unsophisticated than Mr. Wiffin. He united with these qualifications the susceptibility of the poet with the perseverance and discrimination of the faithful historian. His "Memoirs of the House of Russell," which were printed by Mr. Moyes in 1832, will justify these remarks, and will derive further confirmation by his translation of Tasso's "Jerusalem Delivered," with a series of beautifully-executed engravings in wood, also in two smaller volumes. He produced a volume of Miscellaneous Poems, under the title of "Aonian Hours," and other poetry. Mr. Wiffin was Librarian to John, Duke of Bedford, in which honourable office he died, in May 1836, in the prime of life, much beloved by all who knew him. A well-written account of his personal and literary character is preserved in the "Literary Gazette," May 1836. He has been succeeded by John Martin, formerly in partnership with Mr. Rodwell, of Bond Street, and who, in 1834, published "A Bibliographical Catalogue of Privately-printed Books," a handsome and curious volume.

In Bolt Court was the printing-office of Thomas Bensley, which attained marked distinction at the end of the last century and beginning of the present. It was here that Mr. Konig's printing machinery was first employed, and advanced towards perfection; and from this office issued, in 1797, a magnificent royal folio edition of Thomson's "Seasons." Here also were printed Macklin's Bible and many other fine books; likewise my (Britton's) fourth volume of "Architectural Antiquities," and the "History of Redcliffe Church." These premises, like too many other printing-offices of London, suffered by fire: first, on the fifth of November, 1807, when they were much damaged, with several works, by a fire supposed to have been occasioned by careless boys. Again, June 1819, the whole, with their valuable contents, were consumed in or materially injured by another conflagration.

"Red Lion Passage," at the end of the last century and beginning of the present, was familiar to a large class of readers of the "Gentleman's Magazine," and to every topographer and antiquary in England, by the spacious printing-office of John Nichols; and the many publications issuing therefrom. This veteran, respectable, and truly valuable periodical ("Gentleman's Magazine") has continued its monthly course from 1731 to the present time; and it is a singular part of its history that it was commenced by a journeyman printer, and for ninety-six years was continued under the editorship of three. In accordance with the spirit of the times, this venerable journal has now all the freshness, vigour, beauty and interest, which good writing, paper, and typography can impart. I was indulged by my venerated and kind friend, the "Deputy of Farringdon Ward," with the use of any books in his valuable topographical library, but none were to be taken away; for he justly remarked, these were his working-tools almost in daily demand. I found them invaluable to me at a time when my own stock was very small— when the reading-room of the British Museum was not easily accessible, and when I had engaged to write and print "The Beauties of Wiltshire;" and also, in conjunction with my literary coadjutor, Mr. Brayley, "Topographical Accounts of Bedfordshire, Berkshire, and Buckinghamshire," for the first volume of "The Beauties of England." This courtesy, however, proved of great benefit, as was also the personal intercourse and converse with the author of the "History of Leicestershire," in eight folio volumes, his valuable "Literary Anecdotes," in nine volumes, with two of indexes, and of other similar works. Here I occasionally saw Richard Gough, who was a frequent visitor; and here I also had glances of other eminent topographers and antiquaries, who employed the same respected printer and author. Some years afterwards, I was honoured and gratified by friendly intimacy with most of the personages to whom I then looked up with awful respect and admiration. They are all removed from this terrestrial sphere, but have left their names, and varied qualifications, indelibly recorded in the lasting pages of their respective publications. With Mr. Nichols, I continued on friendly terms from the end of the last century to the time of his death, Nov. 26, 1826. By a fall in Red Lion Passage, in January 1807, he fractured a thigh-bone, by which he was lamed for life; and in February of the following year he suffered severely from a calamitous fire, which destroyed his premises, and a large stock of paper, printed books, manuscripts, &c. At the time of my early communion with Mr. Nichols, his son John Bowyer, was taken into partnership, and continued so for nearly a quarter of a century. In such an office and its associations, it is not surprising that he became an antiquary and topographer as well as printer; and that his son, John Gough, should be one of the mose devoted, zealous, and learned amongst the present numerous class of archæologists.

A. J. Valpy, M.A., a son of the learned Dr. Valpy, of Reading School, after being a short time in Tooke's Court, removed to the more spacious offices vacated by Mr. Nichols, in which he executed, besides many other works, "The Delphin Classics," with the Variorum Notes. These extended to 141 volumes, which were charged 18s.

each, and in large paper, £1. 16s. He also printed, for different publishers, many other books, both in Greek and Latin, and not only employed some of the most learned compositors that could be obtained, but several scholars from the Universities, to read and correct the proof-sheets. Hence the Valpy office and press obtained high distinction in the learned world. Mr. Valpy retired from business in the prime of life, to enjoy "otium cum dignitate."

Nearly opposite to the printing-office last referred to was a small house occupied by Stephen Jones, a gentleman with whom I was on familiar terms for many years. He was Secretary to a Freemasons' lodge, and was occasionally employed by some of the publishers to edit and arrange miscellaneous papers, make indexes, &c. He first appeared, in 1791, as abridging Burke's "Reflections;" and two years afterwards his name was attached to an Abridgment of Ward's "Natural History," in 3 vols. In 1796 he produced "A Biographical Dictionary in Miniature," a copy of which he presented me, with his autograph: the first literary work' I had then received, though I can now enumerate more than sixty volumes. He produced several other publications, which are specified in Watt's "Bibliotheca Britannica," the last of which is "A Pronouncing Dictionary of the English Language," a large octavo volume. The third edition of the work, now before me, has the author's autograph, with the date of 1798. He also edited a new edition of the "Biographia Dramatica:" this was harshly criticised, when he published a pamphlet, entitled "Hypercriticism Exposed, in a Letter to the Readers of the Quarterly Review," 8vo. 1812.

Towards the end of his life, my respected friend, a man of mild disposition, strict honesty, great industry, and unblemished character, was embarrassed in circumstances, applied to, and derived pecuniary aid from, the Literary Fund. Dr. N. Drake, in a letter to Cadell and Davies, respecting his large work, "Shakspeare and His Times," says, "S. Jones was the compositor to my Essays on Periodical Literature, and I was perfectly satisfied with his accuracy and attention;" whence he strongly recommended him to those publishers to make the index to his two quarto volumes. It extends to six quarto sheets.

In New Street and New Street Square are the large and famed printing-offices of Strahan, "the King's Printer," who obtained great wealth, and at whose presses an immense number of books have been printed. Among these was the "Cyclopædia," edited by my early and much-loved friend, Dr. A. Rees, and for which I wrote many a colse-ly-packed page. Besides accounts of nearly all the cities, towns, and counties of England, Wales, and Scotland, I wrote separate articles on Avebury and Stonehenge, with illustrative prints, and a memoir of Shakspeare. With copy and proofs I had fre-quent communication with one of the offices, for there were several, and witnessed the order, dis-cipline, and admirable system which prevailed. The liberality and riches of Andrew Strahan, Esq., who died in August 1831, render his name illus-trious in the annals of man. In 1822, he presented £1000 to the Literary Fund, and bequeathed a similar sum after his decease, in the year 1831. He also gave other large sums to different charita-ble societies. He died, in the 83rd year of his age, at the house in New Street, leaving property to the amount of above one million of money; and pre-sented his great printing establishment to his nephew, Andrew Spottiswoode, who married one of the daughters of Mr. T. N. Longman, of Pater-noster Row.

In Chancery Lane, north of Fleet Street, was a shop which William Pickering gave name and note to by publishing many valuable volumes un-der the titles of "Aldine Edition of the Poets;"

"Walton and Cotton's Angler," and other books on the subject; Richardson's Dictionaries of the English Language; Greek, Latin, Italian, and Diamond Classics; and several works on Ecclesiastical, Biblical, and Polemical History; on Anglo-Saxon and Anglo-Norman Literature; "Small Books on Great Subjects, by Well-Wishers to Knowledge;" and last, though not least in merit and popularity, the novel, unique, and original "Bridgewater Treatises," in 12 volumes. These were by Sir Charles Bell, on the "Hand;" the Rev. William Buckland, D.D., on "Geology and Mineralogy;" the Rev. Thomas Chalmers, D.D., on the "Moral and Intellectual Constitution of Man;" John Kidd, M. D., on the "Physical Condition of Man;" the Rev. William Kirby, on the "History, Habits, and Instincts of Animals;" William Prout, M. D., on "Chemistry, Meteorology, and the Function of Digestion;" P. M. Roget, M. D., on "Animal and Vegetable Physiology;" and the Rev. W. Whewell, on "Astronomy and General Physics."

These Essays were written by the respective learned authors, in compliance with a bequest of Francis Henry, Earl of Bridgewater, in February 1829, of £8000. to be paid for eight Treatises "On the Power, Wisdom, and Goodness of God, as

manifested in the Creation." Never, perhaps, in
the annals of the human race, and of testamentary
generosity and rightful application, was a legacy
more wisely and laudably given. It was Mr. Pickering's good fortune to be selected as the publisher
of the series, whence his house and character were
prominently brought under the notice of the reading world. In 1843 he removed to 177, Piccadilly,
where may be seen a house full of rare and valuable books, and where may be obtained many of
those he had printed and published, under the editorial care, learning, and ability of Sir Harris
Nicolas, Basil Montagu, the Rev. W. L. Bowles,
S. W. Singer, the Rev. Alexander Dyce, the Rev.
J. Mitford, J. H. Marsden, Thomas Wright, Robert Roscoe, George Daniel, W. Tooke, the Rev.
Dr. T. F. Dibdin, and many other authors of eminence.

Let us look at a "Pen and Ink Sketch" of Mr.
Pickering by the last-named reverend gentleman,
in his own peculiar style of touch and effect. "How
does Mr. Pickering this morning? and where are
the Caxtons, and Wynkyns, and Pynsons—his Al-
duses, Elzevirs, and Michel Le Noirs? But Mr.
Pickering has a note of louder triumph to sound,
in being publisher of the 'Bridgewater Treatises,'
which bid fair to traverse the whole civilized portion of the globe."—(Reminiscences, p. 904.)

122

From Chancery Lane to High Holborn is a
mere step, and there, at No. 59, is a house, which
was built by Josiah Taylor, the Architectural
Bookseller, with whom I (Britton) became acquainted at the early part of my literary career,
and with whom I fortunately continued on intimate terms to the time of his lamented death, January, 1834. In 1805, I showed him some drawings
of ancient buildings which Mr. Hood thought were
not calculated to adorn the pages, and come under
the title, of "The Beauties of England." After a
little consultation and deliberation, it was agreed
to publish a new quarto work, entitled "The Architectural Antiquities of Great Britain." A plan was
digested, a prospectus was written, Longman and
Co. engaged to take a third share in the work,
and be the publishers. Hence originated a publication, which not only extended to five quarto
volumes, and brought before the public 360 engravings, representing a great variety of old buildings of the country, but many of historical, descriptive, and critical essays. These were not by
my own pen only, but by those of several gentlemen, who thus laid before the reading world much
original and interesting information. This work,
indeed, gave origin to a new school of artists, both
draftsmen and engravers, and to many competing

and rival publications. It obtained great popularity, and was consequently profitable to the publishers and to the author. Had the latter been a little more the man of business, and more anxious to obtain wealth than fame, he might have been enabled to retire from the labours and anxieties of authorship at the age of eighty, with competence to provide all the comforts, and even some of the luxuries of life. His chief solicitude and ambition, throughtout the whole extent of that and other publications, have been to render them truthful, original, correct, and replete with the best artistic illustrations and literary information which he could obtain and impart to the reader. His partners were confiding and kind, upon most occasions; and Mr. Taylor evinced his friendship by a posthumous bequest. Mr. O. Rees· proved himself a warm and even affectionate friend throughout life.

Mr. Taylor was a punctilious, preservering, and honourable man of business, and confined his attention, and publications almost exclusively to those devoted to architecture and engineering. Hence he became acquainted with most of the professional gentlemen of the kingdom, published for many of them, and was connected in business with nearly all. Thus we find that his catalogue of works

contains the following amongst other names: Stuart and Revett, Soane, Malton, G. Richardson, Peter Nicholson, Lugars, Gwilt, Pocock,
Dearn, Gandy, Aikin, Plaw; and the following on
"Gothic Architecture," the Rev. G. D. Whittington,
the Rev. J. Milner, the Rev. James Dallaway, the
Rev. Joseph Warton, James Bentham, Captain
Grose, the Rev. J. Gunn, the Rev. George Millers,
and J. S. Hawkins. The Essays, by Milner, Warton, Bentham, and Grose, were published by Mr.
Taylor in a separate volume, which went through
three editions.

Towards the latter part of his life he purchased
a good house at Stockwell, where he was in the
habit of assembling frequently a succession of
friends around his social board; and there I have
often met, and enjoyed the converse of, some of
the most eminent architects and engineers of London. On those occasions it was his practice to
send a carriage to and from London to convey
two, three, or four gentlemen who did not keep
carriages. In the year 1822 the house and shop,
in Holborn, with their contents, were consumed
by an accidental fire, whereby I sustained a considerable loss. Mr. Taylor died at the age of 73,
in the year 1834, and was buried in Bunhill Fields
cemetery.

"Readings and Music" were popular sources of amusement in London, about fifty years back; and I not only exhibited myself at the place described, but at a large room in Foster Lane, in another at the Globe, Fleet Street, and, lastly, in two others at the Freemasons' Hall, and in the Argyle Rooms. These societies assumed pompous Greek names—"Museodeans," and "Odechorologeans,"—with parade and much etiquette, in aping the operatic customs and manners of theatric and ball-room concerts. The large rooms at both places were crowded with company, every night of performing; and amongst the performers were Miss Brunton, Miss F. Kelly, Miss S. Booth, Miss Bolton, &c.

Part III.

THE STRAND, PALL MALL,
KING STREET.

Part III.

THE STRAND, PALL MALL, KING STREET.

The Strand at the beginning of the Century—Thomas Cadell—The Newspaper Press—George Lane—D. Stuart—John Bell—Rudolph Ackermann and his publications—F. Shoberl, Author and Editor—Annuals—„Dr. Syntax"—Combe—Rowlandson—John and Leigh Hunt—The Literary Gazette—Richardson's Auctions—Geographers—Prince Sanders — Lyceum Theatre—Auctioneers—The Sothebys—Evans—The Christies' Sale-Rooms—Pall Mall—King Street—Covent Garden—Hogarth's Election — P. Luckombe—King and Lochee's Auction Rooms ; their book-sales.

THE STRAND, at the end of the last century and beginning of the present, when a much narrower street than it is now, and when Exeter 'Change occupied a large area of the road-way between the present Lyceum Theatre and Exeter Street, contained several booksellers and publishers of distinction. Amongst these was the house of Alderman Thomas Cadell, which occupied the site of old Jacob Tonson's (the Shakspeare Head).

Andrew Miller, a friend of Thomson, Fielding, Hume, Robertson, was the master of Alderman Cadell.

At the period to which my notes chiefly relate, Alderman Thomas Cadell was living in the Strand, and I had the pleasure of being occasionally in his society. He resigned the business to his Son and to William Davies, jointly, who long traded under the well-known firm of "Cadell and Davies." The Alderman was accustomed to say that he was chiefly indebted for his prosperity to the works of four "Bees,' alluding to four popular publications: "Blair's Sermons," "Blackstone's Commentaries," "Burn's Justice of the Peace," and "Buchan's Domestic Medicine." Johnson's "Dictionary," and Hume and Smollett's "History of England," were also amongst the valuable copyrights belonging to this firm. In reference to the two publications last-mentioned, this establishment, in conjunction with Longman and Co., who were part proprietors with them in those and other works, had to encounter a vigorous opposition from other booksellers when the copyrights expired; but their operations were so judiciously and promptly conducted that they effectually maintained their ground. The "Dictionary" had been published in two costly volumes, folio; and when the copyright was about to expire, an edition in one folio volume was prepared, with great secrecy, by a bookseller in Paternoster Row. The proprietors of the book hearing of that scheme, prepared an edition in two quarto volumes, which, being of a more commodious form, at once became a popular work, and obtained a rapid sale: whereas the rival undertaking involved the speculator in a serious loss. The quarto edition, being published at £5. 5s., produced a considerable profit to the shareholders, who were proportionably tenacious of maintaining its integrity. One of them, however, the managing partner, happening to say vauntingly in the presence of Mr. Childs, an energetic printer at Bungay, that the partners would ruin any one who set up a rival edition, he forthwith stereotyped and reprinted the entire work in a single volume, imperial 8vo. (now currently sold for 18s.) and employing that indefatigable and unscrupulous agent, the late John Ogle Robinson, (formerly of the firm Robinson, Hurst, and Co.) a large and remunerative sale was speedily obtained, and the quarto was consequently much depreciated.

The standard octavo edition of the "History of England" was issued by Cadell and the Longmans, in anticipation of opposition, in periodical numbers, embellished with portraits. Both Cooke and Parsons, nevertheless, entertained the project of duodecimo editions, without prints; but the proprietors forestalled them by a similar edition, with reduced copies of the engravings. The rival publishers proceeded, however, with their respective undertakings, and so great was the sale of the works, that each edition reimbursed its expenses. By a volume of "Autograph Letters and Papers," one of a series now before me, belonging to my friend, Mr. John Wodderspoon, I find that the above-named firm embarked a large capital, at great risk, on Dr. Drake's "Shakspeare and his Times;"Lyson s "Magna Britannica," and Samuels's "Britannia Romana;" G. Chalmers's "Caledonia;" Alexander Chalmers's "British Poets," 21 vols. royal 8vo.; Coxe's Works, (mostly written by Henry Hatcher) Dr. Clarke's Travels, and several other expensive publications. By memoranda amongst this correspondence, it is also evident that they acted with much courtesy and liberality to those authors. Dr. Drake was paid £800 for his two volumes; and in a statement of accounts it seems that the losses were above £900. The works by the Lysonses entailed a great loss on the respectable publishers. Hence we learn that, after their decease, a large stock of unsold books came into the market, and were dispersed at very low prices.

Near the middle part of the ever-crowded, noisy, tumultuous thoroughfare called the Strand, is the very focus—the hot-bed, the forcing-house—of the "Newspaper-Press," now emphatically called "The Fourth Estate." This literary manufactory and news-mart may be almost regarded as exemplifying the perpetual motion. From dawn to night, and thence to dawn again, here is a continued, never-ceasing succession of editors and sub-editors, reporters of various topics, correspondents from foreign states, and from the provinces, merchants and manufacturers, politicians and players, compositors, pressmen, and engineers; also crowds of news-vendors and letter-carriers, with carts and horses to convey loads of wet Papers to railway stations. Could an inquiring and acute foreigner see and appreciate the whole working of this complicated machine, he would marvel, and vainly attempt to give a full and vivid account of it to his distant friends and countrymen. During the sitting of Parliament, and when warmly-contested party questions are under discussion, the activity and excitement in this region are only to be compared to a hive of bees, at the time of swarming. Unlike the generality of London business, that of the News-press is generally conducted during the night, and whilst most people are reposing in bed. Hence we see the windows of the offices fully lighted up, and hear the continued rattle and noise of steam machines and presses in ceaseless operation. I cannot reflect on the comparative and contrasted state of the Newspaper-press, in its mechanical and literary characteristics, as it was at the beginning of the century, when I was occasionally admitted into the editor's "sanctum," and as it is now, when such important reforms have been produced in all departments of paper, type, ink, and particularly in machinery; but still more in the independence and integrity, the vigour and comprehensiveness of editorial writings, without feeling astonished and delighted. It is these improvements and powers which have conspired to gain for the English Press the political title above-named. To the late James Perry, John Walter, Thomas Barnes, and a few other talented and honest men, much of these effects are to be ascribed; and I indulge the hope that others of like powers may continue in the same ranks, and act as substantial checks against every species of tyranny and dishonesty in church and state, in law and commerce, and, indeed, in all gradations of civilized society.

At No. 15, back of St. Clement's, Strand, "The British Press" and "The Globe" first made their public appearance in 1803, "with new and high pretensions," and were ostensibly started by, and intended to promote the views and trading specu- lations of, the publishing booksellers. These had justly complained of the capricious charges made by the Newspaper proprietors for advertisements; and also for the heedless manner in which notices of fine and expensive literary publications were associated with vile and disgusting quack puffs. To remedy such evils, and obtain a medium be- tween themselves and the public, they procured premises, type, an editor, and the combined es- tablishment for conducting a newspaper. George Lane was engaged as editor, who had been on the "Morning Post," and the "Courier," under Daniel Stuart. This gentleman wrote an explanation of the dispute between the publishers and newspaper proprietors in the "Gentleman's Magazine" (Sept. 1838) to vindicate himself and his brothers of the periodical press, and impeach the former. Mr. George Lane, in the same magazine, published a reply and justification of the booksellers. Among the reforms and improvements which the present denizens of London have cause to rejoice in, when compared with their predecessors, who lived amidst and under numerous annoyances of savage warfare, may be specified the relief from ruthless gangs of street news-vendors, who infested the peaceable and nervous inhabitants with noises that surpassed bedlamites broke loose. Tin horns, of different calibre and sounds, mixed with yells and bawling of men and boys, in troops, who paraded the quiet streets proclaiming, "News! Great news! Bloody news! Armies slaughtered by thousands and tens of thousands:—'Currior'! Extraordinary 'Currior'!! Sixth edition of 'The Currior'!!! &c., &c."

By examining some early numbers of the "British Press," I cannot wonder that it failed to secure purchasers, and consequently did not answer the requirements of the speculators. Poor paper, bad printing, tasteless display, and inefficiency of editorship, are conspicuous. Mr. Lane acknowledged that "the actual sale did not exceed two hundred." The "British Press" proved a complete failure, and it was given up. The "Globe" was, however, continued, under new proprietary management, and is still among the diurnal journals.

John Bell, of the Strand.—Not only as an enterprising and spirited publisher, but as an author, this gentleman continued before the public many years, and brought forward a succession of literary and embellished works which gratified and gave profitable employ to numerous writers, artists, printers, stationers, &c. His "British Poets," "British Theatre," part of which includes the plays of Shakspeare; his "Weekly Messenger," commenced May, 1796; the "New Weekly Messenger," a paper of unprecedented quantity and varied literary matter, commenced in 1832; his "New Pantheon, or Historical Dictionary of Heathen Gods, Demi-Gods, Goddesses, &c.," which Lowndes calls "an excellent and useful compilation;" and his "Classical Arrangement of Fugitive Poetry," in 18 vols., were each and all variously popular, and calculated to gratify and improve the minds and taste of readers by their literary and graphic contents. In embellishments, he employed the best artists of the age, both for designs and for engravings. He also produced a monthly periodical called "La Belle Assemblée."

Rudolph Ackermann, from Germany, settled in the Strand, opposite old Exeter 'Change, at the latter part of the last century, as a Printseller; and by perseverance, industry, and skill in business, with some knowledge of art, progressively advanced himself and his establishment to the highest degree of prosperity and credit. When I first became acquainted with him, in 1800, his shop was small, and his first floor was let to my friend, George Holmes, an artist, who was induced by my suggestion to publish, in 1801, an octavo volume, "Sketches of a Tour through the South Part of Ireland.' The artist, though possessed of abilities and of very engaging manners, did not advance in life so fast as his landlord, who soon required and occupied the whole house, and increased his business, family, and fortune. He then moved to larger premises, at No. 101, Strand, which occupied part of the site of the old Fountain Tavern, celebrated in the days of Steele, Addison, Pope, &c. Here was also a famed drawing academy, in which Richard Cosway, F. Wheatley, Shipley, and others, afterwards men of fame, were pupils. The more noted lecture-room of John Thelwall present large and commodious "Repository," at the corner of Beaufort Buildings, from the designs of Mr. Papworth. This building occupies the site of five previous houses. The new edifice was provided with a fine and spacious gallery, at the rear, in which were constantly on view a vast number and variety of works of art. The architect also made many designs, and wrote essays for Ackermann's Magazine. The shop, the staircase, the gallery, &c., were not only lighted but brilliantly

illuminated by night, with gas, which was manu-
factured on the premises, from apparatus which
Mr. Ackermann had invented, and which was supplied with Canal, or Kennel coal, producing the
most vivid light. During the first winter, after
these works were completed, crowds of the nobility, gentry, and artists, were in the habit of visiting
the place every night, to see the splendid novelties. Once a week the proprietor opened his gal-
leries for a Soirée, where I often met many of the
most eminent artists and men of science of our
own and of foreign countries. Amongst numerous interesting articles displayed on these occasions was a copy of the spirited proprietor's work
on Westminster Abbey, printed on vellum and
bound in two large volumes; one containing the
letter-press, printed in Bensley's best manner, the
other comprising proofs of the plates and the original drawings, also skilfully mounted. The binding, of the most sumptuous kind, alone cost Mr.
Ackermann nearly three hundred pounds! This
very splendid work is now in the possession of
John Allnut, Esq., of Clapham, whose gallery of
pictures by English Artists not only reflects honour on his taste and liberality, but on his patriotism.

This article alone serves to give some notion

of the liberal and enterprising disposition of the amiable and estimable German, who manifested a corresponding liberality and enthusiasm in all his business speculations and intercourse with artists and literati. Mr. Shoberl tells me that he paid William Combe at least £400. a year for many successive years, and that he was often a guest at his table; that he proved a friend to him during his last illness, and not only contributed towards, but waited on several of his rich friends to solicit aid in the expenses for the funeral, tomb, &c.

To this improvident, indiscreet man, to T. Rowlandson, to W. H. Pyne, and to several other persons, he was the warm and generous patron. Indeed in all his public dealings, as well as in private life, he displayed generosity, courtesy, frankness, sincerity, and unostentatious benevolence. After the disastrous, murderous, and devasting wars of the French Revolution, the Germans were reduced to the most distressing condition. Poverty and privation pervaded their towns, their villages, and their entire provinces. The English, as usual, afforded many of the emigrants homes and sustenance. To Mr. Ackermann they were indebted for a vast amount of aid and comfort. He took a most active and zealous part in obtaining subscriptions and remitting money to his countrymen. No less than £250,000. were collected for the sufferers in Great Britain, £100,000. of which were voted by Parliament; and as a proof of the effective service of my friend on this occasion, he was rewarded and honoured by the King of Saxony with the Cross of Civil Merit; whilst the King of Prussia, and several of the reigning Dukes of Germany, presented him with handsome testimonials in token of his valuable services.

As Cicerone to Mr. Ackermann's Gallery, my friend, William Henry Pyne, was engaged, and in that capacity was respectably and profitably employed, both for himself and for his worthy master. The former had published, and progressively produced numerous works, both graphic and literary, in all of which, from partialities and experience, Pyne became eminently useful. Hence the artist and the printseller worked in harmony and unison for some years, and jointly completed several publications on the fine arts, topography, and poetry. Besides several lessons, elementary books and prints, for the instruction of young artists, they brought forward a large and expensive work, entitled "The Microcosm of London," 3 vols. royal 4to. with 120 illustrative prints. To Mr. Ackermann we are indebted for the introduction into England, and for effecting many improvements in the new art, of Lithography, by translating and giving publicity to Senefelder's Treatise on the subject; a work that excited much curiosity, speculation, and experiments among the artists. He also imported stones for that novel process, and by adapting presses and paper, and by the employment of competent artists to make drawings, progressively, but slowly, advanced lithography to distinction. The following lines were written by Mr. Combe on the first lithograph stone which Mr. Ackermann printed, when he had prepared everything for working:

" I have been told of one
Who, being ask'd for bread,
In its stead
Return'd a Stone:

" But here we manage better:
The Stone, we ask
To do its task,
And it returns us every letter.
" Wm. Combe, January 23, 1817."

He was the first publisher of a class of books, called "Annuals," by his "Forget-me-Not," which became exceedingly popular, and was a source of employ to numerous artists, authors, and different tradesmen. The "Forget-me-Not" was edited, from its commencement in 1823, to its last volume in 1834, by F. Shoberl, one of the most industrious, persevering, and honourable of the literary fraternity, who has been solely, or mostly, dependant on his profession for a livelihood. Watt, in "Bibliotheca Britannica," has given a long list of his publications, in translations from the French and German, original and compilations, from 1800 to 1814, since which year he has written a further and longer list of works: amongst others I perceive that his name is attached to the histories of the counties of Suffolk, Surrey, and Sussex, forming one of the volumes of "The Beauties of England."

A history of this literary family—"the Annuals" —would embrace much curious anecdote, biography, and exposition of art and artists; of professional and amateur authors; of trade, manufactures, and commerce; of fashion, fame, and frivolity; and last, though not the least, the fluctuation and caprices of taste and ton. The "Annuals," which were so popular and profitable to a Heath, and a Fisher, twenty years ago, are now superseded, and a totally different and new species has been introduced by Messrs. Longman and Co. and by Virtue; in which topography, history, travels, and substantial literature are the basis.

His large and handsome volumes, with illustrations, of Westminster Abbey, of Cambridge, Oxford, and of Public Schools, were amongst the most beautiful topographical works of their class, in paper, typography, and embellishments. The writing, though anonymous, was by William

Combe, one of the most extraordinary men of his age, and who ranks amongst the most prolific of authors.

Though I was never on intimate terms with this talented and eccentric person, I knew him personally by meeting him often at the houses of my friends, the Ackermanns, and James Lonsdale, portrait-painter of Berners Street. Combe was of good family connection, had received a classical education at Eton and Oxford, and very early came into the possession of a large fortune, in ready money. To dash at once into high life, and enact the fashionable gentleman, he (according to his own narration) took a large mansion at "the West End" of London, furnished and filled it with gorgeous articles, and also hired servants, bought carriages, &c., and successively assembled around him a crowd of sycophants and the "beau-monde." This comedy, or rather farce, lasted only for a short time, and it is said that from the commencement to the drop-scene of the ridiculous drama, was not more than one year. Though he fancied this gave him an insight into high life, it is quite evident that the company thus assembled, and thus held together, could only be of a class which ought to rank below the low—gamblers, swindlers, tricksters, imposters, &c. The consequence was

ruin—complete, disgraceful ruin, and Combe fled
from his creditors and from society. We next
hear of him as a common soldier, and recognized
at a public-house with a volume of Greek poetry in
his hand. He was relieved from this degrading
situation, and henceforward, for a long period,
the annals of his life have been pretty fully detailed. The walls of the King's Bench Prison,
and "the Rules" of that famed establishment, were
the limits and sphere of his locomotion; and from
his conduct, manners, and general deportment in
society, they do not appear to have proved causes
of much punishment or lamentation. Horace
Smith, in the Memoirs of his witty and much-ca-
ressed brother, James, says, that Colonel Greville,
with several of his friends, established a Pic-nic
club for theatrical amusements, &c., and published
a newspaper to vindicate their association from
severe strictures that appeared in the daily papers
against them. Our imprisoned hero was appointed the paid editor, and, to suit his peculiarity of situation, the weekly meetings of the writers of articles were held after dark. Horace Smith, who
knew Combe, justly remarks, that "a faithful biography of this singular character might justly be
entitled a romance of real life; so strange were the
adventures and the freaks of fortune of which he

had been a participator and a victim. A ready
writer of all-work for the booksellers, he passed all
the latter portion of his time within 'the Rules,' to
which suburban retreat the present writer was occasionally invited, and never left him without ad-
miring his various acquirements, and the philosophical equanimity with which he endured his re-
verses." Mr. Smith further asserts, that if there
was a lack of matter occasionally to fill up the columns of their paper, "Combe would sit down in
the publisher's back room and extemporize a letter from Sterne at Coxwold, a forgery so well executed that it never excited suspicion." I cannot
but regret that my witty friend had not favoured
us with more anecdotes of, and remarks on, the
character and literary talents of Combe; but I can
easily excuse him when I reflect on the supera-
bundance of material which his memory and his
memoranda must have afforded for the two amusing volumes he had planned of his brother's memorable "sayings and doings." Were I disposed to
dwell on the character of Combe, I could extend
the present description to several pages. He was
born in 1741, and died in June 1814. Subsequent
to his death, a small volume was published, entitled "Letters to Marianne," said to have been written by him after the age of seventy to a young

girl, and, according to the "Literary Gazette," are trivial, silly, puerile. However eventful and amusing may be the adventures and vicissitudes of such a man as Combe, if narrated by a Dickens, a Thackeray, or a Douglas Jerrold, I must resign the task to such vivid writers, or their followers, and merely refer to the "Gentleman's Magazine," for May 1852, for a communication from my friend, Mr. R. Cole, who has a large collection of Autograph Letters and Manuscripts, amongst which is a detailed list of the literary works of, and numerous letters from and to Combe.

The engravings of Westminster Abbey, of Cambridge, Oxford, and of the Public Schools were in aquatint, and coloured in imitation of the original drawings, by Mackenzie, Pugin, W. Westall, F. Nash, W. Turner, and others: many of them represent interior views of the principal public buildings. There are also prints of full-length portraits from drawings by T. Uwins, and etchings by J. Agar, representing the official costume of all the different orders of Officers of the Universities. Mr. Ackermann also brought out a Poetical Magazine, which became the parent of a race of novel publications of unprecedented notoriety. These were a sort of hybrid twins of poetry and art, in the illustrated, or rhyming, ram-

bling, ricketty, and ridiculous poems, "Dr. Syntax's Tour in Search of the Picturesque." The work
not only passed through several editions, of three
Tours, but extended to three volumes; and within
the last few years they have been again brought
before the public at reduced prices by Mr. H. G.
Bohn. "Dr. Syntax" was a lucky and large prize
in the lottery of publication, and was also a novelty
in origin and writing. Instead of the composition
and designs for the illustrations growing out of,
and serving to ornament and give tangible forms,
figures, colours, effects, &c., to the language and
imaginings of the poet, or other writer; the artist,
in the work referred to, preceded the author by
making a series of drawings; in each of which he
exhibited his hero in a succession of places, and
in various associations, calculated to exemplify his
hobby-horsical search for the picturesque. Some
of these drawings, by the versatile and ingenious
artist, Rowlandson, were shown at a dinner-party,
at John Bannister's, in Gower Street, when it was
agreed they should be recommended to Ackermann for publication. That gentleman readily purchased, and handed them by two or three at a
time to Combe, when the latter was in the King's
Bench. He fitted them with rhymes, and they
made their first appearance in the magazine allud-

ed to. Exciting much popularity, the publisher reproduced them in separate volumes, and found demand keep pace with his supply. Hence " Syntax " was succeeded by "The Dance of Life," "The Dance of Death," "Johnny Quæ Genus," and "Tom Raw the Griffin," all of the same class and character, and ultimately extending to two hundred and ninety-five prints, with annotatory poetical letter-press.

Without adverting further, in this place, to the periodical press and publishers, generally, I cannot forbear to notice two weekly journals which had their birth in this locality, and which have proved themselves resolute and powerful advocates of moral, political, and literary reforms: viz., "The Examiner," and the "Literary Gazette." The former was projected and undertaken by two enthusiastic young men, almost boys, John and Leigh Hunt, who thought patriotism and literature were the only thing worth living for; and believing themselves not only slighted, but oppressed by the rulers of the land, thought that it would be glorious, either to obtain emancipation, or suffer martyrdom in the attempt. They paid dearly for their rashness and courage, as may be seen fully set forth, with honest candour and truthfulness, by the latter, in his Auto-Biography, in 3 vols., published in 1850, to which work I can refer the reader, with an assurance that he will find much amusing as well as eloquent and exciting commentary on the popular events and persons of the half-century after the year 1800.

Amongst the literary persons of the present century, that voluminous author ranks in the first class. From boyhood (for he was a precocious poet), up to the present time (1853), his whole time and mental energies appear to have been employed in literature; and the amount, variety, and merits of his numerous published writings are at once manifestations of industry, enthusiasm, zeal, an ardent love of liberty, and of the better productions of genius and talent. His first volume, intituled "Juvenilia," was a series of poems written between the ages of twelve and sixteen. It appeared in the year 1801, when, I believe, he was in "The Blue-Coat School," and a contemporary with the two brilliant intellectual planets in the hemisphere of talent, Coleridge and Lamb. The times when his first volume made its public appearance, when its author sought the approval of critics and patrons, were rife with political excitement and contention. Party spirit was violent and rancorous; and every person who possessed warm feelings and thinking powers became imperceptibly a jacobin, or an anti-jacobin: i. e., a Reformer, or a Tory, opposed to all changes. Mr. Leigh Hunt and his brother John avowed themselves of the former class, and started their "Examiner," as a medium to promulgate their sentiments, and oppose both the opinions and principles of the other party.

The consequence was, State prosecutions and consequent heavy fines, as well as cruel imprisonment. Unintimidated and unflinching, they continued to publish the "Examiner," and also continued to occupy its weekly columns with severe and caustic writings on the malpractices of ministers, and on the vices and follies of those princes, nobles, and commoners, who lived and luxuriated on the revenues of the State.

One department of their paper was devoted to the "Fine Arts," the criticisms and comments on which were mostly written by Robert Hunt, brother of the two partners. Related to Benjamin West, the President of the Royal Academy, and having been educated as an artist, this gentleman rendered his critical articles popular and influential. He wrote two or three Essays for me, which appeared in "The Fine Arts of the English School;" and also produced others for different publications.

"The Literary Gazette," which made its first appearance on the 25th of January, 1817, has proved eminently serviceable in promoting the national literature, as well as its fine arts. It was at first the property of Mr. Colburn, an active and enterprising publisher, who possessed "The New Monthly Magazine," and other works of popularity, and who eagerly availed himself of every channel to attract the notice, and excite the curiosity, of readers. A new medium was found in this Gazette, which not merely professed to advocate, but to bring forward the better specimens of literature, and scout and expose its quackery. It is generally admitted that it was almost constantly kind, generous, and complimentary to young aspirants for fame—in authorship, art, and the drama. I cannot, however, forget, or palliate the severity it manifested towards a youthful Poet of real genius and equal modesty, who ventured to launch a small volume on the "sea of troubles," and which was assailed by the "Literary Gazette" in unqualified terms of reprobation. The principal poem was "Richmond Hill," a site calculated to arouse the most intense admiration in every lover of the fine and beautiful scenery of nature. In his verses on this fascinating prospect, I may safely assert that Charles Ellis evinced ardent feelings as well as genuine sympathies for the beauties of the scene, and also genuine, if not the highest, poetical powers to depict them.

The new periodical ultimately proved a large prize in the lottery of book-speculation, as it progressively rose high in the thermometer of fashion and fame. Its progress and fluctuating annals would afford abundance of interest to the general reader, were they fully and faithfully narrated. Mr. William Jerdan, who tells us in his Auto-Biography that he was its "sole editor and part-proprietor, from its commencement to August 14, 1841," has narrated many particulars of its contents, contributors, proprietors, and changes. To that work I must refer my reader, as well as for an account of the literary career and worldly vicissitudes of an old friend, with whom I have continued in occasional correspondence and personal intercourse for nearly forty years: I cannot, however, help deeply regretting to read his account of the profession of authorship; it being so much at variance with my own experience and opinions. These I have partly explained in the "The Rights of Literature," in "The Authorship of the Letters of Junius Elucidated," and in other parts of my numerous publications. On referring to past volumes of the "Literary Gazette," I always find them replete with valuable and interesting information on the contemporary literature, the fine arts, science, and the drama; also on the manners and customs of the constantly changing times from 1817 to 1850. The recent numbers of this weekly periodical show it to be conducted by an editor of science, candour, and literary talents.

The Strand has long been known as the place of congress of certain learned and eminent national societies, whose "Transactions" have travelled to, and been located and studied in, all the civilized cities of the globe. Those of the Royal, the Antiquaries, and the Astronomical, have free quarters within the government edifice of Somerset House; whilst the Society of Arts, in a noble mansion of its own, has taken root and prospered, in John Street, close to the Strand. The history of each and all of these societies is replete with interesting matter, not merely for the archæologist and scientific, but for the historian of man, in developing the progress of his intellectual qualifications. Mr. Weld has given to the public a well-digested history of that of the Royal, and it is hoped that other authors will shortly produce similar publications on their respective societies.

No. 32 in the Strand was a large print-shop, belonging to Mr. Richardson, whose extensive collection was noted for portraits, topographical and antiquarian prints, and for public sales of that class of property. In February and March, 1800, he sold an amazing collection of British portraits, which continued for thirty-one days, and which appears to have been accumulating for forty years. He was also employed on many other similar occasions to dispose of graphic works. During the winter he frequently had sales in the evening, which I often attended, and as often puchased "lots." Here I met several gentlemen, with whom I became intimate, from congeniality of attachments. Amongst these were Mr. Alexander, of the British Museum, Mr. Baker, of St. Paul's Churchyard, Mr. R. Holford, Mr. Bentham, Mr. Bindley, Dr. Gossett, Mr. Molteno, and several others, whose hoards have since been again brought to the hammer, and distributed to amuse other illustrators. Richardson published several portraits, fac-similes of scarce prints, and also three different-sized prints of the "Felton Shakspeare," as it is usually named. At his rooms were sold by auction the famed collections of Musgrave and of Tighe.

In the Strand were the shops of Mr. Faden, Mr. Cary, and Mr. Smith, who entirely devoted themselves to Geography, by publishing Maps, Charts, Globes, &c. I often visited them to obtain and communicate information. The most important topographical surveys were published by Mr. Faden, but they were too expensive for my pocket. This gentleman has been succeeded by James Wyld, Esq., M. P., who has brought into the business more energy and enterprise than his predecessor, and has consequently produced great changes and improvements in his published works. As a feature of the times in which we live, we find that Mr. Wyld is a member of the Legislature, and a bold competitor with the daring and unparalleled Crystal Palace of 1851, by designing and constructing a building, with an exhibition to display the geographical surface of the terrestrial Globe. The invention and the execution are honourable to his name and country; and it is hoped that it will reward his enterprise.

I always travelled with the best small map I could obtain, and marked in such alterations and corrections as I met with. These were handed over to the publishers, and consequently inserted in new impressions of their respective plates. The Trigonometrical and the Ordnance Surveys were not published when I walked round Wales, into Cornwall, and through some other districts. These truly important national works are now produced, and, being sold at very low prices, are of incalculable value to modern antiquaries and topographers.

Near the western end of the Strand, on the North side, was the house of a Mr. Baxter, having in the rear a large Room, which he let out for private theatricals, for debates, and for readings and music. His wife possessed a fine soprano voice, played well on the piano-forte, and occasionally performed on the stage. At this place I became acquainted with George Saville Carey, who published a small volume called "Balnea, or Sketches of Watering-places," 1799, which, I believe, was the first work that gave a general account of those famed places of fashionable resort; and it would be interesting to show the extent, population, &c., of Bath, Brighton, Leamington, Margate, and Buxton, as they were when that volume was published, and as they now are. Carey wrote a volume on "Mimicry," and was famed for his Imitations of Garrick, Henderson, Kemble, Mrs. Siddons, and others. I have a vivid recollection of the mellow, flexible voice, and expressive intonations of Garrick, as well as the dull, phlegmatic, monotonous tones of Kemble, as Carey displayed them: one was mellifluous to the ear, the other grating and discordant, though not quite so bad as Coleman describes it in his famed Preface to "The Iron Chest"—"a crow in a quinsey." Carey contended that his father wrote "God Save the King;" but his statement is confuted by the Rev. Richard Clark, of Westminster Abbey, who asserts, and has produced authority to show, that it was composed by Dr. John Bull, who wrote it for, and that it was performed at, a public concert at Merchant Tailors' School, London, on the 16th of July, 1607. In Mr. Baxter's room, I occasionally appeared in the reading-desk, and also as one of the speakers, or rather talkers, on some debated question; and I well remember that Mr. Gale Jones, who was the founder and manager of the society, praised me for the matter and manner of my remarks on the subject of the "Slave Trade," then much discussed both in Parliament and in public. I had read a good deal about it, and consequently was ardently prejudiced in the cause. Sermons, Essays, Poetry, History, Debate, were variously and numerously employed to rouse the passions and judgment of the public against the barbarous and horrible traffic. The letters of Sterne and of Ignatius Sancho were familiar to me, and warmed my enthusiasm. The history, amiable character, and literary tact of the latter excited my warmest sympathy, and prepos-

sessed me in behalf of black skin and the ever-
curled hair. I longed to know and love such a
man as Sancho. Experience is the only correction of prejudice. In 1815, I was introduced, at a
Freemasons' Lodge, to Prince Sanders, a complete negro, who was said to be an agent from
Christophe, King of Hayti, and who had obtained
access to, and the patronage of the Duke of Sussex, W. Wilberforce, and other persons of note.
This was a passport even to Freemasons and to
fashionable society. The "Prince" became popular, was lionized in the metropolis, lived in a gay
style, told artists and authors that he was com-
missioned by "his royal master" to engage several
of both classes to emigrate and settle in Hayti,
where the King would confer fortune and fame on
them. Some were tempted to send specimens of
their respective works; and I became one of Mr.
"Prince" Sanders's dupes, by confiding to his
friendly charge fine-paper copies of three volumes, valued at £25. Of these I never heard more;
but found that my new friend, in whom I had no
suspicion of roguery, continued to visit and be visited by several distinguished persons, from the
West End of London. He resided in the vicinity
of Tavistock Square, and one night assembled, at
a Soirée, a large party of nobles, gentry, and la-

dies, amongst whom were the Duke of Sussex, Mr. Wilberforce, and other personages of rank. Before he quitted London, he published an octavo volume, with his portrait engraved by Charles Turner. Its title is: "By Authority. Haytian Papers: A Collection of the very Interesting Proclamations, and other Official Documents; together with some Account of the Rise, Progress, and Present State of the Kingdom of Hayti. With a Preface by Prince Sanders, Esq., Agent for the Haytian Government. London: printed for W. Reed, 17, Fleet Street." 8vo. 1816. This volume is a curiosity. I never heard what became of its editor, after he left London; but I learnt that several other persons, as well as myself, had been imposed on by him.

Connected with the Strand are reminiscences of the Lyceum Theatre, with my public appearance on its stage, and in the stage-box; of Robert Ker Porter's exhibition of Seringapatam and other pictures; of the wonderful mimicry, ventriloquism, and transformations of Monsieur Alexandre, the rival of Mathews; of Phillipstall's Phantasmagoria; and also of the "Sans Pareil Theatre," as it was called in 1806, when Mr. Scott, a colour-maker, built and fitted it up for his daughter, who made her first public appearance there, and gained much applause for songs and recitations. This lady's performances, united with mechanical and optical illusions, gave character to the house, and made the fortune of its proprietor. "Tom and Jerry," by Pierce Egan, afterwards attracted immense crowds, when the name of "Little Adelphi." was given to the theatre. In 1825 Terry and Yates became lessees, but lost money. Charles Mathews joined the latter, and continued to give his popular and profitable "At Home" here for three successive years. It was at this house I first became acquainted with that extraordinary actor, mimic, and man, and continued to meet him frequently afterwards. He was born in 1776, at No. 18 in the Strand, and died in 1835, after a long career of theatrical adventure, vicissitude, and fame. Among the numerous volumes of biography and auto-biography of the heroes and heroines of the sock and buskin, there is not one surpassing in variety, wit, and amusement, that of the eccentric and much-admired Charles Mathews. It is written jointly by the player and his widow, and extends to four volumes. A few pages only of the first are by the pen of the former, and the remainder is admirably executed by the latter.

At No. 145, Strand, were the book-shop and auction-rooms of Messrs. Leigh and Sotheby, at

the beginning of the present century, in which
many choice and costly books were transferred
from one collector to another. Mr. Leigh was established as an auctioneer in King Street, Covent
Garden, in 1744; and from that time to the present
the Catalogues, with prices and purchasers' names,
are preserved by the present respectable firm in
Wellington Street.

After the decease of the first gentleman, the second continued the business for some years in the
same street, and disposed of many celebrated libraries. He has been succeeded by his worthy
Son, who inherits many of the good points of his
much-respected parent, and equally respected partner, retaining the names of both. Since the retirement of Mr. Evans, of Pall Mall, Mr. Samuel
Leigh Sotheby has been most extensively occupied in selling distinguished libraries, and, I
believe, with credit to himself and advantage to his
employers. On comparing one of his recent catalogues, for Samuel Prout, with another printed for
his godfather and father, in 1806, of nine days' sale
of the library of one of my earliest literary friends,
the Rev. Jonathan Boucher, the contrast is
remarkable. The last exhibits bad type,
bad ink, bad paper, and heedless editorship; whilst the former is the reverse in all

these qualities: yet the Boucher Catalogue
is charged 3s. 6d., and that of Prout's Collection was given away. Mr. Sotheby's partner
(John Wilkinson) conducts the selling department
with as much zeal and promptitude as the former
manifests in arrangement, catalogueing, and in
other parts of the business. Their rooms are now
in Wellington Street.

In alluding to the Auction-rooms of the western
part of London, it would seem negligent or invidious were I to omit two which have been justly eminent in credit and respectability for many years
in the early part of the present century: those of
Robert H. Evans, No. 93, Pall Mall, and James
Christie, first in Pall Mall, and afterwards in King
Street, St. James's. Brief notices of the numerous and various sales of books, MSS. and prints
which have been distributed over the world by the
first auctioneer, would extend to a large volume,
and might be made particularly interesting to the
lovers of literature. It would embrace accounts
of a vast variety of valuable and important books,
whose histories involve not merely their own intrinsic merits and peculiarities, but the fluctua-
tions of prices and caprices of purchasers. Some
have been highly prized and hoarded for their
scarcity, (a lamentable criterion, as many of these

"extremely rare" articles are worthless); others
for being a trifle larger in the margin than another
copy which has been pronounced the tallest; whilst
a third quality is the possession of some cancelled
leaf or print, which was originally deemed useless,
or objectionable. I have often seen the large sale-
room crowded by real lovers of literature, by collectors, by bibliographers, and by bibliomaniacs,
and witnessed the enormous prices given for
books, both of intrinsic beauty and merit, and of
capricious worth. The Roxburgh, the Sykes, the
Spencer, the Hibbert, the Dent, the Hoare, and
the Broadley libraries were noted for their extent,
value, scarcity, and for other peculiarities: some
of these have been sold and resold by auction since
their first appearance in a sale-room. Dibdin's
"Library Companion," his "Bibliomania," and his
"Reminiscences," contain much curious information on the subjects here referred to: and I must
not omit to notice my respected friend Mr.
Clarke's "Repertorium Bibliographicum," a large
royal octavo volume of 1819, which contains much
valuable and curious information on celebrated
British libraries, and their choicest book-treas-
ures.

Mr. Christie's Sale-rooms, in Pall Mall and in
King Street, have been noted for more than half

a century, as well for the high respectability and
qualifications of the auctioneers, as for the vast
amount and nature of the property they have exhibited. I have known three generations of the
family, and had reason to esteem each and all.
Though I saw but little of the first, who was
famed for his bland and engaging manners and
voice, as well as for his florid, spontaneous addresses, or panegyrics, yet I never see the ex-
quisite portrait of him, in the counting-house of
King Street, without emotions of admiration of
the artist, and the auctioneer. On referring to a
catalogue of "a most capital and precious assem-
blage of pictures" by Mr. Christie, Sen., whose
"Great Room" was in Pall Mall, June 13th, 1807,
I see a flourishing, and rather a Robins-like account of a small collection of only 44 pictures,
each of which is highly eulogised. One of them,
by Rembrandt, is described as "the finest picture,
without exception, ever painted by that master."
The Catalogue is marked 2s. 6d. George H.
Christie succeeded his parent in 1831, in the same
premises, and in the same career of high character,
and in costly sales of works of art and vertu. In
the same year Peter Coxe, author of "The Social
Day," a poem, sold a small gallery of "original
paintings, the property of Mr. Andrew Wilson,"

the Catalogue of which, marked 2s. 6d., contains a highly coloured advertisement, with comments on each "painting," also praised. He was brother of Archdeacon Coxe, and a popular auctioneer for some years. Amongst other sales was one of the Bowood collection of pictures, out of which I purchased three, by Sir Joshua Reynolds, Romney, and Wright, of Derby. The first and second were transferred to the Marquis of Stafford, and the third, half-length of the Marquis of Granby, to a gentleman of Devonshire.

With the late James Christie I was familiarly acquainted, in his public and private characteristics; and though I occasionally lamented to see him in his auction-rostrum, surrounded by unshaven and rude brokers, and sometimes subjected to the cant language of such "gents," I also saw him in the company of nobles of the land, and commoners of equally noble character. With the latter, my amiable friend seemed "at home," and addressed them in language and manners which could not fail to propitiate their confidence and respect. More than once I have attended his sales, for the purpose of seeing certain fine pictures, and also to bid for some on account of friends. The celebrated series of Hogarth's "Election" I bought for Sir John Soane, at what was thought to be a large sum. The lot excited competition, and the auctioneer made occasional pauses and a few apposite and judicious remarks between the biddings. On knocking it down, he pronounced as neat and pointed an address to the successful candidate as ever was heard at any electioneering contest in the united kingdom. Mr. Christie, Sen., died in 1805; and James Christie, his Son, in 1831, aged 57.

In King Street, Covent Garden, were the Auction-rooms of King and Lochee, chiefly devoted to books, in which I was first tempted to compete for a few topographical articles in 1800. It was the library of Philip Luckombe, who had published a small "History of Printing," in 1771; "A Tour in Ireland, 1783;" and "England's Gazetteer," in 1790, in 3 volumes, 12mo.; also some other works; whence it appears that he had been connected with the press. His library, though small, contained Camden's Britannia, interleaved and illustrated; his own "Gazetteer," interleaved, with MS. Notes; also other topographical books. There being but little competition, I laid out about £20, and carried away a hackney coach load of literary materials for future reference and application.

At the same rooms, the Rev. Dr. Richard Farmer's large library had been sold in 1798; extending over thirty-six days.

My (Britton) earliest aspirations, after engaging to write on Topography, were to cultivate the acquaintance of those persons, who either sold or collected books, prints, or other articles in that class of literature; and that I progressively and ultimately became familiar with most of the bibliopolists, print-sellers, and auction-rooms in the metropolis. My limited funds, however, precluded me from purchasing to a great extent; but I may safely aver that, from the year 1800 to 1850, there was not one Olympic cycle passed without an increase of my library, in books, prints, and drawings. As already remarked, my fit of Bibliomania was first caught at the sale of the library of Philip Luckombe, when I obtained the "Britannia," with printed, manuscript, and graphic accompaniments.

Thenceforward the disease increased in strength, and I continued to frequent nearly all the book sales of London, in which topography and antiquities constituted any distinguished portion. On these occasions, I not only became acquainted with eminent collectors, but also obtained some knowledge of the relative merits and value of books. Unlike many of my associates at these competing marts, I never sought to possess works which were valued and purchased merely from rarity, or dimensions of margin. Fine paper and good prints I coveted, and sometimes bought. Under these influences, and of warm temperament, it is not surprising that my own collection increased to an unwieldly and inconvenient extent. My rooms, boxes, closets, &c., were crowded, whilst the purse collapsed, and I deemed it prudent to commission Mr. Southgate to sell some of the books at his rooms. In June, 1832, I sent enough to make up six days' sale; and subsequently, at different times, have sold a sufficient number to occupy ten more days. Every sale, however, furnished cause of mortification and sorrow; for books, drawings, prints, and objects of vertu, were sold at very low prices.

The following Address was written and printed by Mr. Britton in June, 1832, to accompany Catalogues sent to particular persons; and is reprinted, in this place, as expressive of the feelings and opinions he then experienced and entertained on such a subject.

BOOKS: READING, STUDY.

A man who has been actively engaged for forty years in collecting, and in using Books,—who during that space of time has been economical in all his other expences for the purpose of indulging this "hobby," and who has also been much occupied in the pleasure of writing, and penalties of publishing, will be likely to find the said hobby grow rather too large for his stable, and demand more than common care and labour in "looking after." Though thus overgrown and incommodious, I can truly re-echo the sentiment of Cumberland, who in his "Memoirs" asserts, that his "books and pen have been his never-failing comforters and friends."

From these, and all other earthly ties, a time of parting must arrive; and Books will have failed in one of their important duties, or qualities, if they have not inculcated the lesson of submitting to inevitable events, without unavailing murmur. Philosophy has many pretty maxims, but it has not one among the number to render sensibility insensible. It certainly teaches us "to bear the ills we have," and guard against, or ward off others, which may assail us. Dr. Kitchener instructed "every man to make his own Will"—and he might have taught him, also, to be his own Executor. This would tend to shorten lawyers' bills, and lengthen legacies; would benefit widows and orphans, and abridge posthumous taxation. If there were no other reasons for a man's looking beyond the grave, than a desire of saving litigation, and mulcts to the tax office, these were sufficient; but how often and how effectually can he apply his superfluous property—if he has any—towards the end of his life, if he has resolution and good feelings, to bequeath it to deserving relatives and friends.

Let us hear what Petrarch said of Books, about five hundred years ago, when there were neither Magazines nor Reviews, and when printing and engraving were alike unknown, and let us endeavour to appreciate and profit by his just and philosophical remarks.

"Some people consider the pleasures of the world as their supreme good, and not to be renounced. But I have friends of a very different description (my Books), whose society is far more agreeable to me: they are of all countries, and of all ages; they are distinguished in war, in politics, and in the sciences. It is very easy to see them; they are always at my service. I call for their company, or send them away, whenever I please: they are never troublesome, and immediately answer all my questions. Some relate the events of ages past, others reveal the secrets of nature; these teach me how to live in comfort, those how to die in quiet. In return for all these services, they only require a chamber of me in one corner of my mansion, where they may repose in peace."

If, however, instead of one corner of his mansion, Petrarch had found every room and every closet of his house filled with these dear friends, he might have experienced some inconvenience from their company, and been induced, like myself and many others, to turn some of them out of doors, for the purpose of seeing and enjoying the selected few.

A short account of the rise and progress of the Library, of which a part is now to be disposed of, will "point a moral," if not "adorn a tale." In boyhood I attended the sale of a country 'squire's furniture, &c., and bought a lot of nine books for 1s. One of them was "Robinson Crusoe," which I read with avidity, and longed to be cast on a desert island, with a "Man Friday." This library travelled with me to London, and occupied—with Bailey's Dictionary, a few magazines, some anatomical and medical books, &c.—a small deal box, during six years of miserable apprenticeship, the greater part of which was spent in a murky, damp, and dirty cellar. Sanguine in hopes, and ardently looking forward to emancipation from a sad state of legal slavery, my health gave way, and I became weak, emaciated, and desponding. But

for the "little knowledge" obtained even from my
small library, I should have sunk into an early
grave; from books I acquired some knowledge of
my own constitution, frame of body, and the latent
disease which exhibited evident symptoms of consumption. Thus, I attribute prolongation of life
to reading. At the end of apprenticeship my boy-
library contained twenty-five volumes, and my
purse five guineas. For the ensuing ten years
my stock increased but very slowly; a small nest of
shelves held the whole. Commencing with Mr.
Brayley the "Beauties of England," in 1800, it became necessary to have nearly every printed book
relating to the counties described; but as these
were expensive, they were retained only as long as
wanted, and then sold to purchase others. This
class of reading and writing excited a desire to
possess a library, and every new year not only increased the desire, but also augmented the collection.

In Tavistock Place it occupied three sides of a
small room nine feet square, and I then thought
myself truly rich and happy. Infected with the
"Bibliomania," which raged for some time in London, I was impelled to attend the sale rooms of
King and Lochee—Richardson—Leigh and Sotheby—Evans, and other famed "contagionists"—

where I continued to purchase, as if "increase of appetite grew with what it fed on." Many "curious, choice, and rare articles" have thus come into my possession, which I have seen pass through the hands of three or four "famous" collectors. Here the retrospect is painful, and melancholy; for it brings before imagination the Names, Tales, and varied Characters of the indefatigable and zealous Strutt—the eccentric and enthusiastic Carter—the magnificent Lansdowne—the amiable and learned Boucher—the plodding and laborious Reed—the talented but splenetic Steevens and Ritson—the universally esteemed Alexander—the ostentatious Dent—the historical Coxe, cum multis aliis.

F. Kyte pinx. 1740.   J. Basire sculp.

EDWARD CAVE, PRINTER.

Born in 1691; died in 1754.

Published by J. Nichols & Son, Jan.y 1st 1812.

THE

RISE AND PROGRESS

OF THE

GENTLEMAN'S MAGAZINE,

WITH

ANECDOTES OF THE PROJECTOR

AND HIS EARLY ASSOCIATES.

———

BEING

A PREFATORY INTRODUCTION

TO THE

GENERAL INDEX TO THAT WORK,

FROM 1787 TO 1818

———

By JOHN NICHOLS, F.S.A. LOND. EDIN. & PERTH.

━━━━━━━

LONDON:

PRINTED FOR JOHN NICHOLS AND SON, 25, PARLIAMENT-STREET;
AND J. HARRIS AND SON, AT THE CORNER OF ST. PAUL'S CHURCH-YARD.
1821.

PREFACE.

IN presenting to the numerous and respectable Readers of the GENTLEMAN'S MAGAZINE a General Index to the Volumes from 1787 to 1818, it may not be irrelevant to request their re-perusal of the Preface already given to the First Volume of the former Index; more particularly when they are informed that the greater part of that Preface was written, and the whole of it corrected, by my illustrious Predecessor, Dr. SAMUEL JOHNSON. Whatever interest the public events from 1731 to 1786 might be entitled to claim, those nearer our own times are at least equally important; and very few, it is hoped, of the many remarkable occurrences of so momentous a period are omitted in the present Volumes.

At the advanced age of seventy-six, it will scarcely be expected that I should undertake the extreme labour of so multifarious a compilation. But I have entrusted it, under the immediate superintendance of my Son, to more than one diligent and able Assistant; and have myself, by revising every line in the proof-sheets, been able, from personal recollection, to supply many omissions, and correct some occasional mistakes.

The GENTLEMAN'S MAGAZINE has now for 90 years enjoyed the highly-prized honour of being the repository of communications from many of the most eminent Writers of that long period; and has been uniformly favoured by the patronage of those whose applause is fame. Many of its Rivals and Competitors have "strutted their hour upon the stage," and are now forgotten; whilst the labours of SYLVANUS URBAN, the earliest publication of the kind, still boldly compete with the proudest of similar productions of the present age.

Not to enter too deeply into the *arcana* of a Miscellaneous Publication, the very nature of which depends on a sort of Masonic secresy, it may not be improper to introduce a few anecdotes, and to unfold some particulars, over which concealment is no longer needful. If I should in some instances be thought too minute, let it be attributed to the proper cause, the natural garrulity of age.

This long-established Periodical Miscellany was commenced, in January 1731, by EDWARD CAVE; who, by the admirable Memoir of Dr. JOHNSON, has been consigned to deserved celebrity.

As the great Biographer justly remarks, "few Lives would have more Readers, if all those who received improvement or entertainment from him should retain so much kindness for their Benefactor as to enquire after his conduct and character." From that excellent Memoir, and from the pleasant volumes of Mr. BOSWELL, such extracts shall here be taken as relate to the Magazine; with such particulars as I have otherwise been able to collect respecting the history of CAVE'S darling project.

We learn from the great Biographer, that Edward Cave was born Feb. 29, 1691-2, at Rugby, in Warwickshire; and that he was educated in the Grammar School of that Town, under the Rev. Henry Holyoke.

"After quitting the school, young CAVE was placed with a Collector of the Excise. He used to recount with some pleasure a journey or two which he rode with him as his clerk, and relate the victories he gained over the Excisemen in grammatical disputations. But the insolence of his mistress, who employed him in servile drudgery, quickly disgusted him; and he went up to London in quest of more suitable employment.

"He was recommended to a Timber-merchant at the Bankside, and, while he was there on liking, is said to have given hopes of great mercantile abilities. But this place he soon left, I know not for what reason, and was bound apprentice to Mr. Collins, a Printer of some reputation, and Deputy-alderman; and in only two years attained so much skill in his art, and gained so much the confidence of his master, that he was sent, without any superintendant, to conduct a printing-house at Norwich, and publish a Weekly Newspaper. In this undertaking he met with some opposition, which produced a public controversy, and procured young Cave reputation as a Writer.

"His Master died before his apprenticeship was expired; and, as he was not able to bear the perverseness of his Mistress, he quitted her house upon a stipulated allowance, and married a young widow, with whom he lived at Bow. When his apprenticeship was over, he worked as a journeyman at the printing-house of Mr. Barber, a man much distinguished and employed by the Tories, whose principles had at that time so much prevalence with Cave, that he was for some years a writer in "Mist's Journal," which (though he afterwards obtained, by his wife's interest, a small place in the Post-office) he for some time continued. But, as interest is powerful, and conversation, however mean, in time persuasive, he by degrees inclined to another Party; in which, however, he was always moderate, though steady and determined.

"When he was admitted into the Post-office, he still continued, at his intervals of attendance, to exercise his trade, or to employ himself with some typographical business. He corrected the "Gradus ad Parnassum," and was liberally rewarded by the Company of Stationers. He wrote an account of the Criminals, which had for some time a considerable sale; and published many little pamphlets that accident brought into his hands, of which it would be very difficult to recover the memory. By the Correspondence which his place in the Post-office facilitated, he procured country newspapers, and sold their intelligence to a journalist of London for a guinea a week.

"He was afterwards raised to the office of Clerk of the Franks, in which he acted with great spirit and firmness; and often stopped franks which were given by Members of Parliament to their friends, because he thought such extension of a peculiar right illegal. This raised many complaints; and having stopped, among others, a frank given to the old Duchess of Marlborough by Mr. Walter Plummer, he was cited before the House, as for breach of privilege, and accused, I suppose very unjustly, of opening letters to detect them. He was treated with great harshness and severity; but, declining their questions by pleading his oath of secrecy, was at last dismissed. And it must be recorded to his honour, that when he was ejected from his office, he did not think himself discharged from his trust, but continued to refuse to his nearest friends any information about the management of the office.

"By this constancy of diligence and diversification of employment, he in time collected a sum sufficient for the purchase of a small printing-office, and began THE GENTLEMAN'S MAGAZINE. To this undertaking he owed the affluence in which he passed the last twenty years of his life, and the fortune which he left behind him, which, though large, had been yet larger, had he not rashly and wantonly impaired it by innumerable projects, of which I know not that ever one succeeded.

"The GENTLEMAN'S MAGAZINE, which has already subsisted three and twenty years, and still continues equally to enjoy the favour of the world *, is one of the most successful and lucrative pamphlets which literary history has upon record."

Thus much almost literally from Dr. JOHNSON. I now proceed to more particular details.

The First Number of the Magazine, for January 1731, was "Printed for the Author; and sold at St. John's Gate; by

---

* This was written at the beginning of the year 1754; and it may still with justice be added, that The GENTLEMAN'S MAGAZINE, after a period of ninety years, stands foremost for literary reputation, as the respectable Correspondence it still uniformly continues to enjoy abundantly evinces.

F. Jefferies *, in Ludgate-street ; and all other Booksellers, and by the Persons who serve Gentlemen with the Newspapers."

In a brief Introduction, Mr. Cave thus unfolded his plan :

" It has been unexceptionably advanced, that a good Abridgment of the Law is more intelligible than the Statutes at large : so a nice model is as entertaining as the original, and a true specimen as satisfactory as the whole parcel : this may serve to illustrate the reasonableness of our present undertaking, which in the first place is to give monthly a view of all the pieces of wit, humour, or intelligence, daily offered to the Public in the Newspapers, (which of late are so multiplied, as to render it impossible, unless a man makes it a business, to consult them all,) and in the next place we shall join therewith some other matters of use or amusement that will be communicated to us.

" Upon calculating the number of Newspapers, 'tis found that (besides divers written Accounts) no less than 200 half-sheets *per* month are thrown from the Press only in London, and about as many printed elsewhere in the three Kingdoms ; a considerable part of which constantly exhibit Essays on various subjects for entertainment; and all the rest occasionally oblige their Readers with matters of public concern, communicated to the world by persons of capacity through their means : so that they are become the chief channels of amusement and intelligence. But then being only loose papers, uncertainly scattered about, it often happens that many things deserving attention, contained in them, are only seen by accident, and others not sufficiently published or preserved for universal benefit and information. This consideration has induced several Gentlemen to promote a monthly collection, to treasure up, as in a *Magazine* †, the most remarkable pieces on the subjects abovementioned, or at least impartial abridgments thereof, as a me-

---

* This name was discontinued in 1735.

† "The invention of this new species of publication may be considered as something of an epocha in the Literary History of this Country. The periodical publications before that time were almost wholly confined to political transactions, and to foreign and domestic occurrences. But the Magazines have opened a way for every kind of enquiry and information. The intelligence and discussion contained in them are very extensive and various ; and they have been the means of diffusing a general habit of reading through the Nation ; which, in a certain degree, hath enlarged the public understanding. Many young Authors, who have afterwards risen to considerable eminence in the literary world, have here made their first attempts in composition. Here, too, are preserved a multitude of curious and useful hints, observations, and facts, which otherwise might have never appeared ; or, if they had appeared in a more evanescent form, would have incurred the danger of being lost. If it were not an invidious task, the history of them would be no incurious or unentertaining subject. The Magazines that unite utility with entertainment are undoubtedly preferable to those *(if there have been any such)* which have only a view to idle and frivolous amusement." *Dr. Kippis.*

thod much better calculated to preserve those things that are curious, than that of transcribing *."

From the time of Mr. Cave's first connexion with the News-paper at Norwich, he had conceived a strong idea of the utility of publishing the Parliamentary Debates; and, having been engaged in a situation at the Post-office, had an opportunity, not only of supplying his London Friends with the Provincial Papers, but he also contrived to furnish the Country Printers with those written Minutes of the Proceedings in the Two Houses of Parliament, which within my own remembrance were regularly circulated in the Coffee-houses, before the daily papers were *tacitly permitted* to report the Debates.

The Orders of the House were indeed regularly repeated, and occasionally enforced; and under these, in April 1728, Mr. Cave experienced some inconvenience and expence; having been ordered into the custody of the Serjeant at Arms, for supplying his friend Mr. Robert Raikes with the Minutes of the House, for the use of the Gloucester Journal. After a con-finement of several days, on stating his sorrow for the offence, and pleading that he had a wife and family who suffered much by his imprisonment, he was discharged, with a reprimand, on paying the accustomed fees. In the following year Mr. Raikes again incurred the censure of the House by repeating his offence · but Cave was at that time out of the scrape.

The plan of inserting a regular series of Debates was long in Cave's contemplation before he adventured to put it into practice. At length he boldly dared; and began, in January 1732, by giving only the King's Speech. In June he gave two Pro-tests of the Lords; and, in the Commons, the Speaker's Thanks to Lord Viscount Gage, May 31, 1732, with his Lordship's Reply. But in July, the Parliament being then prorogued, he ventured to introduce the "Proceedings and Debates of the last

---

* So rapid was the sale of the First Volume, that it was frequently re-printed. I have now before me a copy of the FIFTH Edition; in which Mr. Cave says,

"On the re-publication of this Volume, it may be expected we should add something to the foregoing Introduction. All we have to say is, that as this undertaking has met with uncommon success, 'tis but just, and our indispen-sable duty, to pay our most grateful acknowledgments to the Publick from whom we have received such encouragement. We likewise own our obligation to divers ingenious Correspondents, who by furnishing us with several pieces of Poetry, and other useful hints, have not a little contributed to the embellish-ment of the work; and as it has been our endeavour from the beginning to improve our scheme, and store our Magazine with such a variety of matter as might be adapted to the taste and humour of all our Readers, so we shall assidu-ously apply ourselves to what we judge will yield them the best entertainment; and take it as a favour of such persons as will correct any mistakes of the Publick Papers we may possibly fall into; or shall please to communicate any pieces of wit or entertainment proper to be inserted, directing to the Author at St. John's Gate."

Session of Parliament," which were given with the initial and final letters of the names of the several Speakers.

The singular and laborious manner in which Cave most usually obtained the Debates is thus related by Sir John Hawkins: " Taking with him a friend or two, he found means to procure for them and himself admission into the gallery of the House of Commons, or to some concealed station in the other House ; and then they privately took down notes of the several Speeches, and the general tendency and substance of the arguments. Thus furnished, Cave and his associates would adjourn to a neighbouring tavern, and compare and adjust their notes ; by means whereof, and the help of their memories, they became enabled to fix at least the substance of what they had so lately heard and remarked. The reducing this crude matter into form was the work of a future day, and of an abler hand ; Guthrie, the Historian, a Writer for the Booksellers, whom Cave retained for the purpose."

From some of the following Letters to Dr. Birch, it appears that Mr. Cave had better assistance in that department than has been generally supposed ; and that he was indefatigable in getting the Debates made as perfect as was practicable.

" July 21, 1735. I trouble you with the inclosed, because you said you could easily correct what is here given for Lord Chesterfield's Speech*. I beg you will do so as soon as you can for me, because the month is far advanced."

" July 15, 1737. As you *remember*† the Debates so far as to perceive the Speeches already printed are not exact, I beg the favour that you will peruse the inclosed : and, in the best manner your memory will serve, correct the mistaken passages, or add any thing that is omitted. I should be very glad to have something of the Duke of Newcastle's Speech ‡, which would be particularly of service. A Gentleman has Lord Bathurst's Speech §, to add something to."

" Aug. 12, 1738. We still agree on Tuesday; and I think we shall see Claremont, as we did Cannons, and then come to dine at Richmond. Had I best send Mr. Thomson word, that we shall be at such an inn at Richmond by *noon*, his hour of rising ? Your humble servant,   ED. CAVE."

---

* See this Speech in Gent. Mag. 1735, vol. V. p. 445.

† By this it should seem that Dr. Birch was one of the friends who sometimes accompanied Cave when taking Minutes of the Parliamentary Proceedings.

‡ Ibid. vol. VII. p. 377.   § Ibid. p. 379.

" Sept. 9, 1741. I have put Mr. Johnson's Play* into Mr. Gray's † hands, in order to sell it to him, if he is inclined to buy it; but I doubt whether he will or not. He would dispose of the copy, and whatever advantage may be made by acting it. Would your Society ‡, or any gentlemen or body of men that you know, take such a bargain? Both he and I are very unfit to deal with theatrical persons. Fleetwood was to have acted it last season; but Johnson's diffidence or . . . . prevented it. I am, Reverend Sir, your most humble servant, ED. CAVE."

" July 3, 1744. You will see what stupid, low, abominable stuff is put § upon your noble and learned Friend's ‖ character; such as I should quite reject, and endeavour to do something better towards doing justice to the character. But, as I cannot expect to attain my desires in that respect, it would be a great satisfaction, as well as an honour to our Work, to have the favour of the genuine Speech. It is a method that several have been pleased to take, as I could shew — but I think myself under a restraint. I shall say so far, that I have had some by a *third hand*, which I understood well enough to come from the *first;* others by penny-post; and others by the Speakers themselves, who have been pleased to visit St. John's Gate, and shew particular marks of their being pleased."

" Dec. 1747. The Ode to Wisdom, in the second volume of Clarissa, was written by Miss Carter: it had been handed about in MS. I had not permission to print it, though I asked for it personally at Deal; and, though I before then had it in manuscript, it was under a promise not to publish it without leave. ED. CAVE."

" Saturday, Oct. 27, [1750]. I beg that you will send me the pages where Mrs. C's Letters are in the Magazine. Mr. Johnson remembers both the letters; and he says they were the best, and put the affair in a new light to him at that time, and the

---

* By this letter it appears that Johnson's Tragedy of "Irene" had been for some time ready for the press; and that his necessities made him desirous of getting as much as he could for it, without delay. See p. xiv.

† Mr. John Gray, a Bookseller of eminence in London.

‡ Not the Royal Society; but the Society for the Encouragement of Learning, of which Dr. Birch was a leading member. Their object was, to assist authors in printing expensive works. Having incurred a considerable debt, it was in a short time dissolved.

§ In some ephemeral production, now forgotten.

‖ Doubtless, Lord Hardwicke.—Mr. Cave was sometimes favoured with communications by the Hon. Charles Yorke, and his learned and confidential Friend Daniel Wray, Esq.—By the following short note from Mr. Wray to Dr. Birch, it may be fair to presume that the Hurgo *Hickrad's* Speech (vol. XIV. p. 522), in particular was furnished from the fountain-head:

" Sept. 28, 1744. Mr. Yorke equipped me with so huge a packet, that I could not keep it smooth in my pocket. Here you have it, inside and contents unknown to your humble servant.—As you are so near Mr. Cave, you may daily procure, and send me by the bearer, that part of your Neighbour's Literary Correspondence, which has Dr. Perry's Extract."

reasoning excellent. Did Browne Willis, Esq. produce the scheme to the Society of Antiquaries, as said in the Remembrancer ; or is it a joke ? I have procured a *Latin Comus* for *Lauder*, of which I suppose he makes great account."

In 1733 the Magazine had become so warmly patronized, and the Correspondence of respectable Writers so enlarged, that a Supplementary Number became necessary.

Some complimentary verses were prefixed to the Volume of that year ; with the following apologetical remark :

" We are too sensible of our imperfections to assume to ourselves what is so largely advanced in the above pieces to our praise : but, as we could not leave out those poetical heightenings, which otherwise we ought not in modesty to have let pass, without spoiling the lines ; so we can most truly affirm, that our endeavours have been received in such a favourable manner, as to produce a great many Letters of acknowledgment, in which our good-natured Correspondents have expressed themselves in a manner little short of the real meaning of these Poems ; and we may add, that they have also informed us of certain practices made use of to our prejudice, which they condemn with the utmost indignation."

In 1734 the illustrious JOHNSON thus tendered his assistance :

" SIR, *Nov.* 25, 1734.

" As you appear no less sensible than your Readers of the defects of your Poetical Article *, you will not be displeased, if, in order to the improvement of it, I communicate to you the sentiments of a person who will undertake, on reasonable terms, sometimes to fill a column.

" His opinion is, that the publick will not give you a bad reception, if, besides the current wit of the Month, which a critical examination would generally reduce to a narrow compass, you admitted not only Poems, Inscriptions, &c. never printed before, which he will sometimes supply you with ; but likewise short Literary Dissertations in Latin or English, critical remarks on authors antient or modern, forgotten Poems that deserve revival—or loose pieces, like Floyer's †, worth preserving. By this method your Literary Article, for so it might be called, will, he thinks, be better recommended to the publick, than by low jests, aukward buffoonery, or the dull scurrilities of either party. If such a correspondence will be agreeable to

---

* Alluding to the offer noticed in p. xi.

† Sir John Floyer's Treatise on Cold Baths, which was printed in Gent. Mag. 1734, p. 197, was probably sent by Johnson ; who, a very short time before his death, strongly pressed the Writer of this Preface to give to the Publick some account of the life and works of Sir John Floyer, " whose learning and piety," the Doctor said, "deserve recording." An original portrait of Floyer is preserved at Lichfield.

you, be pleased to inform me, in two posts, what the conditions are on which you shall expect it. Your late offer gives me no reason to distrust your generosity.

" If you engage in any literary projects besides this paper, I have other designs to impart, if I could be secure from having others reap the advantage of what I should hint.

" Your Letter, by being directed to *S. Smith*, to be left at the Castle in Birmingham *, Warwickshire, will reach

" Your humble servant."

In July 1735 was published a " Magazine Extraordinary." It contains " several Poems upon Life, Death, Judgment, Heaven, and Hell, sent to the Publisher in consequence of a Proposal made in July 1734, for giving 50*l.* as a Prize for the Poets, to encourage them to write on these important subjects † ; which Proposal was afterwards amended in the Magazine for August and October 1734, and finally adjusted in the Magazine for January and May 1735 ‡."

In December 1735, it was announced, that " a Decision by public votes was not approved by the majority of Candidates ; they thought a certain number of Judges, not less than three, a more eligible method of determination. We have applied accordingly to three proper persons, and begged the favour of them to send their opinions separately to the Rev. Mr. Birch, F. R. S. and Dr. Mortimer, Secretary to the Royal Society ; which two gentlemen will be so good to make the declaration to what Poems the respective Prizes shall be adjudged."—In the February following, the Decision of the Prizes accordingly appears, signed by *Tho. Birch ;* accompanied by an anonymous Letter, containing " the Reasons which might probably have determined the Gentlemen in favour of the Poems they preferred."

In the Supplement for 1735, the Prizes hereafter mentioned were offered : " For the four best Poems, intituled, *The Christian Hero ; viz.* 1. To the Person who shall make the best will be given a GOLD MEDAL (intrinsic value about Ten Pounds) which shall have the Head of the Rt. Hon. the Lady ELIZABETH HASTINGS §

* Mr. Cave has put a note on this Letter, "Answered Dec. 2." But whether any thing was done in consequence of it we are not informed. Mr. Boswell adds, " I am pretty sure Dr. Johnson told me, that Mr. Cave was the first publisher by whom his pen was engaged in London."

† In January 1735, the 50*l.* Prize was repeated, with the addition of " 5*l.* given by a Gentlewoman, for the second in merit ; 5 years Magazines of the large paper, for the third ; 5 years Magazines of the common paper, for the fourth."

‡ In the Title also appears the following Note : " These Poems are thus printed together in one Book *Extraordinary,* at the desire of several of our learned and curious Readers, and not in the least for the sake of lucre, since the profit of the Impression will, as promised, be applied towards raising another Prize for the Poets."—A second Prize of 40*l.* was accordingly afterwards made for the best Poem " On the Divine Attributes." See p. xiii.

§ The above Advertisement, instead of gratifying, gave offence to Lady Elizabeth Hastings, as appears by the following article in February 1736:

" The Donor of the Gold Medal, proposed in our last Supplement, thinks it

on one side, and that of JAMES OGLETHORPE, Esq. on the other,
with this motto,—ENGLAND MAY CHALLENGE THE WORLD, 1736.
—2. To the Author of the Second, a complete Set of Archbishop
Tillotson's Sermons —3. To the Author of the Third, a complete
Set of Archbishop Sharpe's Sermons.—4. To the Author of the
Fourth, a Set of Cooke's Sermons. --In the beginning of October
three eminent Poets shall be solicited to determine the merit of
the Pieces*."

The following Prizes were also offered for the best Epigrams :
1. A Set of Magazines bound; 2. A Set stitched ; 3. Cooke's Sermons, bound ; 4. Ditto, stitched ; 5. Two Histories of the Order
of the Garter ; 6. A dozen Lesser Duties of Man, printed for
Colony of Georgia ; 7. Half a dozen to each Author who has
three Epigrams inserted †."

At the conclusion of the Volume for 1735, Mr. Cave announced his Proposals for publishing Du Halde's Description of
China ‡, in Numbers, once a Fortnight; the price of the whole
not to exceed Three Guineas; and with the following cha-
racteristic Condition : "Whatever number of these Books
there shall be a demand for over the said thousand, during the
progress of the work, the profits thereof shall, at its being finished,
be fairly divided (excepting the few on royal paper) among the
thousand first subscribers, only deducting 50l. to be given to such
his Majesty's British Subject as shall, in the opinion of the Royal
Society, make (from the hints given in this Description of China)

his duty to make this public declaration of his concern, that he has been so unhappy as to give offence by what he intended as an instance of respect and defe-
rence, and humbly asks her Ladyship's pardon for the uneasiness which he has so
unfortunately (but very undesignedly) occasioned. He is, however, desirous that
the Poets should exercise their pens on that sublime subject; and since the lady
will not permit him to do her the justice, to rank her among the first of that
noble and (he fears) small part of mankind, who deserve that illustrious character
(lest he should give a fresh offence by the mention of another living hero) he designs that that side of the medal shall be impressed with the Head of that once
great ornament of the Church of England, Archbishop Tillotson. If any should
charge the Medal with indelicacy, on account of the difference of quality between
the two persons now (and before) intended to be impressed on it; his answer is,
that they, in his opinion, entertain very low notions of Christian Heroism, who
make its excellency consist, or in any wise depend, on the accidental circumstances of birth and talents. He hopes that Mr. Oglethorp will be prevailed upon
to consent that the Medal shall bear his effigies, and that both the lady and he
will be the more readily induced to pardon the liberty he has taken, when they
are assured that it was done with a good intention, by one who has not the honour
to be personally known to either of them, and who is excited to it by the eminence of their characters."

  * Twenty-four Poems were sent in consequence of this Proposal ; two of which
are inserted in June; three in July; two in August; and two others in September, 1736.
  † Several Epigrams sent for the Prizes are printed in the Volume for 1736.
  ‡ This was again announced in September, 1736, under the fuller title of " A
Description of China and Chinese Tartary, with Korea and Tibet ; containing
the Geography, and History, as well Natural as Civil, of those Countries. Lately
published at Paris by Pere Du Halde, Jesuit."

the best and most useful improvement in any beneficial branch of
Art, and exbibit the same to the said Society within three months
after this work is finished."

In June 1736, and again in July, we read as follows :

" At Edial, near Lichfield, in Staffordshire, young gentlemen
are boarded and taught the Latin and Greek Languages by
SAMUEL JOHNSON."

What other communications may have been made by Johnson
to the Magazine in this year is uncertain ; but I believe the following Epigram to be his :

" In locupletissimum ornatissimumque SYL. URB. Thesaurum.

Menstrua concinnat Sylvanus, & Annua *Dona,*
    Quantus ubique Lepos ! quantus ubique Decor !
Apte antiqua novis miscentur, & utile dulci :
    Pallas ubique docet ; ridet ubique Venus.
' *Talis in æterno felix Vertumnus Olympo,
    ' Mille habet Ornatus, mille decenter habet.'
                      RUSTICUS."

In an Advertisement in March 1736, Twenty Pounds, Twelve
Pounds, and Eight Pounds, were severally offered for the three
best Poems on the DIVINE ATTRIBUTES †.—In July (p. 408) two
other chances were offered, a set of Magazines, large paper, for
six years, for the fourth prize, and a set of smaller for the fifth.

The first regular Address to the Reader is prefixed to the volume
for 1737, and contains a plain and manly Answer to Cavillers in the
public Newspapers —In the close of the volume, Mr. Cave says,
" The candid Reader, who knows the difficulty, and sometimes
danger, of publishing Speeches in Parliament, will easily conceive
that it is impossible to do it in the very words of the Speakers.
With regard to the major part, we pretend only to represent the
sense, as near as may be expected in a summary way ; and therefore, as to any little expression being mistaken, which does not
affect the scope of the argument in general, we hope, as not
being done with design, it will be favourably overlooked."

On this subject Cave again thus speaks in February 1738 :
" Such as see into the artifices and interested views of Writers,

* Tibullus, lib. IV.
† The first Poem on this subject is in the numbers for April and May 1737 ;
the second in June the same year.—In April 1738, is the following notice :—
" We expect every post that the Gold Medal, proposed as a Prize for the
Poems on the Christian Hero, will be adjusted. And as there is some prospect,
that the Gentlemen who are to judge and allot the forty pounds proposed as
Prizes for the Poems sent in on the Divine Attributes will now have leisure to
consider them ; we hope it will not be long before those Prizes will be settled,
though there are many Poems to peruse, and one of them equivalent with the
notes to 3000 lines."—A third Poem appeared in May 1738; and a fourth in June.
The Poems on the Divine Attributes being reduced to five, the decision of the
Prizes was finally left to the Authors, by voting among themselves, excepting
their own Poems. See the Number for April 1739, p. 166.

need not to be told that there has been a very strong combination of Booksellers and their dependants, the Authors and Printers of several Newspapers, in order, by ridiculous puffs, paragraphs of buffoonery, and fallacious advertisements, to set the Publick against this Magazine, which is entirely independant of them : but, as a great number of our Country Readers are unacquainted with such arts, we hope to be excused inserting the following remarks in our justification."

For these remarks, which are entirely of a temporary nature, and chiefly relate to personal quarrels, it may be sufficient to refer to the Volume in which they appeared; but a passage of Johnson's shall here be noticed.

" In a few years," says that able Writer, " a multitude of Magazines arose, and perished. Only ' The London Magazine,' supported by a powerful association of Booksellers, and circulated with all the art and all the cunning of Trade, exempted itself from the general fate of Cave's invaders, and obtained, though not an equal, yet a considerable sale *."

The tenor of this narrative requires that the name of Dr. JOHNSON should be prominently brought forward, in his early correspondence with Cave; which led to an uninterrupted friendship, and led ultimately to Johnson's permanent celebrity.

One Letter has been already given in p. x. It was anonymous, and no immediate intercourse appears to have arisen from it : but the following Letters were duly appreciated by Cave.

" SIR,	Greenwich †, next door to the Golden Hart, Church-street, July 12, 1737.

" Having observed in your papers ‡ very uncommon offers of encouragement to Men of Letters, I have chosen, being a stranger in London, to communicate to you the following design, which, I hope, if you join in it, will be of advantage to both of us. The History of the Council of Trent having been lately translated into French, and published with large notes by Dr. Le Courayer, the reputation of that book is so much revived in England, that it is presumed a new Translation of it from the

---

* This was actually the case in 1754; but even this Rival departed in 1785.

† At this time Johnson had written Three Acts of " Irene;" (see p. ix) and (as he told Mr. Boswell) retired for some time to a lodging at Greenwich, where he proceeded in it somewhat farther. He used to compose walking in the Park ; but did not stay long enough in that place to finish it.

‡ " It should seem from this Letter," says Mr. Boswell, " though subscribed with his own name, that he had not yet been introduced to Mr. Cave." Sir John Hawkins observes, that Cave's " temper was phlegmatic : though he assumed, as the Publisher of the Magazine, the name of *Sylvanus Urban*, he had few of those qualities that constitute the character of urbanity. His discernment was also slow , and as he had already at his command some Writers in Prose and Verse who, in the language of Booksellers, are called *good hands*, he was the backwarder in making advances, or courting an intimacy with Johnson."

Italian, together with Le Courayer's Notes from the French, could not fail of a favourable reception.

"If it be answered that the History is already in English, it must be remembered that there was the same objection against Le Courayer's undertaking, with this disadvantage, that the French had a Version by one of their best Translators; whereas you cannot read three pages of the English History* without discovering that the style is capable of great improvements; but whether those improvements are to be expected from the attempt, you must judge from the specimen, which, if you approve the proposal, I shall submit to your examination.

"Suppose the merit of the Versions equal, we may hope that the addition of the Notes will turn the balance in our favour, considering the reputation of the Annotator.

"Be pleased to favour me with a speedy answer, if you are not willing to engage in this scheme†; and appoint me a day to wait upon you if you are. I am, Sir,

"Your humble servant, SAM. JOHNSON."

"SIR, Castle-street, Wednesday morning [1738].

"When I took the liberty of writing to you a few days ago, I did not expect a repetition of the same pleasure so soon; for a pleasure I shall always think it, to converse in any manner with an ingenious and candid man; but, having the inclosed Poem in my hands to dispose of for the benefit of the Author (of whose abilities I shall say nothing, since I send you his performance) I believed I could not procure more advantageous terms from any person than from you, who have so much dis-

* An old Translation, by Sir Nathanael Brent, 1616.

† The recommendation was readily adopted by Mr. Cave; and Proposals were speedily issued (see p. xix) for publishing the Work by Subscription; but another Translation being at the same time announced under the patronage of Dr. (after Bp.) Pearce, the Work was suspended, and the designs of both proved abortive.—The account of Johnson's Translation is accurately stated in Gent. Mag. vol. LIV. p. 891. There were only *six* sheets printed off; and of these the greater part of the impression was converted into waste paper. A few copies were intended to have been reserved; but they were so carefully put by, as to be lost in the mass of Mr. Cave's papers deposited in St. John's Gate. Several years afterwards Bp. Warburton said, "I heartily wish we had a new edition of Father Paul. Such a thing, I remember, was proposed some years ago; but, I know not by what chance, it miscarried. I could wish that Mr. Johnson would give us the original on one side, and his translation on the other. But this will not hit the public taste."

Sir John Hawkins, speaking of Johnson's Translation, says, "Cave's acquiescence in the above Proposal drew Johnson into a close intimacy with him. He was much at St. John's Gate; and taught Garrick the way thither.—Cave had no great relish for mirth, but he could bear it; and having been told by Johnson, that his Friend had talents for the Theatre, and was come to London with a view to the profession of an Actor, expressed a wish to see him in some comic character. Garrick readily complied, and, as Cave himself told me, with a little preparation of the room over the great arch of St. John's Gate, and with the assistance of a few journeymen printers, who were called together for the purpose of reading the other parts, represented with all the graces of comic humour, the principal character in Fielding's farce of The Mock Doctor.

tinguished yourself by your generous encouragement of Poetry;
and whose judgment of that art nothing but your commendation of *my trifle* * can give me any occasion to call in question.

" I do not doubt but you will look over this Poem with another
eye, and reward it in a different manner, from a mercenary
Bookseller, who counts the lines he is to purchase †, and considers nothing but the bulk. I cannot help taking notice, that,
besides what the Author may hope for on account of his abilities, he has likewise another claim to your regard, as he lies
at present under very disadvantageous circumstances of fortune.
I beg, therefore, that you will favour me with a letter to-morrow, that I may know what you can afford to allow him, that
he may either part with it to you, or find out (which I do not
expect) some other way more to his satisfaction ‡.

" I have only to add, that as I am sensible I have transcribed
it very coarsely, which, after having altered it, I was obliged to
do, I will, if you please to transmit the sheets from the press,
correct it for you ; and take the trouble of altering any stroke
of satire which you may dislike. By exerting on this occasion
your usual generosity, you will not only encourage learning,
and relieve distress, but (though it be in comparison of the
other motives of very small account) oblige in a very sensible
manner, Sir, your very humble servant,   SAM. JOHNSON."

" SIR,   Monday, No. 6, Castle-street, April .., 1738.]
    " I am to return you thanks for the present you were so
kind as to send me ; and to intreat that you will be pleased to
inform me by the penny-post, whether you resolve to print the
Poem. If you please to send it me by the post, with a note to
Dodsley, I will go and read the lines to him, that we may have
his consent to put his name in the title-page. As to the printing, if it can be set immediately about, I will be so much the
Author's friend, as not to content myself with mere solicitations

    * His Ode *Ad Urbanum*, printed in vol. VIII. p. 156. A Translation of this
Ode, by an unknown Correspondent, appeared in the Magazine for the May
following.—The Latin Ode is repeated in vol. LIV. Part I; and a very elegant Translation of it by the late William Jackson, esq. of Canterbury in Part II.
    † The Poem mentioned in this and the three following Letters must
doubtless have been our Author's own "London," which was published in May
1738, and is recorded in Gent. Mag. vol. VIII. p. 269, "as being remarkable
for having got to the Second Edition in the space of a week." On a copy of the
First Edition of this Poem Johnson has inserted, "Written in 1738 ;" and, as it
was published in May that year, it is evident that much time was not engaged in
preparing it for the press.
    ‡ Speaking to me in conversation of his own employment on his first arrival
in town, Dr. Johnson observed, that he applied, among others, to Mr. Wilcox,
then a Bookseller of some eminence in the Strand ; who, after surveying Johnson's robust frame, with a significant look said, "Young man, you had better
buy a Porter's knot!"—The great Moralist, far from being offended at the advice
which had been given him, added, "Wilcox was one of my best Friends."—He
added, that Cave was a generous paymaster; but, in bargaining for Poetry, he
contracted for lines by the hundred, and expected the *long hundred*."

in his favour. I propose, if my calculation be near the truth, to engage for the reimbursement of all that you shall lose by an impression of 500; provided, as you very generously propose, that the profit, if any, be set aside for the Author's use, excepting the present you made, which, if he be a gainer, it is fit he should repay. I beg that you will let one of your servants write an exact account of the expence of such an impression, and send it with the Poem, that I may know what I engage for.

" I am very sensible, from your generosity on this occasion, of your regard to Learning, even in its unhappiest state; and cannot but think such a temper deserving of the gratitude of those who suffer so often from a contrary disposition.

" I am, Sir, your humble servant, SAM. JOHNSON."

" SIR, [April, 1738.]

" I waited on you to take the copy to Dodsley *: as I remember the number of lines which it contains, it will be no longer than " Eugenio †," with the quotatiohs, which must be subjoined at the bottom of the page; part of the beauty of the performance (if any beauty be allowed it) consisting in adapting Juvenal's sentiments to modern facts and persons. It will, with those additions, very conveniently make five sheets; and since the expence will be no more, I shall contentedly insure it, as I mentioned in my last. If it be not therefore gone to Dodsley's, I beg it may be sent me by the penny-post, that I may have it in the evening. I have composed a Greek Epigram

* Sir John Hawkins says, that " Johnson and Dodsley were soon agreed; the price asked by one, and assented to by the other was, as I have been informed, Fifty Pounds: a reward for his labour and ingenuity, that induced Johnson ever after to call Dodsley his Patron ;" and adds, " It came abroad in the year above-mentioned, with the name of Cave as the Printer, though without that of the Author."

† " Eugenio, a Virtuous and Happy Life, inscribed to Mr. Pope," published by Dodsley in April 1737. The author of this poem, a work by no means des-titute of public spirit, and which had had the advantage of being corrected by Dean Swift, was Mr. Beach, a wine-merchant at Wrexham, in Denbighshire, a man of learning, of great humanity, of an easy fortune, and much respected. He is said by some to have entertained very blamable notions in religion ; but this appears rather to be a conjecture than a well-established fact. It is certain that he was at times grievously afflicted with a terrible disorder in his head, to which his friends ascribed his melancholy exit. On May 17, 1737, in less than a month after the publication of his poem, he cut his throat with such shocking resolution, that it was reported his head was almost severed from his body. This dreadful catastrophe is thus mentioned by Dr. Herring (then Bp. of Bangor) in one of his letters to Mr. Duncombe, p. 54: " The verses you sent me are very sensible and touching; and the sentiments in them, I doubt not, exhilarated the blood for some time, and suspended the black execution; but his distemper, it may be said, got the better, and carried him off at last. I would willingly put the best construction upon these melancholy accidents, and thus leave the suf-ferers to the Father of Mercies." And an " Epilogue to Cato, for the Scholars at Wrexham, 1735," shews how much better Mr. Beach could think than act.

to Eliza*, and think she ought to be celebrated in as many different languages as Lewis le Grand. Pray send me word when you will begin upon the Poem, for it is a long way to walk †. I would leave my Epigram, but have not day-light to transcribe it. I am, Sir, yours, &c. SAM. JOHNSON."

"SIR,
[April, 1738.]
" I am extremely obliged by your kind Letter; and will not fail to attend you to-morrow with *Irene* ‡, who looks upon you as one of her best friends. I was to-day with Mr. Dodsley, who declares very warmly in favour of the Paper § you sent him, which he desires to have a share in, it being, as he says, a creditable thing to be concerned in. I knew not what answer to make till I had consulted you, nor what to demand on the Author's part; but am very willing that, if you please, he should have a part in it, as he will undoubtedly be more diligent to disperse and promote it. If you can send me word to-morrow what I shall pay to him, I will settle matters, and bring the Poem with me for the press, which, as the town empties, we cannot be too quick with. I am, Sir, yours, &c. SAM. JOHNSON.

"SIR,
Wednesday, September, [1738].
" I did not care to detain your servant while I wrote an answer to your letter, in which you seem to insinuate that I had promised more than I am ready to perform. If I have raised your expectations by any thing that may have escaped my memory, I am sorry; and if you remind me of it, shall thank you for the favour. If I made *fewer alterations* than usual in the Debates ∥, it was only because there appeared, and still appears to be, less need of alteration.

"The verses to Lady Firebrace¶ may be had when you please, for you know that such a subject neither deserves much thought, nor requires it. The Chinese Stories ** may be had folded down when you please to send, in which I do not recollect that you desired any alterations to be made.

"In answer to another query, I am very willing to write; and had consulted with you about it last night if there had been

---

* The Epigram in Greek and Latin, addressed to Miss Elizabeth Carter, printed in the Magazine, vol. VIII. p. 210. Of this Lady see hereafter, p. xx.
† He lived at that time in Castle-street, Cavendish-square.
‡ This Tragedy, though Three Acts of it were written in 1737 (see pages ix. and xiv.) was neither acted nor published till 1749.
§ This alludes to the " History of the Council of Trent;" to the Proposals for which, Mr. Dodsley's name was accordingly added. See p. xix.
∥ At this time Johnson was the Reviser, not the Writer, of the Debates in the Senate of Liliput.
¶ They appeared in the Magazine, vol. VIII. p. 486.—The Life of Father Paul was given in the same volume, p. 581.
** Du Halde's Description of China was then publishing by Mr. Cave in numbers, whence Johnson selected pieces for the embellishment of the Magazine.

time; for I think it the most proper way of inviting such a Correspondence as may be an advantage to the paper, not a load upon it.

"As to the Prize Verses*, a backwardness to determine their degrees of merit is not peculiar to me. You may, if you please, still have what I can say; but I shall engage with little spirit in an affair which I shall hardly end to my own satisfaction, and certainly not to the satisfaction of the parties concerned.

"As to Father Paul, I have not yet been just to my Proposal†; but have met with impediments, which, I hope, are now at an end; and if you find the progress hereafter not such as you have a right to expect, you can easily stimulate a negligent translator. If any or all of these have contributed to your discontent, I will endeavour to remove it; and desire you to propose the question to which you wish for an answer.

I am, Sir, your humble servant,   SAM. JOHNSON."

"SIR,   [October 1738].

"I am pretty much of your opinion, that *the Commentary*‡ cannot be prosecuted with any appearance of success, for as the names of the authors concerned are of more weight in the performance than its own intrinsic merit, the publick will be soon satisfied with it. And I think the *Examen* should be pushed forward with the utmost expedition. Thus, 'This day, &c. An Examen of Mr. Pope's Essay, &c. containing a succinct Account of the Philosophy of Mr. Leibnitz on the System of the Fatalists, with a Confutation of their Opinions, and an Illustration of the

---

* The Prizes are enumerated in p. xiii.

† The following Advertisement, from "The Weekly Miscellany, Oct. 21, 1738," may now be considered as a curiosity: "Just published, Proposals for printing the History of the Council of Trent, translated from the Italian of Father Paul Sarpi; with the Author's Life, and Notes Theological, Historical, and Critical, from the French Edition of Dr. Le Courayer. To which are added, Observations on the History and Notes; and Illustrations from various Authors; both printed and manuscript. By S. Johnson. 1. The work will consist of two hundred sheets, and be two volumes in quarto, printed on good paper and letter. 2. The price will be 18s. each volume, to be paid half a guinea at the time of subscribing, and half a guinea at the delivery of the first volume, and the rest at the delivery of the second volume, in sheets. 3. Two-pence to be abated for every sheet less than two hundred. It may be had on a large paper, in three volumes, at the price of three guineas, one to be paid at the time of subscribing, another at the delivery of the first, and the rest at the delivery of the other volumes. The work is now in the press, and will be diligently prosecuted. Subscriptions are taken in by Mr. Dodsley in Pall Mall, Mr. Rivington in St. St. Paul's Church-yard, by E. Cave at St. John's Gate, and the Translator, at No. 6, in Castle-street, by Cavendish-square."

‡ The work here alluded to was kept back till November 1741, when it appeared under the title of "A Commentary on Mr. Pope's Principles of Morality, and Essay on Man. By Mons. Crousaz. With the Abbé du Resnel's Translation of the Essay into French Verse, and the English interlined; also Observations on the French, Italian, and English Poetry."

Doctrine of Free-will*,' with what else you think proper. It will, above all, be necessary to take notice, that it is a thing distinct from the Commentary.

"I was so far from imagining they *stood still*†, that I conceived them to have a good deal before-hand, and therefore was less anxious in providing them more. But if ever they stand still on my account, it must doubtless be charged to me ; and whatever else shall be reasonable, I shall not oppose; but beg a suspense of judgment till morning, when I must entreat you to send me a dozen Proposals, and you shall then have copy to spare. Pray muster up the Proposals if you can, or let the boy recall them from the Booksellers ‡. I am, Sir,

Yours, *innpransus,*   SAM. JOHNSON."

"It is remarkable," says Boswell, "that this Letter concludes with a fair confession that he had not a dinner §; and it is no less remarkable that, though in this state of want himself, his benevolent heart was not insensible to the necessities of an humble labourer in literature, as appears from the next Letter.

"DEAR SIR,   [No date.]
"You may remember I have formerly talked with you about a Military Dictionary. The eldest Mr. Macbean ‖, who was with Mr. Chambers¶, has very good materials for such a work, which I have seen, and will do it at a very low rate. I think the terms of War and Navigation might be comprised with good explanations in one octavo pica, which he is willing to do for

---

* This Treatise (the production, as it now appears, of the learned Miss Carter), was published, price 2s. in November 1738, under the title of "An Examination of Mr. Pope's Essay on Man; containing a succinct View of the System of the Fatalists, and a Confutation of their Opinions; with an Illustration of the Doctrine of Free-Will, and an Enquiry what View Mr. Pope might have in touching upon the Leibnitzian Philosophy and Fatalism. By Mr. Crousaz, Professor of Philosophy and Mathematicks at Lausanne, &c. Printed for A. Dodd, without Temple Bar, and sold by all the Booksellers. See Gent. Mag. vol. VIII. pp. 608, 664.

† This is a *typographical* phrase; and alludes to the Compositors in Cave's Printing-office, who were then "*standing still*" for want of copy.

‡ 6000 Copies of these Proposals had been dispersed.

§ Might not, however, *impransus* simply mean *before dinner,* or *I have not dined?* The Letter, perhaps, was written in a hurry, late in the day.

‖ Mr. Macbean afterwards published a Dictionary of the Bible; and was employed by the Booksellers in compiling the Poetical Index to Dr. Johnson's Edition of the English Poets. He made also a similar Index to Mr. Nichols's "Select Collection." See in Gent. Mag. vol. LVI. p. 413, a letter from Mr. Ephraim Chambers to Mr. Macbean, directing him to send to *Canqnbury-house* the apparatus he used in correcting the new edition of his "Cyclopædia." In 1780, this useful compiler being oppressed by age and poverty, Dr. Johnson (who had for many years afforded him an asylum) endeavoured to obtain for him an admission into the Charter-house. A very kind letter of Lord Thurlow on this occasion is preserved by Mr. Boswell, Life of Johnson, vol. III. p. 423. Of Mr. Macbean's future history, I have not been able to obtain any particulars.

¶ Mr. Ephraim Chambers, Author of the "Cyclopædia."

twelve shillings a sheet, to be made up a guinea at the second
mpression. If you think on it, I will wait on you with him. I
am, Sir,   Your humble servant,   SAM. JOHNSON.
    " Pray lend me Topsel on Animals."

At this period Cave had the honour, as well as the advantage,
of enrolling the name of JOHNSON as a regular Coadjutor in the
Magazine, which for some years was one of his principal sources
for employment and support.

"The Gentleman's Magazine," says Boswell, " had attracted
the notice and esteem of Johnson, in an eminent degree, before
he came to London as an adventurer in Literature. He told
me that, when he first saw St. John's Gate, the place where that
deservedly popular Miscellany was originally printed, he *beheld
it with reverence.* Johnson has dignified the Magazine by the
importance with which he invests the life of Cave; but he has
given it still greater lustre by the various admirable Essays
which he wrote for it."

His earliest known communication was a copy of Latin verses,
in March 1738, addressed to the Editor* in so happy a style
of compliment, that Cave must have been destitute both of taste
and sensibility, had he not felt himself most abundantly gratified.
In the Magazine also for April are the following lines :

    " *Ad* RICARDUM SAVAGE, *Arm. Humani Generis Amatorem.*
        " Humani studium generis cui pectore fervet,
            O! colat humanum te foveatque genus !"

Numerous are the articles in this Magazine which might now be
traced to Johnson's pen. Some of them he has noticed in the preceding Letters. To these may be added the "Life of Father Paul,"
and the " Life of Boerhaave," in which it will be observed that
he discovers the love of Chemistry, which never forsook him ; an
Epigram, both in Greek and Latin, to Eliza Carter; the English
Verses to the same Lady ; and a Greek Epigram to Dr. Birch.

He wrote also the Preface to that year's Volume; which,
though prefixed to it when bound, is always published with the
Supplement, and is therefore the last composition belonging to
it. The ability and nice adaptation with which he could draw
up a prefatory address was one of his peculiar excellences; and
this Preface particularly demands insertion.

    " The usual design of Addresses of this sort is to implore the
candour of the Publick ; we have always had the more pleasing
province of returning thanks, and making our acknowledgments
for the kind acceptance which our monthly collections have met
with. This, it seems, did not sufficiently appear from the numerous
sale and repeated impressions of our books, which have at once

* An Ode to Mr. Urban. See before, p. xvi.

exceeded our merit and our expectation; but have been still more plainly attested by the clamours, rage, and calumnies of our Competitors, of whom we have seldom taken any notice, not only because it is cruelty to insult the depressed, and folly to engage with desperation, but because we consider all their outcries, menaces, and boasts, as nothing more than advertisements in our favour, being evidently drawn up with the bitterness of baffled malice and disappointed hope; and almost discovering, in plain terms, that the unhappy Authors have SEVENTY THOUSAND *London Magazines* mouldering in their warehouses, returned from all parts of the Kingdom, unsold, unread, and disregarded.

"Our obligations for the encouragement we have so long continued to receive are so much the greater, as no artifices have been omitted to supplant us. Our Adversaries cannot be denied the praise of industry; how far they can be celebrated for an honest industry we leave to the decision of the Publick, and even of their brethren the Booksellers, not including those whose advertisements they obliterated to paste their invectives in our Book.

"The success of the GENTLEMAN'S MAGAZINE has given rise to almost* twenty Imitations of it, which are either all dead, or very little regarded by the World. Before we had published sixteen months, we met with such a general approbation, that a knot of enterprizing Geniuses, and sagacious Inventors, assembled from all parts of the Town, agreed with an unanimity natural to understandings of the same size to seize upon our whole plan, without changing even the title. Some weak objections were indeed made by one of them against the design, as having an air of servility, dishonesty, and piracy; but it was concluded that all these imputations might be avoided by giving the picture of St. Paul's instead of St. John's Gate; it was, however, thought indispensably necessary to add, printed in St. John's-street, though there was then no Printing-house in that place. That these Plagiaries should, after having thus stolen their whole design, charge us with robbery, on any occasion, is a degree of impudence scarcely to be matched, and certainly entitles them to the first rank among false heroes. We have therefore inserted their names at length in our February Magazine, p. 61, being desirous that every man should enjoy the reputation he deserves.

* "The Weekly Magazine, The Gentleman's Magazine and Oracle, The Universal Magazine, The General Magazine, The Oxford Magazine, The Distillers Magazine, The Country Magazine, the Manchester Magazine, The Leeds Magazine, The Dublin Magazine, and The Lady's Magazine, with several other of the like kind, all dwindled to their primitive nothing; to which we may add, The Bee, and Grub Street Journal, that enemy to all works of merit."

" Another attack has been made upon us by the Author of *Common Sense*, an Adversary equally malicious with the former, and equally despicable. What were his views, or what his provocations, we know not, nor have thought him considerable enough to enquire. To make him any further answer, would be to descend too low; but, as he is one of those happy Writers who are best exposed by quoting their own words, we have given his elegant remarks in our Magazine for December at the foot of p. 640, where the Reader may entertain himself at his leisure with an agreeable mixture of scurrility and false grammar.

" For the future, we shall rarely offend him by adopting any of his performances, being unwilling to prolong the life of such pieces as deserve no other fate than to be hissed, torn, and forgotten. However, that the curiosity of our Readers may not be disappointed, we shall, whenever we find him a little excelling himself, perhaps print his dissertations upon our blue covers, that they may be looked over, and stripped off, without disgracing our collection or swelling our volumes.

" We are sorry that, by inserting some of his Essays, we have filled the head of this petty Writer with idle chimeras of applause, laurels, and immortality ; this injury we did not intend, nor suspected the bad effect of our regard for him, till we saw in the Postscript to one of his Papers a wild prediction of the honours to be paid him by future ages*. Should any mention be made of him or his writings by Posterity, it will probably be in words like these : ' In the GENTLEMAN'S MAGAZINE are still preserved some Essays under the specious and inviting title of *Common Sense*. How papers of so little value came to be rescued from the common lot of dulness, we are at this distance of time unable to conceive, but imagine that personal friendship prevailed with URBAN to admit them in opposition to his judgment. If this was the reason, he met afterwards with the treatment which all deserve who patronise stupidity ; for the Writer, instead of acknowledging his favours, complains of injustice, robbery, and mutilation ; but complains in a style so barbarous and indecent, as sufficiently confutes his own calumnies.' In this manner must this Author expect to be mentioned.

" But of him, and our other Adversaries, we beg the Reader's

---

* " I make no doubt but after some grave Historian, 3 or 400 hundred years hence, has described the corruption, the baseness, and the flattery which men run into in these times, he will make the following observation : in the year 1737, a *certain* unknown Author published a *Writing* under the title of *Common Sense*. This *Writing* came out weekly *in* little detached Essays, some of which are political, some moral, and others humourous. By the best judgment that can be formed of a work, the *style* and language of which is become so obsolete, that it is scarcely intelligible, it answers the title well, &c."

Common Sense Journal, March 11, 1738.

pardon for having said so much. We hope it will be remembered in our favour, that it is sometimes necessary to chastise insolence, and that there is a sort of men who cannot distinguish between forbearance and cowardice."

A circumstance occurred in this year, which brought the talents of Johnson into more active service. The Parliamentary Debates had hitherto been given by Cave, with the assistance of Mr. William Guthrie, a man who deserves to be respectfully noticed in the literary history of this country. In this manner all went on smoothly; till, on the 13th of April 1738, a complaint being made to the House, that the publishers of several written and printed News-Letters and Papers had taken upon them to give accounts therein of the Proceedings of the House; it was Resolved, "That it is a high indignity to, and a notorious breach of, the Privileges of this House, for any News-writer, in Letters or other Papers (as Minutes, or under any other denomination), or for any Printer or Publisher of any printed Newspaper of any denomination, to presume to insert in the said Letters or Papers, or to give therein, any account of the Debates, or other Proceedings, of this House, or any Committee thereof, as well during the Recess, as the Sitting of Parliament; and that this House will proceed with the utmost severity against such offenders."

Some expedient was now become necessary; and the *caution* (not the *vanity)* of Cave suggested to him a popular fiction. In June 1738 he prefaced the Debates by what he chose to call "An Appendix to Captain Lemuel Gulliver's Account of the famous Empire of Liliput;" and the Proceedings in Parliament were given as "Debates in the Senate of Liliput," sometimes with feigned denominations of the several speakers, sometimes with denominations formed of the letters of their real names, in the manner of what is called an anagram, so that they might easily be decyphered. Parliament then kept the Press in a kind of mysterious awe, which made it necessary to have recourse to such devices. Not thinking himself perfectly secure, even by this total concealment of the speakers, he did not venture to put his own name to the Title-pages of the Magazine; but published them in the name of a Nephew, "Edward Cave, junior*."

In 1739, besides the share which Johnson took in conjunction with Guthrie in the Parliamentary Debates, and in correcting the labours of other Correspondents, the Magazine for the

* This was continued till the death of that Nephew, at the end of the year 1752. In 1753 Mr. Cave again used his own name; and gave the Debates, as at first, with the initial and final letters of the name of each Speaker.

month of March, was enriched by the following animated " Appeal to the Publick :"

> ' Men' moveat cimex Pantilius ? aut crucier quod
> Vellicet absentem Demetrius ?'   HOR.
> ' Laudat, amat, cantat nostros mea Roma libellos,
> Meque sinus omnes, me manus omnis habet.
> Ecce rubet quidam, pallet, stupet, oscitat, odit.
> Hoc volo, nunc nobis carmina nostra placent.'   MARTIAL.

" It is plain from the conduct of Writers of the first class, that they have esteemed it no derogation from their characters to defend themselves against the censures of Ignorance, or the calumnies of Envy. It is not reasonable to suppose that they always judged their adversaries worthy of a formal confutation, but they concluded it not prudent to neglect the feeblest attacks; they knew that such men have often done hurt, who had not abilities to do good; that the weakest hand, if not timely disarmed, may stab a hero in his sleep; that a worm, however small, may destroy a fleet in the acorn; and that citadels, which have defied armies, have been blown up by rats.

" In imitation of these great examples, we think it not absolutely needless to vindicate ourselves from the virulent aspersions of the *Craftsman* and *Common Sense,* because their accusations, though entirely groundless, and without the least proof, are urged with an air of confidence which the unwary may mistake for consciousness of truth.

" In order to set the proceedings of these calumniators in a proper light, it is necessary to inform such of our Readers as are unacquainted with the artifices of Trade, that we originally incurred the displeasure of the greatest part of the Booksellers by keeping this Magazine wholly in our own hands, without admitting any of that Fraternity into a share of the property. For nothing is more criminal, in the opinion of many of them, than for an Author to enjoy more advantage from his own Works than they are disposed to allow him. This is a principle so well established among them, that we can produce some who threatened Printers with their highest displeasure for their having dared to print Books for those that wrote them.

' Hinc iræ, hinc odia.

" This was the first ground of their animosity, which, for some time, proceeded no farther than private murmurs, and petty discouragements. At length, determining to be no longer debarred from a share in so beneficial a project, a knot of them combined to seize our whole plan; and, without the least attempt to vary or improve it, began with the utmost vigour to print and circulate the *London Magazine,* with such success, that in a few years, while we were printing the fifth edition of some of our earliest Numbers, they had SEVENTY THOUSAND of their Books returned unsold upon their hands.

" It was then time to exert their utmost efforts to put a stop to our progress, and nothing was to be left unattempted that interest could suggest. It will be easily imagined, that their influence among those of their own trade was greater than ours, and that their Collections were therefore more industriously propagated by their brethren ; but this being the natural consequence of such a relation, and therefore excusable, is only mentioned to shew the disadvantages against which we are obliged to struggle, and to convince the Reader, that we who depend so entirely upon his approbation, shall omit nothing to deserve it.

" They then had recourse to Advertisements, in which they sometimes made faint attempts to be witty, and sometimes were content with being merely scurrilous ; but finding that their attacks, while we had an opportunity of returning hostilities, generally procured them such treatment as very little contributed to their reputation, they came at last to a Resolution of excluding us from the Newspapers in which they have any influence ; by this means they can at present insult us with impunity, and without the least danger of confutation.

" Their last, and indeed their most artful expedient, has been to hire and incite the weekly journalists against us. The first weak attempt was made by the *Universal Spectator;* but this we took not the least notice of, as we did not imagine it would ever come to the knowledge of the Publick.

" Whether there was then a confederacy between this journal and *Common Sense,* as at present between *Common Sense* and the *Craftsman,* or whether understandings of the same form receive at certain times the same impressions from the Planets, I know not ; but about that time war was likewise declared against us by the redoubted Author of *Common Sense;* an Adversary not so much to be dreaded for his abilities as for the title of his Paper, behind which he has the art of sheltering himself in perfect security. He defeats all his enemies by calling them *enemies to Common Sense,* and silences the strongest objections and the clearest reasonings, by assuring his readers that *they are contrary to Common Sense.*

" I must confess, to the immortal honour of this great Writer, that I can remember but too instances of a genius able to use a few syllables to such great and so various purposes. One is the old man in *Shadwell,* who seems, by long time and experience, to have attained to equal perfection with our Author ; for, ' when a young fellow began to prate and be pert, says he, I silenced him with my *old word,* TACE *is Latin for a candle.*'

" The other, who seems yet more to resemble this Writer, was one *Goodman,* a horsestealer, who being asked, after having been found guilty by the jury, what he had to offer, to prevent sentence of death from being passed upon him, did not attempt to extenuate his crime, but entreated the judge to beware of hanging a *Good-man.*

"This Writer we thought, however injudiciously, worthy, not indeed of a reply, but of some correction; and in our Magazine for December 1738, and the Preface to the Supplement, treated him in such a manner as he does not seem inclined to forget. From that time, losing all patience, he has exhausted his stores of scurrility upon us; but our Readers will find, upon consulting the passages above-mentioned, that he has received too much provocation to be admitted as an impartial critick.

"In our Magazine for January, p. 24, we made a remark upon the *Craftsman,* and in p. 3 dropped some general observations upon the weekly Writers, by which we did not expect to make them more our friends. Nor, indeed, did we imagine, that this would have inflamed *Caleb* to so high a degree. His resentment has risen so much above the provocation, that we cannot but impute it more to what he fears than what he has felt. He has seen the solecisms of his brother *Common Sense* exposed, and remembers that

—— 'Tua Res agitur, Paries cum proximus ardet.'

He imagines that he shall soon fall under the same censure, and is willing that our criticisms shall appear rather the effects of our resentment than our judgment.

"For this reason I suppose (for I can find no other), he has joined with *Common Sense* to charge us with partiality, and to recommend the *London Magazine,* as drawn up with less regard to interest or party. A favour, which the Authors of that Collection have endeavoured to deserve from them by the most servile adulation. But as we have a higher opinion of the candour of Readers, than to believe that they will condemn us without examination, or give up their right of judging for themselves, we are unconcerned at this charge, though the most atrocious and malignant that can be brought against us. We entreat only to be compared with our Rivals, in full confidence, that not only our innocence, but our superiority will appear."

This was followed by a Letter in the Daily Advertiser of April 18, by the same able hand:

"SIR, It seems now an established custom with the Authors of the *Craftsman* and *White-Fryers Common Sense,* to conclude their Papers with virulent reflections upon the Compilers of the Gentleman's Magazine; and how just soever the reasons are which Urban, in his Appeal to the Publick, at the front of his last Book, has assigned for these their partial and repeated outcries, I cannot but applaud the method which he has taken to obviate any prejudices that might arise from them. He has publicly and seriously exhorted his Readers to compare his Collections with

those of his Rivals, for that no man can have a right to give his
opinion in this dispute without making a comparison, is undeni-
able ; and, from that which I have occasionally made, I am convinced that Urban has consulted his own reputation by proposing
it. I have found, upon an impartial and candid examination,
that in the first part, which contains Debates upon political subjects, Urban abounds in things, and his Rivals in words; that he
has a chain of arguments, and they a flow of periods; that their
style is uniform and diffused ; his, varied, concise, and energetic.

" In the second part, which is the chief subject of dispute, I
cannot discern any instance of partiality in either, or any argument purposely suppressed or obscured ; Urban, indeed, sometimes contracts the weekly Essays to a narrower compass, when
he can do it without any injury to their strength or perspicuity,
and thus he gains room for original Lives, Letters, and Dissertations, in which he confessedly and evidently excels his Competitors.

" In the Poetical part, those who have any taste for that sort
of reading will perceive a manifest difference : the great number of ingenious originals which Urban is constantly supplied
with, give a shameful foil to the crude productions in the other,
which usually exhibits such trash as schoolboys would be whipt
for ; but, on the other hand, the greatest genius might own with
honour many pieces inserted in the Gentleman's Magazine; I
need instance no farther than the last : and, indeed, it would
argue an extreme injustice in poetical writers, if they should
not preferably oblige him with their productions, who had from
time to time proposed and disbursed such large benefactions in
prizes for their encouragement. But although my judgment
may be doubted, which however is impartially given, the balance
must incline to Urban, by the suffrage of all who delight in
musick, since he had added the notes of some curious tunes to
his poetry ; an entertainment not to be met with in the other
Magazine.

" The Historical, which makes the last division of the work, is
for the most part carefully drawn up by both; but, in the Foreign
Article, Urban has of late, by the addition of Maps copied from
the latest drafts, made an improvement of which his Rivals
themselves cannot deny the usefulness or merit. And in his
account of Domestic Transactions, he sometimes not only
inserts curious minutes, but large articles, which, though very
important, are neglected by his Competitors, as the City's Peti-
tion in the Magazine for February, and the Lords' Protest in
that for March."

To the Magazine for 1739 there is no Preface; but that deficiency was supplied by the following appropriate Address to Sylvanus Urban on the conclusion of the Volume * :

" Though hard the task each different taste to please,
'Tis yours that labour to perform with ease ;
Party itself impartial to display,
And charm alike the serious and the gay.
Whoever, anxious for Britannia's fate,
Turns his reflections on affairs of State,
May here the wily Statesman's mazes wind,
And secrets veil'd from vulgar Readers find ;
With *Liliputian* Senators debate,
And in their contests view — the *British* State.
Is there who controversial depths would try ?
Or to th' amazing heights of mystery fly ?
Their different lines, lo ! Martin, Walker, bring,
And Whitefield, Wesley, freely lend their wing.
Here Tales, with pleasure and instruction fraught,
Or shrewd Ænigmas, lure the gay — to thought ;
There sage Philosophy deep-musing tries
T' explore the secrets of earth, air, and skies,
With skill the Geographic Plans displayed
Lend to Historic Page their friendly aid.
And here, if Lyricks are the Reader's choice,
Apt words instruct the mind, apt notes the voice.
While Poesy, divinely-born, prepares
To soothe our passions with her powerful airs,
Or the fair forms displays, in sky-dipt teints,
Which Nature, or which Virtue, strongly paints.

" These, Urban, thy enamell'd Garden show,
Where flowers of every tribe and climate grow.
Whate'er for scent, for beauty, or for use,
Claim most esteem, thy rich parterres produce.
Here lovely Natives of Britannia's soil,
There fair Exotics, nursed with cost and toil,
Delightful mixture, charm the curious sight,
And all the beauties of the World unite.
Hither resort, ye Virtuous, Learn'd, and Fair,
Crop the sweet blooms, and breathe the fragrant air.
But, timely warn'd, a near Inclosure fly,
Whose outward semblance cheats the heedless eye.
The choaking weeds exile the blushing rose,
The poppy there its sleepy influence shows ;
The deadly nightshade breathes infection round,
And sapless stalks o'erspread the tainted ground. BARDUS."

* I should have been glad to have pointed out the Author of these Lines, which I thought might possibly be Johnson's: but they were by an Oxford Correspondent, who had performed a similar act of kindness in 1735 and in 1736.

In 1740, Johnson wrote for the Magazine the Life of Drake;
and the first parts of those of Admiral Blake and Philip Barretier, which he finished in the next year. The following Preface also in that Volume is certainly from his masterly pen:

" Having now concluded our Tenth Volume, we are unwilling
to send it out without a Preface, though none of the common
topicks of Prefaces are now left us. To implore the candour of
the Publick to a Work so well received, would expose us to the
imputation of affected modesty or insatiable avarice. To promise the continuance of that industry, which has hitherto so
generally recommended us, is at least unnecessary; since from
that alone we can expect the continuance of our success. To
criticize the imitations of our Magazine, would be to trample on
the dead, to disturb the dying, or encounter the still-born. To
recommend our undertaking by any encomiums of our own,
would be to suppose mankind have hitherto approved it without
knowing why. And to mention our errors or defects, would be
to do for our rivals what they have never yet been able to do for
themselves. Our Preface had, therefore, been very short, had
not fortune thrown into our hands an ingenious Dissertation,
which we shall impart to our Readers, that they may not look
upon the humble Compilers of a Monthly Chronicle with too
much contempt, when they find such Writers employed to
register the daily transactions of the Roman Heroes. And we
cannot but flatter ourselves with some hope, that it will still
more advance our reputation to shew, what will appear from
the following Essay, that our Magazine is such a collection of
political intelligence as Cicero himself would have approved."

Then follows a very learned Dissertation "on the *Acta Diurna*
of the Romans," undoubtedly by the same able Writer.

A new æra in potiticks bringing on much warmer Parliamentary Debates, required "the pen of a more nervous Writer than
he who had hitherto conducted them;" and "Cave, dismissing
Guthrie, committed the care of this part of his monthly publication to JOHNSON;" who had already given ample specimens
of his ability. But the Lilliputian disguise was still continued,
even beyond the period of Johnson's Debates; [which, as has
been authenticated by his own Diary, began Nov. 19, 1740,
and ended Feb. 23, 1742-3.] And these Debates, which, every
competent judge must allow, exhibit a memorable specimen of
the extent and promptitude of Johnson's faculties, and which
have induced learned Foreigners to compare British with Roman
eloquence, were hastily sketched by Johnson while he was not
yet 32, while he had little acquaintance with life, while he was
struggling, not for distinction, but existence.

Johnson's portion of the " Parliamentary Debates " was collected in 1787 into two octavo volumes; to which the Editor

has substituted the real for the fictitious Speakers. — " The illuminations of Johnson's Oratory," it is there properly ob- served, " were obscured by the jargon which Cave thought it prudent to adopt, to avoid Parliamentary indignation."

Six days only before his death, this incomparable Friend requested to see the present Writer, from whom he had pre- viously borrowed some of the early Volumes of the Magazine, with a professed intention to point out the pieces which he had written in that collection. The books lay on this table, with many leaves doubled down, particularly those which contained his share in the Parliamentary Debates. And such was the goodness of Johnson's heart, that he solemnly declared, " that the only part of his Writings which then gave him any com- punction, was his account of the Debates in the Gentleman's Magazine; but that, at the time he wrote them, he did not think he was imposing on the world. The mode," he said, " was, to fix upon a Speaker's name ; then to make an argument for him ; and to conjure up an answer. He wrote those Debates with more velocity than any other of his productions; often three columns of the Magazine within the hour. He once wrote *ten pages* in a single day, and that not a long one, beginning per- haps at noon, and ending early in the evening.

In 1741 he wrote for the Magazine the Conclusion of the Lives of Blake and Barretier; a free Translation of the Jests of Hierocles, with an Introduction; and (Mr. Boswell suggests) the following pieces : Debate on the Proposal of Parliament to Cromwell, to assume the Title of King, abridged, modified, and di- gested ; Translation of Abbé Gwynn's Dissertation on the Amazons; and a Translation of Fontenelle's Panegyrick on Dr. Morin *.

He concluded this year's assistance by the following Preface :

" We have now completed our Eleventh Volume, with a suc- cess which no other periodical Work ever yet could boast of. The Gentleman's Magazine is read as far as the English lan- guage extends, and we see it re-printed from several presses in Great Britain, Ireland, and the Plantations. Our Debates and Poetical Pieces are copied by some, our Foreign History by others, and the Lives which we have inserted of eminent Men, have been taken into Works of larger size, and, with other parts of our Book, been translated into foreign languages.

" We hope that the mention of these particulars will not be imputed to vanity, but to a proper regard for our Readers and Correspondents; for it is no more than justice to inform each Reader, that what he is pleased to encourage receives the sanc- tion and approbation of the learned and judicious ; and to con- ceal from our Correspondents the satisfaction of knowing that

* Two notes on this article appear undoubtedly to be Johnson's.

what they oblige us with is most effectually diffused, would be an ill return for the preference they have given us : a favour, which will be as gratefully remembered as it has been long and largely experienced.

" All the merit we at first pretended to, and all the share of applause we now claim, is from a diligent and impartial endeavour to exhibit a well-chosen variety of subjects : to render this variety the greater, we resolved to make our Collection *more in quantity* than any other Editor's : what we have promised we have performed, and have besides added many original Pieces.

" How those who profess to be *only Collectors* can be acquitted of imposture, in constantly asserting that they have *more in quantity and greater variety*, when they not only fall short of us more than 70 pages in a Volume, but confine themselves to fewer subjects, we leave the Publick to determine.

" It is no wonder that these men, who can persist in a falsehood so easily to be confuted, should propagate another equally gross, though more malicious—that we are biassed by party considerations ; a calumny which impartiality always receives from the bigots of all parties : nor have we escaped the censure of that very party whose particular interest we are said to espouse.

" As these imputations appear, therefore, to be suggested by the partiality and avarice of the propagators, we have nothing to do but intreat a 'comparison, that those to whom they are suggested may judge from their own inspection and observation. They will, we hope, easily perceive that we pass by no object of laudable curiosity, omit no reigning topick of conversation, and forget no matter that may instruct the present age, or be useful to posterity."

In 1742, on the suggestion of some literary friends, Mr. Cave commenced an interesting publication, under the title of " Miscellaneous Correspondence ; containing Essays, Dissertations, &c. on various Subjects, sent to the Author of The Gentleman's Magazine, which could not be conveniently inserted at length, or properly abridged." This work was continued till 1747, when it was concluded by a ninth number, and a complete Index ; the whole forming a neat octavo volume, which is now exceedingly rare, and to be found in very few sets of the Magazine. It is ornamented with a good portrait of Queen Elizabeth, accompanied by her Translation of a Dialogue of Xenophon, and one whole page in fac-simile of the Queen's hand-writing.

The Miscellaneous Volume is thus briefly prefaced :

" Most of the following Pieces relate to subjects that have been controverted in the course of our Magazine, but could not be conveniently inserted, for the reasons mentioned in vol. x. p. 250. We thought it therefore our duty to make a publication in this manner, which we hope our Correspondents will accept as an instance of our gratitude and willingness to oblige them. We ought indeed to ask their pardon for so long a delay, it being not less than two years since we gave them expectations of seeing their Letters appear. But, after several sheets were printed off, some Dissertations which we mentioned in vol. x. p. 297, were unluckily mislaid. However, should this undertaking meet with a kind reception, we intend a second in a convenient time, and if the Authors of those Dissertations will favour us with new copies, we shall not fail to insert them. Besides those formerly mentioned, we have, towards the next number, been favoured with several Manuscripts too prolix for the Magazine, *viz.* Essays on Biography—On Education—A Comparison between Buchanan and Johnson, &c. &c."

In 1742 Johnson wrote for the Magazine, an Essay on the Account of the Conduct of the Duchess of Marlborough *, then the popular topick of conversation; an Account of the Life of Peter Burman, chiefly taken from foreign publications; the Life of Sydenham, afterwards prefixed to Dr. Swan's Edition of his Works; and the Proposals for printing " *Bibliotheca Harleiana,* or a Catalogue of the Library of the Earl of Oxford †."

His Preface to the Volume for 1742 is well worth attention :

" As continued favours demand repeated acknowledgments, we hope our gratitude will not be thought either ostentatious or troublesome, if we once more express our sense of the kind reception which we have now experienced to the end of the twelfth year. We have still the satisfaction of finding, not only by the applauses of our friends, but by a more certain proof, the continuance of our sale, that our Collections are yet highest in the esteem of the learned, inquisitive, and judicious; that our Debates are considered the most faithful and accurate representations of Senatorial proceedings; that our Extracts from printed Papers are esteemed for their impartiality and perspicuity; that our Poetry finds Advocates among the severest criticks; that our Account of Foreign Affairs is regarded as the best recapitulation of intelligence; and that, where elegance is not to be attained, we are allowed so far the praise of diligence

---

* This Essay is a short but masterly performance. We find him, in No. 13 of his Rambler, censuring a profligate sentiment in that "Account;" and again insisting upon it strenuously in conversation.

† This account of that celebrated collection of books, in which he displays the importance to Literature of what the French call a *Catalogue Raisonée,* when the subjects of it are extensive and various, and it is executed with ability, cannot fail to impress all his readers with admiration of his philological attainments. It was afterwards prefixed to the first volume of the Catalogue, in which the Latin accounts of books were written by him. He was employed in this business by Mr. Thomas Osborne, the bookseller, who purchased the Library for 13,000l. a sum which Mr. Oldys says, in one of his manuscripts, was not more than the binding of the books cost; yet, as Dr. Johnson assured me, the slowness of the sale was such, that there was not much gained by it.

and fidelity, that our Papers are consulted as the most copious repositories of Domestic Occurrences.

" Among the many original Pieces which we have inserted, the Lives of celebrated men have been thought worthy of particular attention, and it shall be our endeavour to preserve it, by continuing our inquiries on that head. That we have hitherto oftener entertained our Readers with accounts of foreigners than our own countrymen, is not to be imputed to partiality, but to the care with which other nations preserve the memories of those to whom they are indebted for discoveries in science or works of genius.

" It would afford us no small degree of satisfaction to free our own country from the censure of ingratitude to such as have extended its reputation, beyond the progress of our arms, or of our commerce, and therefore entreat those who have been acquainted with any circumstances of the lives of learned or remarkable men, to transmit them to us, that they may be added to those which we may obtain from other hands, or at least be treasured in our Collections, as materials for future Biographers.

" If any thing farther be thought, by our Correspondents, necessary to complete our plan, to which we have from year to year made additions, we continue to hope for advice and information; for we are not yet so much elated by success, as to imagine that we have attained perfection.

" Among those who have already favoured us with such hints, we cannot but pay a particular acknowledgment to the Author of the judicious proposal of an *Introduction* to our Magazine, which we hope to compile with that candour and impartiality which he has been pleased to commend in our past productions, and to comprise it in less compass than he appears to expect.

" As we doubt not but the favour of the Publick will be preserved by the same conduct which obtained it, we shall endeavour to show, that applause has rather increased than relaxed our application, and that victory has not lulled us in security, but excited us to vigilance."

In the Magazine for 1743, Johnson wrote " Considerations on the Dispute, between Crousaz and Warburton, on Pope's Essay on Man;" in which, while he defends Crousaz, he shews an admirable metaphysical acutenes, and temperance in controversy; " Ad Lauram parituram Epigramma;" and " A Latin Translation of Pope's Verses on his Grotto*;" and, as he could employ his pen with equal success upon a small matter as a great, I suppose him to be the Author of an Advertisement for Osborne, concerning the great Harleian Catalogue. Two other

* Mr. Hector was present when this Epigram was made *impromptu.* The first line was proposed by Dr. James, and Johnson was called upon by the company to finish it, which he instantly did.

Poems by him in this year's Magazine, both written in early life, deserve particular notice. The first of them, "Ad Ornatissimam Puellam," is ascribed to him on the authority of the late James Bindley, Esq.; the other, "Friendship, an Ode," on that of Mr. Hector.

To this Volume of the Magazine he also furnished a Preface:

"It has been for many years lamented, by those who are most eminent among us for their understanding and politeness, that the struggles of opposite parties have engrossed the attention of the Publick, and that all subjects of conversation, and all kinds of Learning, have given way to Politicks.

"Though under a form of Government like ours, which makes almost every man a secondary Legislator, politicks may justly claim a more general attention than where the people have no other duty to practise than obedience, and where to examine the conduct of their superiors would be to disturb their own quiet, without advantage, yet it must be owned that life requires many other considerations, and that politicks may be said to usurp the mind, when they leave no room for any other subject. For this reason, we have taken care to diversify our Work, and have thought ourselves by no means negligent of the public happiness, when we interspersed political controversies with dissertations on morality, commerce, and philosophy.

"The most important part of our commerce arises from the manufacture of our wool; we have, therefore, distinguished it by a proportionate regard, and have collected and abridged all the schemes that have been proposed for preventing its exportation; we have not only preserved many from being lost, but have drawn attention upon others which would, by their length, have discouraged many from perusing them, and, by inserting them all in our Volumes, have facilitated the task of comparing them. On this subject, as well as others, we have published many curious Letters, which the reputation of our Work has procured us from Correspondents eminent in all parts of knowledge, who have been pleased to consider this Magazine as the great Canal of intelligence, by which their sentiments may be most expeditiously transmitted to the world. To these favours we thankfully attribute much of the esteem with which the Publick has distinguished us; and hope to secure the continuance of them by the diligence and impartiality that first obtained them."

That Johnson was busily employed during the whole of 1743, is evident from the following Letters to Mr. Cave; and that he was struggling hard for an humble maintenance, from one to Mr. Levett, which will be found in page xl.

" SIR, [No date nor signature, but written in 1743].

" You did not tell me your determination about the ' Soldier's Letter *;' which I am confident was never printed. I think it will not do by itself, or in any other place so well as the Magazine Extraordinary. If you will have it at all, I believe you do not think I set it high ; and I will be glad if what you give, you will give quickly.

" You need not be in care about something to print ; for I have got the State Trials †, and shall extract Layer, Atterbury, and Macclesfield, from them, and shall bring them to you in a fortnight ; after which I will try to get the South Sea Report."

" Mr. URBAN, [August ..., 1743.]

" As your Collections show how often you have owed the ornaments of your poetical pages to the Correspondence of the unfortunate and ingenious Mr. Savage ‡, I doubt not but you have so much regard to his memory as to encourage any design that may have a tendency to the preservation of it from insults or calumnies, and therefore with some degree of assurance intreat you to inform the Publick, that his Life will speedily be published by a person who was favoured with his confidence, and received from himself an account of most of the transactions which he proposes to mention, to the time of his retirement to Swansey, in Wales. From that period to his death in the prison of Bristol, the account will be continued from materials still less liable to objection, his own Letters and those of his Friends ; some of which will be inserted in the work, and abstracts of others subjoined in the margin. It may be reasonably imagined that others may have the same design, but as it is not credible that they can obtain the same materials, it must be expected that they will supply from invention the want of intelligence, and that under the title of the Life of Savage they will publish only a novel filled with romantic adventures, and imaginary amours. You may therefore perhaps gratify the lovers of truth and wit, by giving me leave to inform them in your Magazine, that my Account will be published in 8vo. by Mr. Roberts, in Warwick Lane §."

* This must have been something of a friend of Johnson's, recommended by him to Cave. Had it been his own, he would not have said, " I am confident was never printed ;" and I suspect it was never printed at all.

† The "State Trials and Proceedings for High Treason, from Richard II. to the 14th of George II." were published, in folio, 1742.

‡ Savage's " Volunteer Laureats " were printed in the Magazine at the times when they were written. He died August 5, 1743, in his 45th year.

§ This was Johnson's first announcement of the Life of Savage ; and which he soon after completed, as appears by the next Letter, and by the following Memorandum : " The 14th day of December, 1743, Received of Mr. Ed. Cave the sum of Fifteen Guineas, in full, for compiling and writing ' The Life of Richard Savage, Esq.' deceased ; and in full for all materials thereto applied, and not found by the said Edward Cave. I say, received by me SAM. JOHNSON."

" Sir, [No date; but written in 1743.]

" I believe I am going to write a long Letter, and have therefore taken a whole sheet of paper.

" The first thing to be written about is our Historical Design.

" You mentioned the proposal of printing in numbers as an alteration in the scheme; but I believe you mistook, some way or other, my meaning. I had no other view than that you might rather print too many of five sheets, than of five-and-thirty.

" With regard to what I shall say on the manner of proceeding, I would have it understood as wholly indifferent to me; and my opinion only, not my resolution, *Emptoris sit eligere.*

" I think the insertion of the exact dates of the most important events in the margin, or of so many events as may enable the reader to regulate the order of facts with exactness, the proper medium between a Journal, which has regard only to time, and a History, which ranges facts according to their dependence on each other, and postpones or anticipates according to the convenience of narration. I think the work ought to partake of the spirit of history, which is contrary to minute exactness, and of the regularity of a Journal, which is inconsistent with spirit. For this reason, I neither admit numbers or dates, nor reject them.

" I am of your opinion with regard to placing most of the Resolutions, &c. in the margin, and think we shall give the most complete account of Parliamentary proceedings that can be contrived. The naked papers, without any historical treatise interwoven, require some other book to make them understood. I will date the succeeding facts with some exactness, but I think in the margin.

" You told me on Saturday that I had received money on this work, and found set down 13*l.* 2*s.* 6*d.* reckoning the half-guinea of last Saturday. As you hinted to me that you had many calls for money, I would not press you too hard, and therefore shall desire only, as I send it in, two guineas for a sheet of copy, the rest you may pay me when it may be more convenient; and even by this sheet-payment I shall, for some time, be very expensive *.

" The Life of Savage I am ready to go upon; and in Great Primer, and Pica notes, I reckon on sending in half a sheet a day; but the money for that shall likewise lie by in your hands

---

* What the "Historical Design" was, has not hitherto been ascertained. It is evident from this Letter that the subject was Parliamentary; and that it was a Work on which Johnson was employed by Cave. That he was zealous in the task is evinced by the following Letter to Dr. Birch, dated Sept. 29, 1743 :

" Sir, I hope you will excuse me for troubling you on an occasion on which I know not whom else I can apply to. I am at a loss for the Lives and Characters of Earl Stanhope, the two Craggs, and the Minister Sunderland ; and beg

e 3

till it is done. With the Debates, shall not I have business
enough — if I had but good pens?

" Towards Mr. Savage's Life * what more have you got?
I would willingly have his 'Trial,' &c. and know whether his
' Defence†' be at Bristol; and would have his 'Collection of

you will inform me where I may find them, and send any pamphlets, &c.
relating to them to Mr. Cave, to be perused for a few days by, Sir,
                        " Your most humble servant,   " SAM. JOHNSON."
    From the peculiar manner in which the following Advertisement appears in
the Magazine for July 1744, p. 400, I was induced to conjecture that the Work
in question was, "On the Use and Abuse of Parliaments; in Two Historical
Discourses; viz. 1. A general View of Government in Europe. 2. A Detection
of the Parliament of England for the Year 1660." No Author's or Publisher's
Name is introduced; and, thinking I had made a very important discovery, I
eagerly sought for the book, which I had not before seen, and instantly perceived
that I was on a wrong scent; that mysterious Work being in reality the production of James Ralph, a powerful, but violent Party-writer. What Johnson's "Historical Design " was, therefore, still remains to be discovered. Cave's Proposals
for publishing the Hon. Anchitel Gray's Debates, did not appear till March 1745.
    * Of this Life, Dr. Johnson told me, he wrote 48 octavo pages in one day;
but that day included the night, for he sat up all the night to do it. It was
published early in February 1743-4; and in the Magazine for that month
appeared this Letter to Mr. Urban:
    " There are some reasons to believe that your giving place to the Letter in
your Magazine for August last, concerning a design to publish the Life of Mr.
Richard Savage, from authentic materials, has prevented several from writing on
that subject; but I conceive that in this you have not done any injury but a
service to the Publick, since the performance promised in that Letter has by the
judicious Author of the *Champion* been thought worthy of the following character:
" The Pamphlet, entitled, An Account of the Life of Mr. Savage, Son of E.
Rivers, is, without flattery to its author, as just and well-written a piece as, of
its kind, I ever saw; so that at the same time that it highly deserves, it certainly
stands very little in need of this recommendation.
    " As to the history of the unfortunate Person whose Memoirs compose this
Work, it is certainly penned with equal accuracy and spirit, of which I am so
much the better judge, as I know many of the facts mentioned in it to be
strictly true, and very fairly related. Besides, it is not only the story of Mr.
Savage, but innumerable incidents relating to other persons and other affairs,
which render this a very amusing, and withal a very instructive and valuable
performance. The Author's Observations are short, significant, and just, as his
narrative is remarkably smooth, and well disposed. His reflections open to us all
the recesses of the human heart, and in a word, a more just or pleasant, a more
nagaging or a more improving treatise on the excellencies and defects of human
nature, is scarce to be found in our own, or perhaps in any other language."
    This character of the Life of Savage was not written, as has been supposed, by
Fielding—but by Ralph, who, as appears from the Minutes of the Partners in
"The Champion," in the possession of the late Mr. Reed, succeeded Fielding
in his share of the Paper before the date of this eulogium.
    † Soon after the publication of this Life, which was anonymous, Mr. Walter
Herte, dining with Mr. Cave at St. John's Gate, took occasion to speak very
handsomely of the work. Cave told Harte, when they next met, that he had
made a man very happy the other day at his house, by the encomiums he bestowed on the author of Savage's Life. "How could that be?" Cave replied,
"You might observe I sent a plate of victuals behind the skreen. There
skulked the Biographer, one Johnson, whose dress was so shabby that he durst
not make his appearance. He overheard our conversation; and your applauding
his performance delighted him exceedingly."

Poems,' on account of the Preface ;—' The Plain Dealer*;'—all the Magazines that have any thing of his, or relating to him †.

"The boy found me writing this almost in the dark, when I could not quite easily read yours.

"I have read the *Italian* ‡—nothing in it is well.

"I had no notion of having any thing for the *Inscription* §. I hope you do not think I kept it to extort a price. I could think of nothing, till to-day. If you could spare me another guinea for the *History*, I should take it very kindly, to-night; but if you do not, I shall not think it an injury.—I am almost well again.

"I thought my Letter would be long; but it is now ended; and I am, Sir,   Yours, &c.   SAM. JOHNSON."

I once possessed a paper, in Johnson's hand-writing, which I gave to Mr. Boswell, intituled, "Account between Mr. Edward Cave and Sam. Johnson, in relation to a version of Father Paul, &c. begun Aug. 2, 1738;" by which it appears, that from that day to April 21, 1739, Johnson received for that work 49*l.* 7*s.* in sums of one, two, three, and sometimes four guineas at a time, most frequently two. And it is curious to observe the minute and scrupulous accuracy with which Johnson has pasted upon it a slip of paper, which he has intituled "Small Account," and which contains one article, " Sept. 9, Mr. Cave laid down 2*s.* 6*d.*" There is subjoined to this account a list of some sub-scribers to the work, partly in Johnson's hand-writing, partly in that of another person; and there follows a leaf or two, of characters which have the appearance of a short-hand, which, perhaps, Johnson was then endeavouring to learn.

* Published in 1724, and containing some account of Savage.
† Savage's Tragedy of " Sir Thomas Overbury" was acted at Drury Lane in 1723, and printed in 1724. During his retirement in Wales, he had begun a second Tragedy on the same subject, which, at the time of his death, was left in pawn with the Gaoler in Bristol, with whom it remained when Savage died. After that event it was bought by Mr. Cave, and laid by among his own papers, where it was found many years after. It was then put into the hands of Mr. William Woodfall, who made some alterations in it himself, and re-ceived others from both Mr. Garrick and Mr. Colman. These, however, con-sisted chiefly of transpositions. When completed, it was produced at Covent Garden in 1777, and acted with applause.
The following Letter was from an eminent Bookseller at Bristol, who was an Uncle of the late Alderman Cadell :
"Mr. CAVE,   *Bristol, March* 17, 1740.
" According to your request, I have purchased Savage's Play, and have here sent it you with a receipt inclosed. The person of whom I purchased the Play is a particular friend of mine : he assures me, the play is perfect, and never was copied. I hope you will find it to your satisfaction. Please to give my account credit for the Five Guineas. I am, Sir, your humble servant, THO. CADELL."
‡ Some article intended for the Magazine.
§ This, Mr. Malone thinks, might *perhaps* have been the Runic Inscription, Gent. Mag. XII. 132. But I doubt it, though unable to ascertain what it was.

"To Mr. Levett, in Lichfield.

"SIR, December 1, 1743.

"I am extremely sorry we have encroached so much upon your forbearance with respect to the interest, which a great perplexity of affairs hindered me from thinking of with that attention that I ought, and which I am not immediately able to remit to you, but will pay it (I think twelve pounds) in two months. I look upon this, and on the future interest of that mortgage as my own debt; and beg that you will be pleased to give me directions how to pay it, and not mention it to my dear Mother. If it be necessary to pay this in less time, I believe I can do it; but I take two months for certainty, and beg an answer whether you can allow me so much time. I think myself very much obliged to your forbearance, and shall esteem it a great happiness to be able to serve you. I have great opportunities of dispersing any thing that you may think it proper to make public. I will give a note for the money, payable at the time mentioned, to any one here that you shall appoint. I am, Sir, Your most obedient and most humble servant, SAM. JOHNSON, at Mr. Osborne's, Bookseller, in Gray's Inn."

In 1744, Johnson appears to have been almost wholly occupied by his engagement with Osborne on the Harleian Catalogue; but Cave re-printed the Life of Barretier in a separate pamphlet; and was favoured by Johnson with the following Preface to the Magazine:

"Having now suspended controversy, and left our Antagonists to struggle for a time without interruption, under the weight of an undertaking to which they are by no means equal*, we shall confine ourselves to the acknowledgment of our obligations to the Publick, and to our ingenious Correspondents, whose contributions have increased so much that we have found it necessary to open new receptacles, in two more periodical pamphlets.

"Of these one (to be published quarterly) is to be appropriated to the Mathematicks †; which, however, will not be so far excluded the Magazine, but that any useful discoveries will be taken notice of, though not in such manner as to disgust that part of Readers who delight in a different kind of amusement.

"The other is an occasional Collection of the Miscellaneous Correspondence, of which we have already published three numbers, and which we shall continue, that we may afford the ingenious that convenience of publication which could not be allowed in

* "This inability they in effect confess by the perpetual repetition of a shameless falsehood, in affirming in their title-pages and advertisements that they *have more in quantity*, when every one who can compute may see that they have less by above one Magazine in the year."

† This plan proved abortive; for which Cave apologized in the next Preface.

the Magazine. This instance of regard has been acknowledged, and rewarded by fresh contributions, particularly those of an accurate writer, who has favoured us with a plan and specimen, both of a Supplement and a new Edition to the Cyclopædia: and it has been so well received that many letters of approbation are come to hand, with some few objections, which will be answered in No. IV. to be published in February; so that we need only say here, that the specimen for abbreviating Mr. Chambers, in case of a new edition, is universally commended.

"We hope that a public benefit will arise from a general communication of sentiments among the Learned, to which we have the pleasure of contributing in several ways, and that we shall be able soon to congratulate the world on a new literary undertaking by several good hands, of which we shall not fail, from time to time, to give specimens in our Magazine."

During the years 1745 and 1746 the communications of Dr. Johnson are rarely to be traced in the Magazine; which, however, had now attained the height of its well-earned fame; and, from the impartial fidelity with which the unhappy public disturbances of 1745 were detailed, the circulation was very considerably extended; and this to so great a degree, that Mr. Cave patriotically concludes his Preface by "declaring a truth that may seem a paradox; we have sold more of our books than we desire for several months past; and are heartily sorry for the occasion of it, the present troubles."

The Debates were still continued under the Liliputian disguise; and in March this year appeared in the body of the Magazine, "Proposals for publishing the Debates of the House of Commons, from the year 1667 to the year 1694. Collected by the Hon. Anchitell Grey, Esq. who was thirty years Representative of the Town of Derby, Chairman of several Committees, and decyphered Coleman's Letters for the use of the House."

The Debates in the Senate of Liliput were occasionally given in 1746; but it was only on matters of very extraordinary interest; and in the two following years, when at all noticed, it was only as an article of news.

On the 3d of April 1747, a complaint having been made in the House of Lords, against Edward Cave and Thomas Astley, for printing in their respective Magazines an account of the Trial of Simon Lord Lovat; they were both ordered into the custody of the Gentleman Usher of the Black Rod. On the 10th of April, Mr. Cave, in custody, petitioned the House; expressing his sorrow for his offence; begging pardon for the same; promising never to offend again in the like manner; and praying to be discharged. On the 30th of April, the Lord Raymond reported from the Committee appointed to consider of the offences of Astley and Cave, "That they had ordered Cave to be brought before them; and the book complained of being shewn to him, he owned that he printed and published it. Being asked, "how he came to publish an account of Lord Lovat's Trial, and from whom he had the account so published?" he said, "it was done inadvertently; he was very sorry for having offended; that he published the said Account of the Trial from a printed Paper which was left at his house, directed to him; but he does not know from whom it came." Being asked, "how long he has been a Publisher of *The Gentleman's Magazine?*" he said, "that it is about sixteen years since it was first published: that he was concerned in it at first with his Nephew; and, since the death of his Nephew, he has done it entirely himself." Notice being taken to him, "that the said books have contained Debates in Parliament;" he said, "he had left off the Debates — that he had not published any Debates relative to this House above these twelve months—that there was a Speech or two relating to the other House, put in about the latter end of last year." Being asked, "how he came to take upon him to publish Debates in Parliament?" he said, "he was extremely sorry for it; that it was a very great presumption; but he was led into it by custom, and the practice of other people: That there was a monthly book, published before the Magazines, called *The Political State,* which contained Debates in Parliament; and that he never heard, till lately, that any persons were punished for printing those books." Being asked, "how he came by the Speeches which he printed in *The Gentleman's Magazine?*" he said, "he got into the House, and heard them, and made use of a black-lead pencil, and only took notes of some remarkable passages; and, from his memory, he put them together himself." Notice being taken to him, "that some of the Speeches were very long, consisting of several pages:" he said, "he wrote them himself, from notes which he took, assisted by his memory." Being asked, "whether he printed no Speeches but such as were so put together by himself, from his own notes?" he said, "Sometimes he has had Speeches sent him by very eminent persons; that he has had Speeches sent him by the Members themselves; and has had assistance from some Members, who have taken notes of other Members' Speeches." Being asked, "if he ever had any person whom he kept in pay, to make Speeches for him?" he said, "he never had."

Though Johnson's personal assistance in the Magazine was unavoidably suspended, his regard for Mr. Cave continued undiminished; and to his advice Cave constantly resorted.

In 1747 he occasionally afforded his powerful assistance to the Magazine; and though many entire pieces cannot be ascertained to have come from his pen, he was frequently, if not constantly, employed to superintend the materials of the Maga-

zine; and several introductory passages may be pointed out
which bear evident marks of his composition. The time, indeed of the great Lexicographer was now most unremittingly
devoted to the stupendous labour of his matchless Dictionary; but the Magazine for the year 1747 was enriched by
Johnson with five short poetical pieces, distinguished by three
asterisks: 1. "A Paraphrase Latin Epitaph on Sir Thomas Han-
mer." 2. "To Miss ———— on her giving the Author a Gold
and Silver Net-work Purse of her own weaving." 3. "The
Winter's Walk." 4. "An Ode." 5. "To Lyce, an elderly
Lady."

In this year the first Emblematic Frontispiece was introduced,
which were continued through ten volumes.

In 1748 Johnson wrote a Life of Roscommon, with notes,
which he afterwards much improved, converted the notes into
text, and inserted it amongst his Lives of the English Poets.

In November 1749, the Debates were restored, in "A Letter
from a Member of Parliament to his Country Friend."

In this year the second Imitation of Juvenal *, under the title
of "The Vanity of Human Wishes," was printed at *St. John's Gate;*
as was "Irene †," in the following month.

But Cave's press was destined to higher honours.

Early in 1750 he was not only the Printer, but the earliest
Patron‡ of THE RAMBLER; of which the First Number was published March 20, 1749-50, and the last March 17, 1752; and,
notwithstanding the Author's constitutional depression of spirits,
and his labour in carrying on his Dictionary, he answered the
calls of the press twice a week from the stores of his mind,
during all that time; having received no assistance, except four
billets in No. 10, by Mrs. Mulso, afterwards Mrs. Chapone; No.
30, by Mrs. Catherine Talbot; No. 97, by Mr. Samuel Richard-
son§; and Nos. 44 and 100, by Mrs. Elizabeth Carter. Posterity

* Notwithstanding the reputation which Johnson had by this time acquired,
the remuneration for it was far less than he had obtained for the former Poem,
as the following document will testify:
"Nov. 25, 1748. I received of Mr. Dodsley fifteen guineas, for which I assign
him the right of copy of an Imitation of the Tenth Satire of Juvenal, written
by me; reserving to myself the right of printing one edition. SAM. JOHNSON."
Sir John Hawkins represents this Poem as a consequence of the indifferent
reception of his Tragedy. But the fact is, that the Poem was published on
the 9th of January, and Irene was not acted till the 6th of February.
† The progress of this Tragedy has been noticed in Johnson's Letter, pp. ix.
xiv. and his Friend Garrick having now become the Proprietor of Drury Lane
Theatre, Irene was there performed, but without much success, although the
Manager contrived to have it played long enough to entitle the Author to his
profits of his three nights; and Dodsley bought the copyright for an hundred
pounds. It has ever been admired in the closet, for the propriety of its sentiments, and the elegance of its language.
‡ See the Assignment in p. xliv.
§ This communication by Richardson was six months subsequent to the Letter here printed, at which time the name of the Author was a secret.

will be astonished when they are told, upon the authority of Johnson himself, that many of these Discourses, which we should suppose had been laboured with all the slow attention of literary leisure, were written in haste as the moment pressed, without even being read over by him before they were printed.

Johnson appears to have entered on "The Rambler" without any communication with his friends, or desire of assistance. Whether he proposed the scheme himself is uncertain, but he was fortunate in forming a connexion with Mr. John Payne, a bookseller in Paternoster-row, and afterwards chief accountant in the Bank of England, a man with whom he lived many years in habits of friendship, and who on the present occasion treated him with great liberality. He engaged to pay him two guineas for each paper, or four guineas *per* week, which at that time must have been to Johnson a very considerable sum; and he admitted him to a share of the future profits of the work, when it should be collected into volumes *; this share Johnson afterwards sold.

The following Letters may here be not unaptly introduced:

"Mr. CAVE,
                                                    Aug. 9, 1750.
"Though I have constantly been a purchaser of the Ramblers from the first five that you was so kind as to present me with, yet I have not had time to read any farther than those first five, till within these two or three days past. But I can go no farther than the thirteenth, now before me, till I have acquainted you, that I am inexpressibly pleased with them. I remember not any thing in the Spectators, in those Spectators that I read, for I never found time—(alas! my life has been a trifling busy one) to read them all, that half so much struck me; and yet I think of them highly.

* This appears by the following indisputable document:
"To all people to whom these presents shall come, I Samuel Johnson, of Gough-square, London, gentleman, send greeting. Whereas Edward Cave, Citizen and Stationer of London, has bought paper and printed for me an edition, in folio, of a Periodical Work called 'The Rambler,' and is now about to reprint Seventy Numbers of the same Work, in twelves, at his own expence: Now know ye, that I, the said Samuel Johnson, do hereby authorize and impower the said Edward Cave to sell and dispose of the second edition of 'The Rambler,' in twelves, and to receive and apply to his own use so much of the money arising from such sale as shall fully repay and reimburse to him such sums as upon a just reckoning he shall appear to have expended on account of the said work; provided that the names of John Payne and Joseph Bouquet be inserted in the new edition in twelves, as the persons for whom the said edition is printed, as is inserted in the said folio edition. In witness whereof, I, the said Samuel Johnson, have to these presents set my hand and seal, this first day of April, in the twenty-fourth year of the reign of our Sovereign Lord George the Second, by the grace of God, of Great Britain, France, and Ireland, King, Defender of the Faith, and in the year of our Lord one thousand seven hundred and fifty-nine.   SAM. JOHNSON.
" Sealed and delivered, being first duly stamped, in the presence of
                          " DAVID HENRY, JOHN HAWKESWORTH."

" I hope the world tastes them ; for its own sake, I hope the world tastes them ! The Author I can only guess at. There is but *one man*, I think, that could write them; I desire not to know his name ; but I should rejoice to hear that they succeed ; for I would not, for any consideration, that they should be laid down through discouragement.

" I have, from the first five, spoke of them with honour. I have the vanity to think that I have procured them admirers; that is to say, readers. And I am vexed that I have not taken larger draughts of them before, that my zeal for their merit might have been as glowing as now I find it. Excuse the over-flowing of a heart highly delighted with the subject; and believe me to be an equal friend to Mr. Cave and the Rambler, as well as their most humble servant, S. RICHARDSON."

" DEAR SIR, St. John's Gate, Aug. 29, 1750.
" I received the pleasure of your letter of the 9th instant at Gloucester; and did intend to answer it from that city, though I had but one sound hand (the cold and rain on my journey having given me the gout); but as soon as I could ride, I went to Whitminster, the seat of Mr. Cambridge, who entertained the Prince there, and, in his boat, on the Severn. He kept me one night, and took me down part of his river to the Severn, where I sailed in one of his boats, and took a view of another of a peculiar make, having two keels, or being rather two long canoes connected by a floor or stage. I was then towed back again to sup and repose. Next morning he explained to me the contrivance of some waterfalls, which seem to come from a piece of water which is four feet lower. The three following days I spent in returning to town, and could not find time to write in an inn.

" I need not tell you that the Prince * appeared highly pleased with every thing that Mr. Cambridge shewed, though he called him upon the deck often to be seen by the people on the shore, who came in prodigious crowds, and thronged from place to place, to have a view as often as they could, not satisfied with one ; so that many who came between the towing-line and the bank of the river were thrown into it; and his Royal Highness could scarce forbear laughing ; but sedately said to them, 'I am sorry for your condition.'

" Excuse this ramble from the purpose of your letter. I return to answer, that Mr. *Johnson* is the Great Rambler, being, as you observe, the only man who can furnish two such papers in a week, besides his other great business—and has not been assisted with above three.

" I may discover to you, that the world is not so kind to itself as you wish it. The encouragement, as to sale, is not in pro-portion to the high character given to the work by the judicious, not to say the raptures expressed by the few who do read it.

* The Prince of Wales. See Gent. Mag. 1750, p. 331.

But its being thus relished in numbers gives hopes that the sets must go off, as it is a fine paper, and, considering the late hour of having the copy, tolerably printed *

"When the Author was to be kept private (which was the first scheme) two gentlemen belonging to the Prince's Court came to me to enquire his name, in order to do him service; and also brought a list of seven gentlemen to be served with the Rambler. As I was not at liberty, an inference was drawn that I was desirous to keep to myself so excellent a Writer. Soon after, Mr. Dodington* sent a Letter directed to the Rambler, inviting him to his house, when he should be disposed to enlarge his acquaintance. In a subsequent Number a kind of excuse was made, with a hint that a good Writer might not appear to advantage in conversation†. Since that time, several other circumstances, and Mr. Garrick and others, who knew the Author's powers and style from the first, unadvisedly asserting their (but) suspicions, overturned the scheme of secrecy. (About which there is also one paper.)

"I have had Letters of approbation from Dr. Young, Dr. Hartley, Dr. Sharpe, Miss Carter, &c. &c.; most of them, like you, setting them in a rank equal, and some superior, to the Spectators (of which I have not read many, for the reasons which you assign): but, notwithstanding such recommendation, whether the price of *two-pence*, or the unfavourable season of their first publication, hinders the demand, no boast can be made of it. The Author (who thinks highly of your writings) is obliged to you for contributing your endeavours; and so is, for several marks of your friendship, good Sir,

"Your admirer, and very humble servant,   ED. CAVE."

The Preface to the Magazine for the year 1750 notices a new swarm of Imitators, the very titles of which would have been lost, had they not been thus recorded: "The Polite and General Entertainer;" "The Kapelion, or Poetical Ordinary;"

---

* The sale was very inconsiderable, and seldom more than 500; and it is very remarkable, and a most curious *trait* of the age, that the only paper which had a prosperous sale, and may be said to have been popular, was one which Dr. Johnson did *not* write. This was No. 97, Feb. 19, 1750-1, written by Richardson, as I was assured by Mr. John Payne, the original publisher. Dr. Johnson indeed introduces it to his Readers with an elegant compliment, as "the production of an Author from whom the age has received greater favours, who has enlarged the knowledge of human nature, and taught the passions to move at the command of virtue."

* The celebrated George Bubb Dodington, afterwards Lord Melcombe.

† No. XIII, May 1, 1750, treats expressly on "the Duty of Secrecy;" and No. XIV, May 5, on "the Difference between an Author's Writings and his Conversation," ends thus: "A transition from an Author's Book to his Conversation is too often like an entrance into a large City after a distant prospect. Remotely, we see nothing but Spires of Temples and Turrets of Palaces; and imagine it the residence of splendour, grandeur, and magnificence: but, when we have passed the gates, we find it perplexed with narrow passages, disgraced with despicable cottages, embarrassed with obstructions, and clouded with smoke."

"The Magazine of Magazines;" "The Grand Magazine;" "The Living World;" "The Traveller's Magazine;" "The Prisoner's Magazine;" "The Theological Magazine;" "The Quaker's Magazine;" "The Religious Magazine;" "The Royal Magazine;" "The British Magazine;" "The Lady's;" "The Old Woman's," &c.

In 1751, Johnson was carrying on his "Dictionary" and "The Rambler;" and, besides some occasional contributions to the Magazine, assisted in the detection of Lauder, who had imposed on him and on the world by advancing forged evidence that Milton was a gross plagiary.

About this period a material change took place in the compilation of the Miscellaneous part of the Magazine. Selections from other periodical Publications were gradually laid aside, and the Miscellany was rendered in a great degree an original work. This (as is observed in the Preface for the year 1752) " was effected chiefly by the favours received from a large number of ingenious and learned Contributors, by whom many subjects of the highest importance are treated with accuracy, spirit, and candour. While so many men of unquestionable erudition and abilities, too elevated to be bribed, too distant to be courted, unite in one design of propagating science by our vehicle, we have little to dread from competitors," &c.

In 1752 the Proceedings in Parliament were reported briefly, in the shape of a Letter, thus introduced :

" The following heads of Speeches in the H—— of C—— were given me by a Gentleman, who is of opinion, that Members of Parliament are accountable to their Constituents for what they say, as well as what they do, in their Legislative capacity—that no honest man, who is intrusted with the liberties and purses of the people, will be ever unwilling to have his whole conduct laid before those who so intrusted him, without disguise—that, if every Gentleman acted upon this just, this honourable, this constitutional principle, the Electors themselves only would be to blame, if they re-elected a person guilty of a breach of so important a trust.—But let the arguments speak for themselves. Thus much only may be necessary to premise, that, as the state of public affairs was, in a great measure, the same both last year and this, I send you a Speech, in the Committee of Supply, upon the number of Standing Forces for the year 1751, and also another, in the last Session of Parliament, for the year 1752. You may be assured they are really genuine, and not such an imposition upon the Speakers and the Publick, as some that have appeared in other Monthly Collections*."

* From the above period, the Debates were regularly given, as formerly, with the initial letters of the several Speakers, till the end of 1782: subsequently to

Not long before Mr. Cave's death, he was busily employed in preparing and printing a General Index to the first Twenty Volumes of the Gentleman's Magazine, which was published in 1753, with a Preface* by his incomparable Friend; whose regard was still farther evinced by the following affectionate paragraph, which concludes his Memoir of Mr. Cave :

" He continued to improve his Magazine†, and had the satisfaction of seeing its success proportionate to his diligence, till in the year 1751 his wife died of an asthma ‡; with which, though he seemed not at first much affected, yet in a few days he lost his sleep and his appetite; and, lingering two years, fell, by drinking acid liquor, into a diarrhœa, and afterwards into a kind of lethargic insensibility, in which one of the last acts of reason he exerted, was *fondly to press the hand that is now writing this little narrative.* He died on January 10, 1754, æt. 63, having just concluded the twenty-third annual collection."

Again, some years later, Jan. 14, 1756, Johnson says, " To every joy is appended a sorrow. The name of Mrs. Carter introduces the memory of Cave.—Poor dear Cave ! I owed him much : for to him I owed that I have known you. He died, I am afraid, unexpectedly to himself : yet surely unburthened with any great crime ; and for the positive duties of Religion, I have no reason to condemn him for neglect."

Mr. Pennington, in his Life of Mrs. Carter, adds : " Mr. Cave was much connected with the Literary World ; and his friendship for Mrs. Carter was the means of introducing her to many Authors and Scholars of note ; among these there was Mr. (afterwards Dr.) Johnson §."

which, they have been printed without the least affectation of disguise ; and form, in the whole, a complete and impartial report for nearly NINETY years.

* Re-printed in the First Volume of the General Index.

† Mr. Cave had this so much at heart, that it was hardly possible to miss the good effects of such a temper. If he heard of the loss of a single customer, he would say, " Let us be sure to look up something, taking of the best, for the next month."

‡ Prefixed to the Volume for 1735, is a *jeu d'esprit* under the title of " *Mrs. Cave's* Lecture," which (under the signature of SUSAN URBAN) pleasantly banters her husband's fondness for new Projects, particularly his then proposed publication of Du Halde's China ; and the various Prizes he had offered for good Poetry. His own personal habits of life are also agreeably depicted.

§ By a Letter from Mr. Cave to Dr. Birch, Nov. 28, 1739, we find that " Johnson advised Mrs. Carter to undertake a translation of ' Boethius de Consolatione,' because there is prose and verse ; and to put her name to it when published." This advice was not followed ; probably from an apprehension that the work was not sufficiently popular for an extensive sale.—Mr. Cave was, in 1739, the Printer and Publisher of "Sir Isaac Newton's Philosophy explained, for the Use of the Ladies ; in Six Dialogues on Light and Colours ; from the Italian of Algarotti ; translated by Miss Carter ;" 2 vols. 12mo. A handsome complimentary Poem to Miss Carter on this publication, by Dr. J. Swan, appeared in the Magazine for 1739, p. 322.

A good Portrait of Mr. Cave, by Worlidge, after the manner of Rembrandt, appeared in the Magazine for 1754, from which the Portrait prefixed to this volume is copied.

There is another Portrait of him, by Grignion, with emblematic devices, thus inscribed :

"EDWARD CAVE, ob. 10 Jan. 1754, ætat. 62.
The first Projector of the Monthly Magazines.
Th' Invention all admired, and each how he
To be th' Inventor miss'd."

Mr. Cave was buried in the Church of St. James, Clerkenwell: but the following inscription, to the memory of his Father and himself, which was written by Dr. Hawkesworth, is placed on a table monument in the church-yard at Rugby:

"Near this place lies the body of
JOSEPH CAVE, late of this parish,
who departed this life Nov. 18, 1747, aged 80 years.
He was placed by Providence in a humble station :
but INDUSTRY abundantly supplied his wants,
and TEMPERANCE blest him with
CONTENT and HEALTH.
As he was an affectionate Father,
he was made happy in the decline of life
by the deserved eminence of his eldest Son,
EDWARD CAVE ;
who, without interest, fortune, or connexions,
by the native force of his own Genius,
assisted only by a Classical Education,
which he received in the Grammar-school
of this Town,
planned, executed, and established
a Literary Work, called
THE GENTLEMAN'S MAGAZINE ;
whereby he acquired an ample Fortune,
the whole of which devolved to his Family.

Here also lies the body of ESTHER his wife,
who died Dec. 30, 1734, aged 69 years."

On the North side of the same tomb :

"Here also lies
the body of WILLIAM CAVE,
second son of the said JOSEPH and ESTHER CAVE,
who died May 2, 1757, aged 62 years ;
and who, having survived his elder Brother
EDWARD CAVE,
inherited from him a competent estate ;
and, in gratitude to his Benefactor,
ordered this Monument, to perpetuate his memory.

He liv'd a Patriarch in his numerous race,
And shew'd in charity a Christian's grace :
Whate'er a Friend or Parent feels, he knew ;
His hand was open, and his heart was true ;
In what he gain'd and gave, he taught mankind,
A grateful always is a generous mind.
Here rest his clay ! His soul must more than rest ;
Who blest when living, dying must be blest."

Sir John Hawkins, who in early life was a frequent visitor at St. John's Gate, thus characterizes his old Friend Edward Cave :

"On the first appearance of a stranger, his practice was to continue sitting, a posture in which he was ever to be found, and, for a few minutes, to continue silent: if at any time he was inclined to begin the discourse, it was generally by putting a leaf of the Magazine then in the press into the hands of his visitor, and asking his opinion of it. He was so incompetent a judge of Johnson's abilities, that, meaning at one time to dazzle him with the splendour of some of those Luminaries in Literature who favoured him with their correspondence, he told him that, if he would, in the evening, be at a certain alehouse in the neighbourhood of Clerkenwell, he might have a chance of seeing Mr. Browne and another or two of the persons mentioned in the subsequent pages : Johnson accepted the invitation ; and being introduced by Cave, dressed in a loose horse-man's coat, and such a great bushy uncombed wig as he constantly wore, to the sight of Mr. Browne, whom he found sitting at the upper end of a long table, in a cloud of tobacco-smoke, had his curiosity gratified. Johnson saw very clearly those offensive particulars that made a part of Cave's character ; but, as he was one of the most quick-sighted men I ever knew in discovering the good and amiable qualities of others, a faculty which he has displayed, as well in the Life of Cave, as in that of Savage, so was he ever inclined to palliate their defects ; and though he was above courting the patronage of a man whom, in respect to mental endowments, he considered much inferior, he disdained not to accept it when tendered with any degree of complacency.

"Cave manifested his good fortune by buying an old coach and a pair of older horses ; and, that he might avoid the suspicion of pride in setting up an equipage, he displayed to the world the source of his affluence, by a representation of St. John's Gate, instead of his arms, on the door-pannels. This he told me himself, was the reason of distinguishing his carriage from others, by what some might think a whimsical device, and also for causing it to be engraven on all his plate.

"It might seem that between men so different in their endowments and tempers as Johnson and Cave were, little of true friendship could subsist; but the contrary was the case. Cave, though a man of saturnine disposition, had a sagacity which had long been exercised in the discrimination of men, in searching into the recesses of their minds, and finding out what they were fit for ; and a liberality of sentiment and action, which, under proper restrictions, inclined him not only to encourage genius and merit, but to esteem and even to venerate the possessors of those qualities as often as he met with them : it cannot, there-fore, be supposed but that he entertained a high regard for such a man as Johnson, and, having had a long experience of his abilities and integrity, that he had improved this disposition into friendship. Johnson, on his part, sought for other qualities in those with whom he meant to form connexions. Had he deter-mined to make only those his friends whose endowments were equal to his own, his life would have been that of a Carthusian. He was therefore more solicitous to contract friendships with men of probity and integrity, and endued with good moral qua-lities, than with those whose intellectual powers, or literary at-tainments, were the most conspicuous part of their character; and of the former, Cave had a share, sufficient to justify his choice. On this mutual regard for each other, as on a solid basis, rested the friendship between Johnson and Cave. It was therefore with a degree of sorrow proportioned to his feelings towards his friends, which were ever tender, that Johnson re-flected on the loss he had to sustain, and became the narrator of the most important incidents of his life. In the account which he has given of his death, it will be readily believed that what he had related respecting the constancy of his friendship is true, and that when, as the last act of reason, he fondly pressed the hand that was afterwards employed in recording his memory, his affection was sincere."

The following brief notices of the early Friends and Corre-spondents of Mr. Cave are given by Sir John Hawkins, who was himself an Honorary Member of that Literary Fraternity :

" Rev. *Moses Browne*, originally a pen-cutter, was, so far as concerned the poetical part of it, the chief support of the Ma-gazine, which he fed with many a nourishing morsel. This per-son, being a lover of Angling, wrote Piscatory Eclogues ; and was a candidate for the fifty-pound prize mentioned in John-son's first letter to Cave, and for other prizes which Cave en-gaged to pay him who should write the best Poem on certain subjects ; in all or most of which competitions Mr. Browne had the good fortune to succeed. He published these and other Poems of his writing in an octavo volume, London, 1739 ; and has therein given proofs of an exuberant fancy and a happy in-vention. Some years after, he entered into holy orders. A far-ther account of him may be seen in the Biographia Dramatica, to a place in which work he seems to have acquired a title by some juvenile compositions for the Stage. Being a person of a religious turn, he also published in verse a series of devout contemplations, called *Sunday Thoughts.* Johnson, who often expressed his dislike of Religious Poetry, and who, for the purpose of Religious meditation, seemed to think one day as proper as another, read them with cold approbation, and said, he had a great mind to write and publish *Monday Thoughts.*— To the proofs above adduced of the coarseness of Cave's manners, let me add the following: he had undertaken, at his own risk, to publish a Translation of Du Halde's History of China, in which were contained sundry geographical and other plates. Each of these he inscribed to one or other of his friends; and, among the rest, one to *Moses Browne.* With this blunt and familiar designation of his person, Mr. Browne was justly offended. To appease him, Cave directed an engraver, to introduce with a *caret* under the line *Mr.*; and thought, that in so doing, he had made ample amends to Mr. Browne for the indignity done him.

" Mr. *John Duick,* also a pen-cutter, and a near neighbour of Cave, was a frequent contributor to the Magazine, of short poems, written with spirit and ease. He was a kinsman of Browne, and author of a good copy of encomiastic verses prefixed to the collection of Browne's Poems above mentioned.

" Mr. *Foster Webb,* a young man who had received his education in Mr. Watkins's academy in Spital-square, and afterwards became clerk to a merchant in the city, was at first a contributor to the Magazine, of Enigmas, a species of poetry in which he then delighted, but was dissuaded from it by the following lines, which appeared in the Magazine for October 1740, after a few successful essays in that kind of writing:

  ' Too modest Bard, with enigmatic veil
No longer let thy Muse her charms conceal;
Though oft the Sun in clouds his face disguise,
Still he looks nobler when he gilds the skies.
Do thou, like him, avow thy native flame,
Burst through the gloom, and brighten into fame.'

" After this friendly exhortation, Mr. Webb, in those hours of leisure which business afforded, amused himself with translating from the Latin Classics, particularly Ovid and Horace: from the latter of these he rendered into English verse, with better success than any that had before attempted it, the Odes, " Quis multa gracilis te, puer, in rosa;" " Solvitur in acris hyems grata vice veris, et Favoni;" " Parens Deorum cultor et infrequens;" and " Diffugêre nives, redeunt jam gramina campis;" all which are inserted in Cave's Magazine. His signature was sometimes *Telarius,* at others *Vedastus.* He was a modest, in-

PREFACE. liii

genious, and sober young man; but a consumption defeated the hopes of his friends, and took him off in the twenty-second year of his age.

" Mr. *John Smith*, another of Mr. Watkins's pupils, was a writer in the Magazine, of prose essays, chiefly on religious and moral subjects, and died of a decline about the same time.

" Mr. *John Canton*, apprenticed to the above-named Mr. Watkins, and also his successor in his academy, was a contributor to the Magazine, of verses, and afterwards, of papers on philosophical and mathematical subjects. The discoveries he made in Electricity and Magnetism are well known, and are recorded in the Transactions of the Royal Society, of which he afterwards became a member.

" Rev. *William Rider*, bred in the same prolific seminary, was a writer in the Magazine, of verses signed *Philargyrus*. He went from school to Jesus College, Oxford, and, some years after his leaving the same, entered into holy orders, and became sur-master of St. Paul's school, in which office he continued many years, but at length was obliged to quit this employment by reason of his deafness. [This industrious Divine was also Lecturer of St. Vedast, Foster Lane, Curate of St. Faith's, and was the author of a " History of England to the year 1763 inclusive," in fifty pocket volumes ; a " Commentary on the Bible ;" an " English Dictionary ;" and other works. He died March 30, 1785.]

" Mr. *Adam Calamy*, son of Dr: Edmund Calamy, an eminent Non-conformist Divine; and author of the Abridgement of Mr. Baxter's History of his Life and Times, was another of Mr. Watkins's pupils, that wrote in the Magazine ; the subjects on which he chiefly exercised his pen were essays in polemical theology and republican politics ; and he distinguished them by the assumed signature of *A consistent Protestant*. He was bred to the profession of an attorney, and was brother to Mr. Edmund Calamy, a Dissenting teacher, of eminence for his worth and learning.

" A seminary, of a higher order than that above mentioned, *viz.* the academy of *John Eames* in Moor-fields, furnished the Magazine with a number of other Correspondents in mathematics and other branches of science and polite literature. This was an institution, supported by the Dissenters, the design whereof was to qualify young men for their Ministry. Mr. Eames was formerly the Continuator of the Abridgement of the Philosophical Transactions begun by Jones and Lowthorp, and was a man of great knowledge, and a very able tutor. Under him were bred many young men who afterwards became eminently distinguished for learning and abilities; among them were the late Mr. Parry, of Cirencester, the late Dr. Furneaux, and Dr. Gibbons ; and, if I mistake not, Dr. Price. The pupils of this

academy had heads that teemed with knowledge, which, as fast
as they acquired it, they were prompted by a juvenile and laudable ambition to communicate in letters to Mr. Urban.

" The Rev. *Samuel Pegge* [then resident in Kent], who, by an
ingenious transposition of the letters of his name, formed the
plausible signature of *Paul Gemsege*." [After his removal into Der-
byshire, he signed *T. Row*, the initials of 'The Rector Of Whittington.'—This venerable Antiquary commenced his Correspondence with Mr. Cave in 1746, and continued it with his successors till 1795. He died Feb. 14, 1796, at the advanced age of 92.]

To this account of Cave's Correspondents Sir John Hawkins
adds the names of Dr. *Akenside* ; Mr. *Luck*, of Barnstaple in Devonshire; Mr. *Henry Price*, of Pool in Dorsetshire; Mr. *Richard
Yate*, of Chively in Shropshire ; Mr. *John Bancks* ; and that
industrious and prolific genius, Mr. *John Lockman*.

To this list should also be added the unhappy *Richard Savage* ;
and the ingenious but unfortunate *Samuel Boyse*, of whom the following melancholy particulars were related to the present Writer
by Dr. Johnson, not long before his own death.

" By addicting himself to low vices, among which were glut-
tony and extravagance, Boyse rendered himself so contempt-
ible and wretched, that he frequently was without the least sub-
sistence for days together. After squandering away in a dirty
manner any money which he acquired, he has been known to
pawn all his apparel. Dr. Johnson once collected a sum of money to redeem his cloaths, which in two days after were pawned
again. "This," said the Doctor, " was when my acquaintances
were few, and most of them as poor as myself. The money was
collected by shillings." In that state he was frequently confined
to his bed, sitting up with his arms through holes in a blanket,
writing verses in order to procure the means of existence. It
seems hardly credible, but it is certainly true, that he was more
than once in that deplorable situation, and to the end of his life
never derived any advantage from the experience of his past sufferings. Mr. Boyse translated well from the French ; but, if any
one employed him, by the time one sheet of the work was done,
he pawned the original. If the employer redeemed it, a second
sheet would be completed, and the book again be pawned ; and
this perpetually. He had very little learning ; but wrote verse
with great facility, as fast as most would write prose. He was
constantly employed by Mr. Cave, who paid him by the hundred
lines, which, after a while, his employer wanted to make what is
called the *long* hundred.—A late Collector of Poems (Mr. Giles)
says, he was informed by Mr. Sandby the Bookseller, that this
unhappy man at last was found dead in bed, with a pen in his
hand, and in the act of writing, in the same manner as above
described. This circumstance Dr. Johnson assured me was not

true; it being supposed that, in a fit of intoxication, he was run over by a coach; at least, he was brought home in such a condition as to make this probable, but too far gone to give any account of the accident."

Of Mr. Boyse's principal Poem, intituled, "The Deity," an account was sent to the Magazine; and although not inserted, it was probably the means of Boyse's first introduction to Cave, from whom he obtained some supplies for writing and translating in that Miscellany between the years 1741 and 1743. The usual signature for his Poems was either Y. or *Alcæus*.

When in a spunging-house in Grocers'-alley, in the Poultry, he wrote the following Letter to Cave, which was communicated by the late Mr. Astle to the late Dr. Kippis.

<blockquote>
"Inscription for St. Lazarus' Cave.

"Hodie, teste cœlo summo,
Sine panno, sine nummo,
Sorte positus infestè,
Scribo tibi dolens mœstè:
Fame, bile tumet jecur,
URBANE, mitte opem, precor;
Tibi enim cor humanum
Non à malis alienum:
Mihi mens nec malè grata,
Pro à te favore data.
</blockquote>

Ex gehennâ debitoriâ,   ALCÆUS."
vulgò domo *spongiatoriâ*.

"SIR, I wrote you yesterday an account of my unhappy case. I am every moment threatened to be turned out here, because I have not money to pay for my bed two nights past, which is usually paid before-hand, and I am loth to go into the Compter, till I can see if my affair can possibly be made up: I hope, therefore, you will have the humanity to send me half a guinea for support, till I finish your papers in my hands.—The Ode to the British Nation * I hope to have done to-day, and want a proof copy of that part of Stowe† you design for the present Magazine, that it may be improved as far as possible from your assistance. Your papers are but ill transcribed. I agree with you respecting St. Augustine's Cave. I humbly entreat your answer, having not tasted any thing since Tuesday evening I came here; and my coat will be taken off my back for the

---

* The Ode on the British Nation, mentioned here, is a Translation from Van Haren, a Dutch Poet, from whose works he translated some other passages.
† The "part of Stowe" was a part of his Poem on Lord Cobham's Gardens.

charge of the bed, so that I must go into prison naked, which is too shocking for me to think of.   I am, with sincere regard, Sir,
    Your unfortunate humble servant,   S. BOYSE."
Crown Coffee-house, Grocers-
    alley, Poultry, July 21, 1742.
  " I send Mr. Van Haren's Ode on Britain.
  " To Mr. Cave, at St. John's Gate, Clerkenwell.
  " July 21, 1742.   Received from Mr. Cave the sum of half a guinea, by me, in confinement.   S. BOYSE."

The greater number of the Poems which Boyse wrote for the Gentleman's Magazine during the years above mentioned, are re-printed in Mr. Alexander Chalmers's late Edition of the English Poets; but all his fugitive pieces were not written for the Magazine, some of them having been composed long before he had formed a connexion with Cave, and, as there is reason to believe, were sent in manuscript to such persons as were likely to make him a pecuniary return.   Mr. Boyse died in May 1749.

In 1754 a new æra in the publication of the Magazine commenced, under the immediate guidance of Mr. DAVID HENRY, an ingenious young Printer, who in 1736 had married Mary, the Sister of Edward Cave; and by him, in conjunction with Mr. RICHARD CAVE, a Nephew of the original Projector, the Magazine was jointly edited, printed, and published, at St. John's Gate.

The new Firm continued to receive the countenance, and occasionally the assistance, of JOHNSON, and of many other of their Uncle's Literary Friends, to which were soon added the names of many new and highly-respectable Correspondents.

Among these were some eminent Physicians; particularly the well-known Sir *John Hill;* and the not less celebrated Dr. *James,* whose memory Dr. Johnson so handsomely eulogizes, as " having lengthened life," and who was the inventor of the matchless Fever-Powders that still bear his name.

Mr. *Christopher Smart* was also a Contributor; as was Mr. *Ephraim Chambers;* and their mutual friend Mr. *John Newbery,* the truly-philanthropic projector of entertaining little books for the Juvenile Students, and who purchased a small share in the property of the Magazine, which still remains in his Family.

Many other names might be added; but it may be sufficient to mention Dr. JOHN HAWKESWORTH, who wrote the Epitaph printed in p. xlix; and who, in April 1765, superadded to the monthly list of books, which had been regularly given, at first his own concise, but valuable critical remarks, and afterwards a regular Review.

In 1757 the Friends to the Magazine were thus addressed :
  " To our Correspondents we impute our superiority, not only

with pleasure, but with pride; for we are more flattered by the contributions which we receive from others, than we could be by any success that might attend what was our own."

This language, after an interval of more than sixty years, is equally applicable to the Magazine at the present day.

In the Preface to the year 1761 is given an Epitome of the Contents contained in each Number of that Volume; which was continued through twenty-three Volumes, with the exception of the years 1774 and 1777; in the former of which is an interesting account of the rise of Humane Societies for the Recovery of Persons apparently drowned.

Mr. Richard Cave * died in December 1766; and in 1767 the name of *Francis Newbery* (Nephew of the before-mentioned Mr. John Newbery) appeared in the title-page †.

On the death of Richard Cave, Mr. Henry relinquished the actual profession of a Printer; and employed, as his agent at St. John's Gate, Mr. David Bond, who was so continued till the end of 1778 — when, a considerable share of the Proprietorship having been purchased by the Writer of this Preface, the Magazine was for the next two years printed partly at St. John's Gate, and partly in Red Lion Passage, Fleet Street : but this arrangement having been found inconve-

---

* The following inscription, on a flat stone in the old church of St. James Clerkenwell, was written by Mr. Cave's worthy Friend and Partner David Henry, whose laudable exertions long supported and increased the original credit of what Mr. Burke styled " one of the most chaste and valuable Miscellanies of the age."

" Sacred to the memory
of RICHARD and SARAH CAVE,
late of St. John's Gate.
He died December 8, 1766; she, December 1776.
" Reader, if native worth may claim a tear,
Or the sad tale of death affect thy ear,
Heave from thy breast one sympathising sigh,.
Since here such fair examples mouldering lie.
Here lies a pair, whom Honesty approv'd,
In death lamented, and in life belov'd ;
Who never meant a neighbour to offend ;
Who never made a Foe, nor lost a Friend ;
Whose only strife was who should act the best ;
Whose only hope to rise among the blest. '
" In grateful remembrance of their many virtues and parental tenderness, their only daughter has caused this small tribute to be erected to
the memory of her dear Parents."
Miss Mary Cave, the daughter above mentioned, an amiable and worthy woman, of elegant manners, died in June 1811.
† Where it continued till his death in 1780. From that period till 1800 the Magazine was regularly published by his Widow, Mrs. Elizabeth Newbery; and since her relinquishing business, at the close of the Eighteenth Century, by the present respectable Bookseller, Mr. John Harris; with the addition, in 1819, of his Son.

nient, the printing was in 1781 entirely removed to Cicero's Head *.

The more important avocations of Dr. Hawkesworth (who had been elected an East India Director, and who was afterwards appointed by the Admiralty to be the Editor of Captain Cook's Voyages) having engrosed his whole attention ; the department of the Review of Books in the Magazine was readily undertaken, and for several years very creditably performed, by the Rev. JOHN DUNCOMBE, a Gentleman of great literary reputation, and highly estimable in every relation of life.   Mr. Duncombe was also a valuable and regular Correspondent, both in the Miscellaneous and Poetical Departments; and furnished many of the introductory Prefaces, particularly that of 1780, from which, as peculiarly adapted to the present subject, an extract is given :

" Half a century, a large proportion of the life of man, having now elapsed since we first engaged in the pleasing but arduous task of *instructing and amusing*, we think it expedient, for the convenience of our numerous readers, in some measure to complete this part of our Work, by subjoining a General Index to the last Thirty †, as has been done to the first Twenty Volumes; but, as this will be a work of much labour, and will require great care and accuracy, our Readers cannot expect it to be hastily executed.   Those who have complete Sets may then easily refer to any former volume, and those who chuse to begin *de novo* may consider the Gentleman's Magazine for January 1781, as the commencement of a new Work, which in due time will be closed in the same manner, with this material advantage over every new compilation, and indeed over all our Competitors, that our long-established reputation has procured us so many Friends and Correspondents in all parts of the British Dominions, that we have often reason to say, with the fanciful Poet of Sulmo, *Inopes nos copia fecit*, we are often at a loss what to adopt, and what to reject ; and, in general, instead of extracting honey, as at first, from the fugitive flowers and blossoms of the month, or poison (as is the manner of some) from the baneful hemlock of the day, have little more merit than the industrious Husbandman or Gardener, who sows good seed in his ground, and clears it from weeds and vermin.   Our Biographical Memoirs have been generally esteemed, and frequently copied.   Our Antiquarian Researches have received a very flattering commendation ; and many other eulogiums might be mentioned that do us equal honour.   But for the importance of the subjects discussed, we shall refer (as usual)

* Where the Magazine continued regularly to be printed till March 1820 ; when, for the convenience of printing the Votes of the House of Commons more expeditiously, the extensive Establishment of " Nichols and Son, " as Printers and Booksellers, was removed to No. 25, Parliament Street, Westminster.

† This was postponed till the " Thirty " became " Thirty-six."

to the principal contents of each month ; and shall conclude with observing, that, instead of relaxing in our speed, the encouragement which we receive and gratefully acknowledge, and the rivalry which our success has excited, shall only quicken our endeavours to deserve the one, and to counteract the other."

From the extensive literary connexions of the present Editor, the Correspondence with Mr. Urban so considerably increased, that a more ample field of action soon became indispensable, which at the end of 1782 was thus announced.

"The Gentleman's Magazine is so well known, and the conduct of it so generally approved, that room only is wanting to render our plan complete. We have the pleasing satisfaction to receive commendations from every quarter, with requests to enlarge our limits for the admission of favours, which the Virtuous and the Learned most liberally communicate, and which we with pain most unwillingly suppress.

"Our Readers, we believe, will do us the justice to acknowledge, that no means have been left unattempted to make room for variety, nor a line left void that could be usefully filled. The chief complaints of our purchasers are the smallness of the type, and the compression of the subjects.

"Among other inconveniences attending our narrow limits, not the least has been the unavoidable procrastination of the Parliamentary Debates. Those of the first Session are completed in the Supplement to the present Volume; the second Session shall be soon closed; and in future we shall be enabled to comprise the whole within the year to which they immediately belong.

"The great and important events of 1782 have been so various and diffuse, and have crowded upon us so copiously and rapidly, that, though we collected them with care, we were not able to arrange them with precision. Where all could not be admitted, the chain was necessarily broken; nor could it be resumed, as the same cause subsisted the second that obstructed the first; and thus, month after month, in proportion as matter increased, room diminished, till at length we are overwhelmed with an accumulation of various kinds, which we can no otherwise discharge than by enlarging our limits, and in consequence increasing our price. We may truly say that this is our last resort. Hardly any subject has escaped our retrenching hands; naked argument has been preferred to florid declamation; bare facts to long details : yet, with all our care, we have not been able to keep within our usual bounds."

The new plan commenced in January 1783; and at the same time a considerable number of imperfect sets of the Magazine, then remaining at the old warehouse at St. John's Gate (of which, though no longer a Printing-office, Mr. Henry was still the pro-

prietor) ; it was determined to re-print a few copies of the early
Volumes, and to continue the General Index ; and the following
notification was accordingly given.

" Though the reputation which the Gentleman's Magazine
has maintained for more than Fifty Years renders all other recommendation unnecessary—yet that it was the first that laid
the plan which has been followed by so many imitators ; that it
is read and approved wherever the English language is understood ; and that the Learned of all nations are occasionally its
correspondents, may, we hope, be urged as an additional proof of
its intrinsic merit.

" The inestimable value of a Periodical Work formed and
continued for more than Half a Century, on the plan of the
Gentleman's Magazine, if executed with tolerable accuracy,
must be obvious to every man, conversant with the world, at first
sight. In the wide range of Literature, there is not a subject that
the most fertile genius can suggest, but must, in the course of so
many years, come before the tribunal of the Publick tó be discussed, and consequently furnish materials for such a Work ;
nor is there an invention, or a discovery of importance to the
improvement of science, or the advantage of mankind, that does
not serve to increase the same stock.

" In the Work we now offer to the Publick, the original Compiler is known to have made every thing that was new the first
object of his care ; nor have those who succeeded him been less
attentive. There has scarcely a new subject been started, a new
invention introduced, or a discovery of any kind, either by land
or sea, of which a satisfactory account is not to be found in the
Gentleman's Magazine.

" Nor are these the only materials of which the Compilers
have availed themselves. The great controversial subjects, in
which the Publick have borne a part, are all to be found impartially stated, whether respecting individuals, as Rundle, Hoadly,
Canning, Blandy, Dodd, &c. &c. ; or those in which whole bo-
dies of men, and even States, have been involved, as Churchmen
and Dissenters, Britain and her Colonies, &c. To these may be
added the lesser controversies that have arisen concerning the
interpretation of doubtful passages in the Sacred Text, of which
there is hardly one to be met with in Scripture that has not either
been explained or elucidated. The mineral and fossil Kingdoms
have likewise contributed largely to enrich this compilation ;
and the rare productions which they exhibit, together with
the obvious utility of maps, furnished the first hint for embel-
lishing and illustrating it with copper-plates.

" Other materials are, a profusion of Prescriptions in the Medical Art, so liberally interspersed, that there is scarcely a disease
or disorder to which the human frame is subject, for which a re-

medy is not to be found in the Gentleman's Magazine; in which likewise many of the most celebrated Nostrums are analysed, and the ingredients of which they are compounded laid open for the benefit of the publick. Extraordinary cases in Surgery likewise abound, which are not less interesting to the Faculty in general, than instructive to the young Practitioner.

" The rudiments of almost every Science, as deduced from first principles, will also be found so clearly explained, that those who are bent on improvement, either in language or art, need no other tutor. Physics and Metaphysics are occasionally introduced; Mathematical Questions resolved; and the Phænomena of Nature, according to the systems of antient and modern times, accounted for, and scientifically demonstrated.

" The Antiquary who may purchase these Volumes will find materials sufficient to gratify the amplest curiosity. The Memorials of antient Families; the Antiquities of particular Cities, Churches, and Monasteries; the Topography of Provinces, Counties, and Parishes; with the Laws, Customs, and Prescriptions peculiar to each, that are interspersed in these Volumes, are innumerable. Nor will those who read for entertainment only have cause to regret their too scanty allotment. Affecting Narratives, interesting Stories, Novels, Tales, Poetry, and Plays, take up their full proportion of that room in which the whole is necessarily comprized. Add to these the Lives of Eminent Men, the recital of whose illustrious actions, at the same time that it fires the mind to virtuous emulation, cannot but fill it with the most refined pleasure. Even those who have transmitted their memories with infamy to posterity, and who have rendered themselves notorious for acts of transcendant villainy, are not wholly excluded, but are recorded as examples of atrocious vice, to deter others from like enormities.

" But the materials of greatest National Concern remain still to be noticed. The Parliamentary Proceedings, during those periods in which the Debates in both Houses were carried on with the most spirited opposition, will be found amply recorded, and stated with the strictest regard to truth. By a curious inspection, the gradations by which the National Debt has risen from the moderate sum of Sixteen Millions (the Debt due at the accession of the present Royal Family of Hanover to the Throne) to the enormous sum of Two Hundred and Twenty Millions, the Debt due at the end of 1782*, may be traced, and all the fallacious pretences that have from time to time been urged by successive Ministers to increase it, developed.

" The Revolutions that have happened in the Political Systems of Europe, in the course of the period included in these Volumes, will be apt to bring to the Reader's mind the uncer-

* The present amount of the National Debt (1821) is estimated at 835 millions!

tainty of all human affairs. The Nations whose interests were
thought to be inseparable, will be seen warring against each
other; while those, on whose opposition the Balance of Power
was thought to depend, are now connected in the closest amity;
nay, so strange are the vicissitudes which the short period of
Fifty Years has produced, that neither the people on this side
the Globe, nor the other, seem actuated or governed by the
same political principles.

" Nor will this revolution in Politicks be found much more remarkable than the Revolution that has happened in Religion.
From an abhorrence of Popery, which marked the Reigns of the
two first Georges, the mild Reign of George the Third has set
the example of Tolerance and Moderation to every Sect, and to
the people of every persuasion. At the same time may be observed that lenient spirit spreading wide and far among Nations
the most intolerant. Even the Pope himself has felt its influence.

" An attentive enquirer, enlightened by the means which these
Volumes will furnish, will be able to trace the spring of all these
Revolutions to its source; and will probably be inclined to conclude, that the same Power that produced all these astonishing
alterations, in the short period of Half a Century, will in time
bring forth still greater changes, of which human foresight can
have no conception.—To make this Work of the greater value
to the Purchasers, no more than One Hundred Sets will be
perfected by the Proprietors; but a few single Volumes are
printed over, to perfect the Sets of former Purchasers."

The reprinting proceeded to the Twentieth Volume.

The enlargement of the Magazine, which was most favourably
received, was thus noticed, by the present Writer, in the Preface
to the year 1783.

" Having now for a year experienced the advantages of our enlarged plan, our Readers, we flatter ourselves, will allow its ex-
pediency. If our price is increased, so is our Volume in the
same proportion, and by this means we have been enabled to
admit many valuable communications, which must otherwise
have been consigned to oblivion. And our example has been
followed by much the oldest and most respectable of our competitors. Encouraged by the approbation that it has generally
received, we are determined to pursue our plan with redoubled
vigour, and doubt not that, though

' Years following years steal something every day'

from the pleasures and friendships of human life, they will add
to the reputation and the friends which the Gentleman's Magazine has so long enjoyed. We have only to desire them to continue their kind contributions, and to believe that though they
may even now be sometimes unavoidably postponed, they will

not be omitted, unless for reasons of which they will allow us to
be the judges, and then (if desired) they shall be returned."

To the Volume for 1784 the Editor took the liberty of pre-
fixing this sonnet:

> URBAN, thy skill matur'd by mellowing Time,
>   Thy pleasing toil, thy well-conducted page,
> Through Britain's Realms, and many a Foreign Clime,
>   Have charm'd the last, and charm the present age.
>
> Unnumber'd Rivals, urg'd by thy renown,
>   To match thy useful labours oft have tried;
> In vain they tried; unnotic'd and unknown,
>   In cold Oblivion's shade they sunk, and died.
>
> Chear'd by the fostering beams of public praise,
>   Continue still " to profit and delight * :"
> Whilst Learning all her ample store displays,
>   Her " varying" charms at thy command " unite †."
> Hence future Hawkesworths, Wartons, Grays, may sing,
> Where virtuous JOHNSON ‡ plum'd his eagle wing.   J. N.

In the Preface to 1784 allusion is made to a plan (in the
Number for September, p. 653) for an extensive "Repertory
of Antiquity, or a Register of Communications, and Notices of
Discoveries, of Matters as yet undescribed, Points as yet unex-
plained, or not hitherto discussed, &c." A valuable description of the *sorts of materials* of which it should consist is then
given; which we are tempted to transcribe, as pointing out the
nature of those communications which are now, as they were
then, thought very desirable.

" Notice and information of matters or things respecting antient topography, or geography; of changes and alterations
which the face of any country hath undergone in its mountains,
rivers, ports, harbours, particularly, as far as may be collected
from history, record, or tradition, or traced by any vestiges of antiquity; of the drowning of any country; of eruptions; of
countries becoming drained from failure of waters which before
flooded them; of the growing of soil, as marshes beyond the antient sea-shores and banks, or of fens within land; the changes of
the courses of rivers, and the apparent effect of them; antient accounts of tides, where they differed from the present state of things.

" Accounts and information of the antient inhabitancy in its
successive inhabitants, by colony or conquest; remains of their

---

* " Prodesse et delectare."   † " E pluribus unum."
  ‡ To whom the Writer of these Lines had the pleasure of shewing them in
the last interview with which he was honoured by this illustrious pattern of true
piety.—" Take care of your eternal salvation," and " Remember to observe the
Sabbath; let it not be a day of business, nor wholly a day of dissipation;" were
parts of his last solemn farewell. " Let my words have their due weight," he
added; " they are those of a dying man."

mode of living and dwelling : Britons ; Scots ; Picts ; Saxons ; Anglo-Danes ; Normans ; their respective peculiarities as to the point of inhabitancy ; the progress and improvements in house-building, as to the materials and form ; remains of public dwellings and inhabitancy ; Pictish, British, Roman, Saxon, Norman, Gothic, Moorish, or Arabesque, or of the beginnings of the introduction of the Grecian and Roman architecture ; of pavings, tesselated, brick, tile, plaster, or the introduction of wood-flooring ; of ceilings, and specimens or accounts of antient painted ceilings or walls.

" Specimens or accounts of antient furniture, worthy of notice, so far as it may tend to mark the change of manners, or the progress of what is called Refinement and Fashion.

" Specimens or accounts of clothing, cookery, brewery, confectionery, in general ; the table of medicines, which may tend to illustrate the changes and progression of customs, or may recall to memory any thing *useful*, which may have been lost, or disused from mere caprice and love of change, perhaps for the worse, of which many instances will occur, and some very material ones might here be specified.

" Any thing which may recall to memory antient modes of farming in tillage or grazing, used and useful under former circumstances of the country, and which, though now disusen, may become again useful, should the country, by loss of foreign trade, or oppression of taxes, and an emigration or decrease of inhabitants, fall back, in any degree, to its former state.

" The antient modes of internal carriage, by land or by water ; therein of river and canal navigation from the time of the Romans. There is a curious clue by which this investigation may be carried back to much earlier times. Notices and information of marine carriage ; as also of the progress of marine architecture, and of the nature of the antient marine navigation.

" All notices, or specimens, of antient mechanics, and mechanic trades and handicrafts ; antient tools (as, for one instance, how and when the chissel succeeded the adze in working stone) ; of antient machines, which, though now disused in practice, may not be wholly unuseful, at least to be known ; accounts of antient manufactures, and specimens of their fabrics.

" Accounts, or any specimens, of the refined arts in jewellery, embroidery, knitting, and frame-weaving ; statuary, painting, and engraving ; particularly the illuminator's art.

" Antient musick ; psalmody ; musical instruments ; poetry ; and stage-plays.

" Any thing which may give precedents or explanations of our constitution under the Saxons or Danes, or of the revival of it in later times.

" State of our constitutional customs, and our modes of the

administration and execution of law, and in the usage and maintenance of rights. The state of these matters as found in the
law courts, and other jurisdictions, either general and public,
or peculiars of local courts, such as ampts, bailliages, loes, and
other inferior leets and jurisdictions. Any accounts marking, at
various periods, the state of our military, and our art of war; our
arms, defensive and offensive ; our artillery, before and since the
use of gunpowder. I should here mention our antient mode of
fortification, but that Mr. King, in his very curious and very
learned Dissertation on Antient Castles, has almost exhausted
that subject.

" Local and town customs, antiently established, distinguishing those which were grounded in wise policy from those which
are derived from the caprice of insolent fœdal despotism.

" State, at various periods of time, of our internal trade, markets, and marts ; of our external commerce and navigation ;
places to which we traded ; manner in which such was conducted ;
articles of such commerce in each place respectively.

" Heraldry ; such as marks the alliances and descendants of
our Sovereigns, which in part comes under the head of Diplo-
matic Information ; such as marks the history of any family or
person, having any reference to the clearing-up any point of
history.

" Notices of any materials which lie buried in unnoticed places
of record, in the treasuries of courts, churches, chapters, or libraries ; materials which remain obscure and unnoticed in the several places of our public records.

" Articles of biography, respecting the lives of men of any
description ; of such who have been of any use during their lives,
or by their works ; of men whose conduct or fate in life recorded,
may become useful examples, encouragement, or warning to
others."

It will not, we trust, be deemed presumptuous to say, that
the Gentleman's Magazine has in a great measure fulfilled the
prediction of the learned and ingenious Antiquary, and has proved
itself " one of the most useful Repositories of the species of
knowledge above recommended, any where to be met with ; its
pages having been always eagerly opened to facts, and observations upon facts, respecting the History and Antiquities of our
Country ; precedents and explanations of our ancient and glorious Constitution ; with useful discoveries of every kind."

" But it is not to the Antiquary alone, however respectable,
that the Editors have devoted their attention. The Philosopher,
the Historian, the Physician, the Critic, the Poet, the Divine,
and above all the PUBLICK, have in turn shared the utmost ex-
ertion of their abilities."

In the Preface to 1785, instead of recapitulating the principal

Contents of the Volume, a new plan was struck out, of introducing an "INDEX INDICATORIUS;" or, an Explanatory Index of Papers, which our limits would not admit in the course of the preceding year; and this MINOR CORRESPONDENCE was found so useful an addition to the Magazine, that it was soon after continued *monthly*, instead of annually.

By the death of the Rev. JOHN DUNCOMBE*, the Magazine lost a Correspondent, whose communications, in Biography, Poetry, and Criticism, during the last twenty years of his life, were frequent and valuable. Many of them are without a name; but his miscellaneous communications are usually distinguished by the signature of CRITO.

And this may be a proper place to mention the considerable assistance which the Magazine received from the kindness of RICHARD GOUGH †, Esq. which cannot be better mentioned than in his own words:

" He opened a correspondence with Mr. Urban in 1767, with an account of the village of Aldfriston in Sussex, under the signature of D. H.; which signature be retained to the last, but not altogether uniformly; nor is another signature in some later Volumes with the same letters to be mistaken for his. And on the death of his Fellow Collegian, Mr. Duncombe, in 1786, the department of the Review in that valuable Miscellany was, for the most part, committed to him. If he criticised with warmth and severity certain innovations attempted in Church and State, he wrote his sentiments with sincerity and impartiality—in the fulness of a heart deeply impressed with a sense of the excellence and happiness of the English Constitution both in Church and State."

On the 7th of May 1786, a considerable number of the Volumes of the Magazine, from 1781 inclusive, were unfortunately consumed by a Fire, which began in Ludgate Street, and extended its ravages to Mrs. Newbery's dwelling-house and warehouse, in St. Paul's Church-yard.

The Two Volumes of a General Index, from 1731 to 1786 inclusive, were published in 1789. They were compiled by a laborious and worthy Divine, the Rev. Samuel Ayscough, many years Assistant Librarian in the British Museum, where his multifarious labours, more particularly in arranging and cataloguing the undescribed Manuscripts, the very numerous and scarce single Tracts, and especially the many original Charters, will long bear testimony to his uncommon industry. He died Oct. 30, 1804, in his 59th year ‡.

---

* This worthy Divine died January 18, 1786. See Vol. LXVI. p. 85.
† This not less respectable Correspondent, and benevolent Friend, died Feb. 20, 1809. See Vol. LXXIX. pp. 190, 195.
‡ See his Epitaph, with a Portrait of him, in General Index, Vol. V. p. viii.

In 1789, a copious and accurate Diary was given of his late Majesty's Visit to Weymouth and Plymouth; as were also, in subsequent years, of the Sovereign's various Excursions to Weymouth, Portland, Portsmouth, Cheltenham, Worcester, Hartlebury, &c.; from which some future Historian of Royal Progresses may find some useful materials; or some future necromantic Romancer (if another Sir Walter Scott should arise) may dilate on the Princely Pleasures of Weymouth, and its delightful Vicinity.

In 1790 Mr. Urban thus addressed his Readers:

" On the completion of a Sixtieth Volume, we may again be allowed to make the most grateful acknowledgments for that succession of favour, which has so long enabled us to stand conspicuous in the foremost rank of Monthly Journalists.

" We assume no merit beyond that of being the brief, but faithful, reporters of the Chronicle of the Times; and of selecting from the variety of excellent contributions which we receive what, in our best judgment, we think most conducive to the general fund of public entertainment and instruction. It is to our correspondents that the Reader is principally indebted for the valuable materials with which our pages are constantly filled, by Writers of the first eminence.

" Useful inventions and improvements in all branches of science, and even the record of unsuccessful projects, have regularly been registered in our Miscellany. The admirers of Biography, which has become a favourite amusement of the present age, will find here the most copious stores of information; and that very frequently in the truest picture that can be given, by the genuine Letters of such eminent characters as best deserve to be perpetuated. The Natural Historian, the Antiquary, the Philosopher, and the Studious in Polite Literature of every description, may also meet with their favourite object of research, and mutually give and receive that instruction which we are proud of being the instruments of conveying to public notice.

" In Politicks, the present year has been pregnant with events of the highest importance both to Church and State; and those it has been our study to detail with the strictest impartiality. And in this Volume, we may confidently assert, will be found a satisfactory narrative of the proceedings of the National Assembly of France, and of that ever-memorable Federation, which an elegant Female Writer, who went to Paris on purpose to be a spectator of it, calls ' the most sublime Spectacle that ever was represented on the Theatre of the Earth.'

When the preceding extract was written no reasonable man could have contemplated the lamentable proceedings which so speedily followed the dawnings of happiness in France, by the total demolition, not only of the visionary fabrick which had been erected, but of the very Government itself, and of all that was sacred and venerable.

The change was duly noticed in the Preface of 1791 :

" That the Sixty-first Volume of the Gentleman's Magazine meets the public eye, at the close of the year 1791, survivor to so many of its Contemporaries, is acknowledged with every grateful sentiment by the Compiler, whom it encourages to flatter himself, that, out of the heterogeneous mass of matter that offers itself to his ingenuity, he has served up some dishes at least suitable to the various palates of his Readers.

" When the world around him is in confusion ; when 'the nations rage, and the people imagine a vain thing, the Kings of the earth set themselves, and the Princes take counsel together ;' with astonishment and an impartial eye he sees the absurd doctrine of the Rights of Man, and of turning loose into a state of equality men who have no more idea of liberty than infants have of being left to go alone, or are no more to be trusted than the tenants of Bedlam or Newgate. For of this axiom he is firmly convinced, that the torpid Greenlander, the indolent Turk, the placid Hindoo, the ferocious Cossack, and the stupid Negro, the more flippant Frenchman, and the self-sufficient Chinese, have not the same idea of liberty, or the same talents for using or improving it, with his brave and generous Countrymen ;—consequently, all men are not equal in their natural or acquired advantages. He considers too, that it is not the obtruding of private opinions or vagaries, whether by secret or open artifice, that will weary a whole people out of their received and well-founded systems, to which they are convinced no better can be substituted. In giving his sentiments on these topicks with freedom, he has borne his testimony as a true friend to the Constitution of his Country, which, he hopes and prays, will not be subverted, or even shaken, at the caprice of every visionary, or the clamours of every incendiary.

" It is the glory of the Gentleman's Magazine to be founded on true Protestantism and true Patriotism, superior to the clamours of the day, whether extorted by mistaken humanity, misguided faith, or interested policy. Thus its Conductor condemns the total and instantaneous abolition of the Slave Trade, and thinks himself warranted by the horrors of St. Domingo ; he deprecates such a Revolution as has happened in France, when he contemplates the successors to the first National Assembly, the miseries of the bulk of emancipated Twenty-five millions, who have more liberty than they know what to do with, and the rapid approaches of a civil war ; and, sincerely as he commiserates the sufferers by riot and outrage in his own Country, he feels and laments, that they brought their sufferings on themselves, and persist in their attempts to provoke them with unrelenting resentment.

" So much for the speculations which administer (we heartily wish the term could be avoided) *fuel* to controversy, religious or political: but we may surely be allowed to claim a merit from endeavouring to damp, if we cannot extinguish, the fire; and to hope for the concurrence of good men of all denominations, inspired by genuine Christian Charity and Peace."

In 1792 the subject was thus resumed:

" The Editor of the Gentleman's Magazine contemplates the completion of its Sixty-second Volume with delight and gratitude. This delight and this gratitude is the more increased from the recollection, that the competitors for the favours of the publick become every day more and more numerous; he has, therefore, the greater reason to be satisfied that his well-meant endeavours retain, what they ever have been exerted to deserve, their proper share of the public countenance and esteem.

" We have yet again lived to see turbulent and perilous times; but we do not fear that we shall still continue to behold the solid good sense of Englishmen dispel the mists of sophistry and vain philosophy; we still hope to know that vice and folly can never triumph over virtue and wisdom; and we are fully convinced that the blessings and advantages of the British Constitution are as permanent in themselves, and as equally diffused, as the infirmities of human kind will warrant, or its reasonable faculties enjoy.

" To the Constitution, they whose labours are devoted to the Gentleman's Magazine have ever been firm, consistent, and systematic friends: we may defy those who have been most envious of our success to prove, that we have in any instance deviated from the integrity of Englishmen, to favour any prejudices of any party, at the expence of our general duty to the publick. To this conduct we shall adhere with steady perseverance, uninfluenced, and unintimidated. We stand on the firm base of our Countrymen's good opinion; and we well know they will never remove us from it as long as we shall continue to vindicate their true and proper interests.

" We are compelled also to avow the melancholy truth, that we have beheld the cause of Religion, and consequently the best hopes of man, audaciously attacked by some, and insidiously undermined by others. In this respect we may venture to claim to ourselves some portion of applause. We have been vigilant in counteracting these attacks, in whatever form, and from whatever quarter, they came; being well assured that we could not better serve or promote the genuine happiness of our fellow-beings, than by averting all contamination from those springs, which, rising in the First Principles of Things, are to terminate only in Eternity."

One more extract shall be given as it expresses the sentiments of the present Writer in 1794:

" Again the period returns, when with honest exultation we

acknowledge that uniform patronage, which for sixty-four years we have thankfully experienced; and which, though it may be difficult to find words that will vary the expressions of gratitude, is now acknowledged with the truest sensibility of the obligation.

" The unparalleled events of the past year have crowded on each other with such rapidity, and form such a memorable epoch in the historic page, that we look back with astonishment on the stupendous facts which we have recorded; facts which have set at defiance the most profound speculations of the politician, and such as the most visionary projector could not dare to have predicted. We forbear to dwell on the painful recital of slaughtered armies; or on other and still more afflicting devastations of cruelty, where the numerous victims were either of the softer sex, or, from infancy or age, unable to resist the ferocity of their assailants. Whatever may be the termination, these are events which stamp an indelible disgrace on the perpetrators; of whom very many have in their turns already expiated their crimes under the hands of public justice; and that in such a rapid succession as must astonish the most inattentive observer. Having felt it our duty to relate with fidelity these melancholy events as they have arisen; we look to the Great Disposer of Events, in humble hope that the signal mercies which have hitherto attended this favoured Country, may long be continued to it. Happily preserved by our insular situation from the more immediate scene of War; may we be truly sensible of the blessing; and may our inestimable Constitution long remain impregnable to the attacks of every assailant, and be transmitted inviolate to the latest posterity! Wishing most sincerely to draw a veil over whatever might tend to keep open dissentions which we hope are now for ever closed; it will be sufficient to recall to recollection the excellence of our Laws, and the purity with which they are administered.—The Reader will pardon this effusion, not wholly undigressive.

" To our numerous and very learned Correspondents we have to pay those thanks which their own ingenuous hearts will dictate to them in the warmest terms, without over-rating our sentiments. To them alone it is owing that the Gentleman's Magazine has so long preserved its Literary Reputation. Their contributions unite to form an aggregate of entertainment and instruction. With pride and Pleasure we look round to some of the brightest ornaments of Church and State—to the Bar, the Pulpit, and the Senate—and see in every department names of the first distinction who have sent their early shafts from our *Ulysses's Bow*. And it is with conscious satisfaction we reflect that, whenever the impetuosity of controversy has led our Correspondents to a greater degree of warmth than cooler prudence may have suggested, our columns have ever been open to the vindication of every person who has thought himself aggrieved; and in some cases even to an insertion of a direct attack upon ourselves. Let this, however, be a hint to our friends, not to indulge too freely in the satiric vein. We wish to hold out an olive-branch both in Literature and Politicks; and that an armistice may take place in the territories of Mr. Urban, even if it should fail on the Continent of Europe.

"In one department of our Miscellany it is not arrogant to assert, that we stand unrivalled. The Obituary forms a Body of Biography, which posterity will look back to with a satisfaction which any one may conceive who for a moment considers the defects of similar annals in preceding periods. In this branch of our labours, we have to acknowledge the assistance of many friends. At the same time we request those who in future may be inclined to favour us with intelligence of this kind to confine themselves in general to dates and facts, and to avoid expatiating on that which, arising from circumstances of private knowledge, or a local nature, may serve equally for thousands, as the favourite individual to whom it is promiscuously applied.

"The most difficult part of our ask remains; an apology to those who may feel hurt at their productions not appearing in print. To such we can only say, that, in cases where articles are *wholly improper*, we regularly point them out; but that all others are *intended* to be used, till the press of fresh correspondence becomes so great, that, large and crowded as our pages are, and small as is our type, we are often unable to find room for what we estem truly valuable. We have, therefore, to request indulgence on this head; and to beg that our friends will be as concise as the subject will admit, and avoid, wherever they can, superfluous controversy. We consider ourselves as caterers for the publick; and wishing, to the best of our abilities, to furnish them with instruction and delight, we trust they will give us credit for endeavouring at least to perform our task with impartiality, and with some of the advantages obtained from long experience."

After this period, the Prefaces have for the most part been the productions of more able Writers; but these, as some of them are still living ornaments of the present age, it would be impertinent to particularize, though the mention of two deceased Friends, Mr. GOUGH and Mr. BELOE, it would be unpardonable to conceal. It may safely, however, be said, that their general and constant tenour, in the stormy events of a most eventful period, has been to inculcate the purest principles of Religion and Morality; and to inculcate a due reverence for the Constituted Authorities in Church and State, as settled by Magna Charta, and confirmed by the glorious Revolution of 1688.

In 1792 the present Writer had occasion to lament the loss of his old and excellent Friend, Mr. HENRY, his very able associate in the Magazine, of which he was the principal Proprietor *, and of whom in this place some notice seems necessary.

Mr. David Henry was born in the neighbourhood of Aberdeen, in 1710, which place he left at the age of fourteen; and, coming to London, became connected with Edward Cave, whose sister (as stated in p. lvi) he married in 1736; and began business at Reading, where he established a provincial Paper for the use of that town, and of Winchester, where he had likewise a Printing-office. In 1754 his name was used in the Magazine, as partner with Richard Cave (see p. lvi.) at St. John's Gate, where he continued to reside for many years with great reputation : and he possessed the freehold property of the Gate and its appurtenances at the time of his death. Besides taking an active part in the management of the Magazine for more than half a century, Mr. Henry's separate literary labours were such as do credit to his judgment and industry. The only printed Volume that we recollect, which bears his name, was a compilation, while he lived at Reading, under the patronage of Dr. Bolton, Dean of Carlisle, entitled, " Twenty Discourses — abridged from Archbishop Tillotson, &c." of which a second edition was published in 1763, and a fourth in 1779. Those useful and popular publications which describe the Curiosities of Westminster Abbey, St. Paul's, and the Tower, &c. were originally compiled by Mr. Henry, and were improved by him through many successive impressions. He wrote also, " The Complete English Farmer, or a Practical System of Husbandry," a science which he cultivated on his farm at Beckenham in Kent; and " An Historical Account of all the Voyages round the World, performed by English Navigators," 1774, 4 vols. 8vo ; to which he afterwards added two more, including Captain Cook's Voyages ; all remarkable for being comprehensive, perspicuous, and accurate. He was a man of sound understanding, well acquainted with the literary history of his time, and agreeably communicative of what he knew.

In the Magazine for 1792, is a Letter signed N. L. L. (I forget from whom) in which are several particulars respecting Mr. David Henry and his various Publications.

In January 1794, soon after the death of the celebrated Mr. *Gibbon*, a letter from that elegant Historian was printed in the Magazine, vol. LXIV. p. 5, in which he strongly advised the Writer of this Preface to publish a Selection of the many important articles of the Magazine. From other numerous and pressing avocations, Mr. Nichols never had the opportunity of availing himself of this friendly hint ; but the idea was afterwards

* Mr. Henry's shares in the Magazine became the property of his Widow ; and are still possessed by her Family.

adopted, and successfully acted upon, by a Gentleman of the University of Oxford.

In 1799, in consequence of a considerable advance in the duties on paper, imposed by Parliament, and at the same time a considerable increase in the price of labour, the Proprietors of the Magazine were under the necessity of raising the price to eighteen pence; and in 1809 to two shillings.

The Preface to the year 1800, written by Mr. Gough, on occasion of the conclusion of the Eighteenth Century, is well worthy of particular notice. In it is given a list of the Sovereigns who flourished during the course of the Century; and in a curious supplementary article in Feb. 1803, Mr. Gough drew up, with great attention, a List of such departed Worthies as had effectually served their Country in Church and State, or distinguished themselves in Literature or in Arms, arranged under the heads of "Ministers and Statesmen, Stateswomen; Lawyers, Judges; Warriors, Admirals and Seamen; Learned Divines of the English and Irish Church, Dissenters, and Foreigners; Historians, Antiquaries, Writers, Critics, Grammarians, Poets, Mathematicians, Painters, Architects, Statuaries, Engravers, Printers, Letter-founders, Wood-cutters, Travellers, Physicians, Surgeons and Chemists, Botanists and Gardeners, Naturalists, Actors, and Musicians."

On the night of Feb. 8, 1808, a calamitous event (at which the present Writer still trembles whilst recording it) in a few short hours demolished the accumulated stock of half a century. His extensive printing-office and warehouses, with their valuable contents, were rapidly consumed; and, amongst other articles of still more intrinsic literary as well as pecuniary interest, were the unsold Numbers of the Gentleman's Magazine, from 1783 to 1807; with the exception of a very few copies, which were in the Publisher's warehouse; and so fiercely did the Fire rage, that many hundred copper-plates (and amongst them those of the Magazine) were totally spoiled, and some actually melted.

From this period * is to be dated the "New Series" of the Magazine; which may still be regularly had, or almost any single Number, at Messrs. Harris and Son's, in St. Paul's Church-yard.

Of the very numerous Engravings which embellish the Magazines (not less than TWO THOUSAND, exclusive of the Wood-cuts) it may be sufficient to refer the Reader to a slight account of them in an Advertisement prefixed to the "Complete List of the Plates and Wood-cuts in the Gentleman's Magazine, and Index thereto," which forms the Fifth Volume of these General Indexes; and for which the Publishers are highly indebted to its ingenious Compiler, CHARLES ST. BARBE, jun. Esq. F. S. A.

* Earlier Volumes, or single Numbers, are occasionally to be had from various Booksellers, by whom they are treasured whenever they are found in Libraries.

⁎ In the preceding pages the names have been enumerated of some of the *earliest Correspondents* of the Magazine ; and it is with equal pride and pleasure that the following List is subjoined of Contributors of a later date, formed principally from a *memoriter* recollection of departed Friends and Patrons—and which might be most considerably enlarged, were the pages of the different Volumes turned over for that particular purpose.

William Alexander, Esq.
George Allan, Esq. Darlington.
Rev. Richard Amner.
Mr. Henry Andrews, Astrologer.
James Pettit Andrews, Esq.
Rev. George Ashby.
Thomas Astle, Esq.
Benjamin Aylett, Esq. Surgeon.
Sir Joseph Ayloffe, Bart.
Rev. Samuel Ayscough.
John Bacon, Esq. First Fruits Office.
John Bacon, Esq. Architect.
Rev. Dr. Phanuel Bacon.
Rev. Samuel Badcock.
Chambers Hyde Badger, Esq.
Mr. William Baker, Reading.
Rev. Roger Baldwin.
Rev. Dr. Thomas Balguy.
Sir Joseph Banks, Bart.
Thomas Barker, Esq. Lyndon.
Rev. Stephen Barrett.
Mr. William Barrett, Bristol.
Mr. Thomas Barritt, Manchester.
Hon. Daines Barrington.
Mr. Benjamin Bartlett.
Rev. Julius Bate, Deptford.
John Baynes, Esq.
Rev. Dr. Osmund Beauvoir.
Mr. Thomas Beckwith, York.
Rev. William Beloe.
Dr. W. Bennet, Bishop of Cloyne.
Rev. James Bentham.
Mr. Samuel Bentley, Uttoxeter.
Mrs. Eliza Berkeley.
John Berkenhout, M. D.
Sir Thomas Bernard, Bart.
William Bernard, Esq.
Rev. William Bickerstaffe, Leicester.
Ralph Bigland, Esq. Garter.
Rev. George Bingham.
John Birch, Esq. Surgeon.
Rev. Samuel Bishop.
Dr. Robert Bisset.
Rev. F. Blackburne, Archdeacon.
Mr. Thomas Bland, of Norwich
(*A Friend to Accuracy.*)

Rev. Dr. Benjamin Blayney.
Mr. Richard Bond, Gloucester.
William Boscawen, Esq.
James Boswell, Esq.
Rev. Jonathan Boucher.
Rev. John Bowle, Idmiston.
John Bowles, Esq.
Rev. St. George Bowles.
Mr. W. Bowyer, (learned Printer).
William Boys, Esq. Sandwich.
Abraham Bragge, Esq. Surgeon.
Rev. John Brand, Sec. A. S.
Rev. John Brand, Southwark.
Edward Bridgen, Esq.
Richard Brocklesby, M. D.
John Charles Brooke, Esq. Herald.
Alderman T. Broster, Chester.
John Hawkins Browne, Esq.
Jacob Bryant, Esq.
William Buchan, M. D.
Mr. Joseph Buckmaster, Lambeth.
Joseph Budworth, Esq. afterwards
    Palmer *(A Rambler).*
William Burdon, Esq.
Rev. Dr. And. Burnaby, Archdeacon.
Rev. Dr. Charles Burney.
Sir William Burrell, Bart.
Mr. E. Burton *(Ruben D'Moundt).*
Rev. Thomas Butler, Child Ockford.
Rev. William Dejovas Byrche.
John Cade, Esq. Gainford, Durham.
Hon. and Rev. W. Bromley Cadogan.
Rev. Dr. John Calder.
Sir John Call, Bart.
Dr. John Carr, Hertford.
Francis Carter, Esq.
Mr. John Carter, Architect.
Mr. George Saville Cary.
Tiberius Cavallo, Esq.
Rev. William Chafin, Chettle.
Mr. James Chalmers, Aberdeen.
Mrs. Chapone.
John Charnock, Esq.
William Chisholme, Esq.
Thomas Christie, Esq.
Rev. Edward Clarke, Buxted.

Rev. William Clarke, Chichester.
Rev. Charles Coates.
Thomas Cogan, M. D.
Rev. Dr. Thomas Coke.
Charles Nalson Cole, Esq.
Rev. William Cole, Mliton.
William Collins, Esq. Greenwich.
Michael Collinson, Esq.
Peter Collinson, Esq.
Thomas Collinson, Esq.
Patrick Colquhoun, LL.D.
John Coltman, Esq. Leicester.
Charles Combe, M. D.
Rt. hon. W. Burton Conyngham.
Rev. William Cooke.
Rev. Oliver St. John Cooper.
Rev. George Costard.
Mrs. Cowley.
William Cowper, Esq. the Poet.
J. Crane, M. D. Wells.
Rev. Sir Herbert Croft, Bart.
Rev. Sir John Cullum, Bart. F. R.S.
Richard Cumberland, Esq.
William Cuming, M. D.
Mr. William Cuningham.
Mr. William Curtis, Botanist.
Mr. Emanuel Mendez Da Costa.
Alexander Dalrymple, Esq.
David Dalrymple, Lord Hailes.
Richard Dalton, Esq.
Erasmus Darwin, M. D.
Mr. Lockyer Davis.
Mr. Thomas Davies.
Mr. Benjamin Dawson, Bath.
Rev. C. E. De Coetlogon.
Lieut.-colonel De la Motte.
John Louis De Lolme.
Rev. Samuel Denne (*W.* and *D.*)
Rev. Dr. John Disney.
Rev. Dr. Philip Doddridge.
Josiah Dornford, LL. D.
Rev. James Douglas.
Dr. John Douglas, Bp. of Salisbury.
John Dovaston, Esq.
Hugh Downman, M. D.
Rev. Wm. Drake, Isleworth.
Matthew Duane, Esq.
Andrew Coltee Ducarel, D. C. L.
Mrs. S. Duncombe, Canterbury.
Rev. Charles Dunster.
Rev. Lewis Dutens.
Rev. Henry Dimock, Hebraist.
Mr. Edward Easton, Salisbury.
Bryan Edwards, Esq.
John Elderton, Esq. Bath.

Mr. Deputy Ellis.
Peter Elmsly, Esq.
Mr. Henry Emlyn, Architect.
Rev. Dr. Wm. Enfield.
Mr. James Essex, Architect.
Rev. Edward Evanson.
Francis Eyre, Esq.
Rev. Dr. Richard Farmer.
J. Feltham, Esq.
Sir John Fenn.
John Forbes, Esq. Stanmore.
Mr. Theodosius Forrest.
Rev. Benjamin Forster, Boconnoc.
Edward Forster, Esq. Walthamstow.
John Reinhold Forster, LL. D.
William Forsyth, Esq. Kensington.
John Fothergill, M. D.
Anthony Fothergill, M. D.
Mr. Richard Fowke, Elmesthorpe.
Rev. Dr. Thomas Francklin.
Dr. Benjamin Franklin.
Rev. Dr. John Free.
Fielding Best Fynney, Esq.
Rev. Robert Burd Gabriel.
Rev. Dr. Alexander Geddies.
Edward Gibbon, Esq. the Historian.
Rev. Dr. Andrew Giffard.
Rev. Richard Gifford, Duffield.
Rev. William Gilpin.
Rev. Dr. Samuel Glasse.
Rev. George-Henry Glasse.
Richard Glover, Esq.
Rev. Edward Goodwin, Sheffield.
Rev. Dr. John Gordon, Lincoln.
Rev. Dr. Isaac Gosset.
Rev. William Gostling, Canterbury.
Foote Gower, M. D.
Rev. James Granger.
Rev. Richard Graves.
Rev. Stephen Greenaway.
Edward Burnaby Greene, Esq.
Mr. Richard Greene, Lichfield.
Rev. Francis Gregory.
Rev. Dr. George Gregory.
Mr. Samuel H. Grimm, Artist.
Captain Francis Grose.
William Grove, Esq. LL.D.
Rev. Philip Hacket.
Sir William Hamilton, K. B.
Jonas Hanway, Esq.
Hon. Mr. Justice Hardinge.
Mr. E. Hargrove, Knaresborough.
Robert Harrington, M. D.
John Harriott, Esq.
David Hartley, Esq.

Rev. Dr. Edward Harwood.
Edward Hasted, Esq. Kent.
William Hawes, M. D.
Sir John Hawkins.
Mr. B. B. Hayden, Plymouth.
William Hayley, Esq.
Rev. Henry Headley *(T. C. O.)*
Rev. Dr. Ralph Heathcote.
William Heberden, M. D.
Mr. John Hedger.
Rev. John Henderson, Oxford.
Rev. Dr. Samuel Henley.
Mr. John Henn, Appleby School.
Rev. Samuel Henshall.
Rob. Henson, Esq. Bainton House.
Mr. Wm. Herbert, Cheshunt.
John Herrick, Esq. Beaumanor Park.
Joseph Highmore, Esq.
John Hinckley, Esq.
Thomas Ford Hill, Esq.
Francis Hiorne, Esq. Warwick.
Rev. Henry Hodgson, M. D. LL.D.
Rev. Richard Hole.
John Holliday, Esq. Lincoln's Inn.
Rev. Edward Holmes.
Rev. Dr. Robert Holmes.
Mr. John Holt, Liverpool.
Rev. Henry Homer.
John Hoole, Esq.
Dr. G. Horne, Bp. of Norwich.
Dr. S. Horsley, Bp. of St. Asaph.
John Howard, Esq. Philanthropist.
Rev. James Hurdis.
William Hutchinson, Esq. Durham.
William Hutton, Esq. Birmingham.
William Jackson, Esq. Canterbury.
Edward Jacob, Esq. Faversham.
Rev. Richard Jago.
Rev. T. Jeffreys.
David Jennings, Esq. Hawkhurst.
Mr. Joseph Jennings.
Edward Jerningham, Esq.
Rev. Robert Ingram.
Thomas Johnes, Esq. Hafod.
Rev. Edward Jones, Loddington.
Rev. John Jones.
Rev. W. Jones, Nayland.
Sir William Jones.
Mr. J. Jordan, Stratford-upon-Avon.
Edward Ironside, Esq.
John Ives, Esq.
George Keate, Esq.
Robert Kelham, Esq.
Rev. Dr. Benjamin Kennicott.
Rev. Dr. Andrew Kippis.

Thomas Kirkland, M. D.
Mrs. Mary Knowles, Fair Quaker.
Mr. John Knox, Bookseller.
Rev. John Kynaston.
Rev. Thomas Langley.
Bennet Langton, Esq.
The Most Noble William Petty, the first Marquis of Lansdown.
Mr. J. Laskey, Crediton.
William Latham, M. D.
French Laurence, D. C. L.
Rev. Francis Leighton.
Mr. Henry Lemoine.
John Coakley Lettsom, M. D.
Sir Ashton Lever.
Mr. David Levi.
Rev. Dr. Lickorish, Hockley.
Rev. John Lightfoot.
Rev. Theophilus Lindsey.
Mr. Robert Loder, Woodbridge.
Edward Long, Esq. Jamaica.
Mr. Barak Longmate.
Dr. J. Lorimer.
Rev. Dr. Michael Lort.
Dr. Robert Lowth, Bp. of London.
John Loveday, Esq. Caversham.
John Loveday, D.C.L. *(Antiquarius, Academicus,* and *Scrutator).*
Rev. Thomas Ludlam.
Rev. William Ludlam.
Rev. John Lyon, Dover.
Samuel Lysons, Esq.
Dr. Charles Lyttelton, Bp. of Exeter.
Rev. Aulay Macaulay, Vicar of Rothley *(Clericus Leicestrensis.)*
Rev. Dr. Archibald Maclaine.
Dr. S. Madan, Bp. of Peterborough.
J. Hyacinth de Magelhaens, Esq.
Mr. James Peller Malcolm.
Edmund Malone, Esq.
The Abbé Mann, Brussels.
Rev. Owen Manning.
Dr. W. Lort Mansel, Bp. of Bristol.
Rev. Dr. Rt. Markham, Whitechapel.
Jeremiah Markland, Esq. M. A.
Rev. Edmund Marshall.
Rev. William Mason.
George Mason, Esq.
Rev. Robert Masters.
Mr. James Matthews, Librarian at Shelburne House.
Rev. Paul Henry Maty.
Israel Mauduit, Esq.
Sir Joseph Mawbey, Bart.
Rev. Henry Meen.

William Melmoth, Esq.
Mr. Richard E. Mercier, Dublin.
Rev. Henry Michell.
Mr. Julius Mickle.
Mr. Richard Miles, Numismatist.
Edward Miller, Mus. D.
Dr. Jeremiah Milles, Dean of Exeter.
Rev. J. Mills, Cowbit.
Rev. Thomas Monro.
Rev. James Knight Moor.
James Moore, Esq.
Samuel More, Esq.
Rev. Dr. Thomas Morell.
Rev. Thomas Morgan.
Thomas Mortimer, Esq.
Charles Morton, M. D.
Benjamin Moseley, M. D.
Joseph Moser, Esq.
Rev. William Mounsey, Sproxton.
Peter Muilman, Esq.
Thomas Mulso, Esq.
Arthur Murphy, Esq.
S. Musgrave, M. D.
Robert Mylne, Esq. Architect.
Rev. Dr. Treadway Russell Nash.
Rev. Dr. James Nasmith.
Rev. Dr. Timothy Neve.
Dr. W. Newcomb, Abp. of Armagh.
Rev. Peter Newcome.
James Neild, Esq. Visitor of Prisons.
Rev. Dr. R. Boucher Nickolls, Dean
    of Middleham.
Rev. Ralph Nicholson.
Rev. Dr. Matthew Norton, Hinckley.
Rev. Francis Oakley, Northampton.
General Oglethorpe.
Mr. S. Marsh Oram, Shaftesbury.
Rev. Dr. Henry Owen.
Rev. John Owsley, Blaston.
Rev. Dr. William Paley, Archdeacon.
Rev. John Parkhurst.
James Parsons, M. D.
Dr. J. Parsons, Bp. of Peterborough.
Rev. Philip Parsons, Kent.
John Paterson, Esq. Deputy.
Mr. Samuel Paterson, Book Auc-
    tioneer.
Mr. George Paton, Edinburgh.
Sir George Onesiphorus Paul, Bart.
Rev. Dr. Edward Pearson.
Samuel Pegge, Esq. (L. E. and Paul
    Gemsege, jun.)
Thomas Pennant, Esq.
Dr. Thomas Percy, Bp. of Dromore.
Rev. Thomas Percy, LL. D.

Tho. Percival, M. D. Manchester.
William Perfect, M. D.
Mr. Alderman Pickett.
Francis Pigott, Esq. Barrister.
Mr. Richard Porson, Greek Professor.
Dr. Beilby Porteus, Bp. of London.
Rev. Robert Potter.
John Pownall, Esq.
Governor Thomas Pownall.
Samuel Jackson Pratt, Esq.
Sir John Prestwich.
Rev. John Price, Bodleian Library.
Rev. Dr. Richard Price.
Rev. Dr. Joseph Priestley.
Mr. Daniel Prince, Oxford.
Sir John Pringle, Bart.
Rev. John Prior.
Rev. John Newell Puddicombe.
Richard Pulteney, M. D.
Henry James Pye, Esq.
Robert Raikes, Esq.
Mr. Charles Rathband.
Isaac Reed, Esq.
Sir Joshua Reynolds.
Mr. Thomas Cox Reynolds.
Rev. Dr. W. Richardson, Ireland.
Rev. Dr. Gloster Ridley.
Edward Rigby, Esq. Norwich.
Joseph Ritson, Esq.
John Peter Roberdeau, Esq.
Henry Townley Roberdeau, Esq.
Barré-Charles Roberts, Esq.
Rev. Joseph Robertson.
Mr. John Robinson, Hinckley.
Rev. Robert Robinson, Cambridge.
Charles Rogers, Esq.
Rev. William Romaine.
Major Hayman Rooke.
Right Hon. George Rose.
Samuel Rose, Esq.
Rev. Thomas Rotheram.
William Rowley, M. D.
Major-gen. William Roy.
Rev. Rogers Ruding.
Benjamin Rush, M. D. Philadelphia.
Rev. Sambrook Nicholas Russell.
Rev. Thomas Russell.
John Ryland, Esq.
Mr. Jacob Schnebbelie.
Isaac Schomberg, M. D.
Rev. Dr. James Scott.
John Scott, Esq. Amwell.
Miss Anna Seward.
Rev. Thomas Seward.
William Seward, Esq.

Granville Sharp, Esq.
Mr. James Sharp, Mechanist.
George Shaw, M. D.
Rev. Stebbing Shaw.
Mr. C. Shepherd, Gray's Inn.
Rev. Dr. R. Shepherd, Archdeacon.
Rev. Martin Sherlock.
Samuel Foart Simmons, M. D.
James Sims, M. D.
James Six, Esq. Canterbury.
Rev. James Six.
Mr. Matthew Skinner, Pentonville.
Henry Smeathman, Esq.
Mrs. Charlotte Smith.
Southern Faunist *(Q. Who?)*
Rev. Richard Southgate.
Rev. John Spicer, Reading.
George Steevens, Esq.
Rev. Percival Stockdale.
Rev. Sir James Stonehouse.
Lieut. John Stoyle, R. N.
Rev. Dr. John Strachey, Archdeacon.
John Strange, Esq.
Mr. Joseph Strutt, Engraver.
Rev. Dr. John Sturges.
Rev. Charles Sturges.
Deane Swift, Esq.
Henry Swinburne, Esq. *(Porcustus.)*
Mr. John Tailby, Slawston.
Miss Catharine Talbot.
Mr. Isaac Tarrat.
Rev. William Tasker.
Rev. Anthony Temple.
Rev. Giles Templeman.
Philip Thicknesse, Esq. *(Polyxena, P. T.* and *A Wanderer.)*
Rev. Josiah Thomas, Archdeacon.
Mr. Nathaniel Thomas.
Mrs. Thomas, of Newbold.
Sir B. Thompson, Count of Rumford.
John Thorpe, Esq. Bexley.
Mr. John Throsby, Leicester.
Rev. William Tooke.
John Topham, Esq.
Rev. Joshua Toulmin, Taunton.
Rev. Dr. Joseph Towers.
Rev. Micajah Towgood.
Rev. James Townley.
Francis Townsend, Esq. Herald.
Rev. Dr. Thomas Townson.
Rev. George Travis, Archdeacon.
Rev. Dr. John Trusler.
Rev. Dr. Josiah Tucker, Dean of Gloucester.
Marmaduke Cuthbert Tunstall, Esq.
Mark Cephas Tutet, Esq.

Rev. Thomas Twining.
Thomas Tyers, Esq.
Thomas Tyrwhitt, Esq.
Rev. Michael Tyson.
H. W. Tytler, M. D.
General Charles Vallancey.
Rev. Dr. William Vincent, Dean of Westminster.
Rev. Gilbert Wakefield.
Mr. Francis Godolphin Waldron.
Adam Walker, Esq.
Mr. John Walker, Grammarian.
Joseph Cooper Walker, Esq.
Rev. John Wallis.
Hon. Horace Walpole, E. of Orford.
John Ward, LL. D.
Dr. Edward Waring, Professor.
Rev. Dr. John Warner.
Dr. John Warren, Bishop of Bangor.
Rev. Dr. Joseph Warton.
Rev. Thomas Warton.
Rev. John Watson, Halifax.
Sir William Watson, M. D.
Francis Webb, Esq.
D. Wells, Esq. Burbach *(Observator)*.
William Charles Wells, M. D.
Rev. John Wesley.
Mr. Joseph Weston, Solihull.
Mr. Richard Weston, Botanist.
Rev. Peter Whalley.
Rev. John Whitaker, Manchester.
Samuel Whitbread, Esq.
Thomas White, Esq. Naturalist.
Rev. Gilbert White, Selborne.
Rev. Joseph White, D. D. Professor.
Caleb Whitefoord, Esq.
William Whitehead, Esq.
John Wilkes, Esq.
John Eardley Wilmot, Esq.
Ralph Willett, Esq.
David Williams, Esq.
John Williamson, Esq.
Benjamin Wilson, Esq.
Mr. George Witchell, Portsmouth.
William Withering, M. D.
Michael Wodhull, Esq. *(L. L.)*
Rev. Dr. C. G. Woide.
Mr. Isaac Wood, Shrewsbury.
Mr. William Woodfall.
Samuel Pipe Wolferstan, Esq.
Rev. William Woolston, Adderbury.
Mr. William Woty.
Daniel Wray, Esq.
Rev. Dr. Paul Wright.
Arthur Young, Esq.
Rev. Dr. Zouch.

In p. xvii. I have mentioned, on the authority of Sir John Hawkins, that the price given by Mr. Robert Dodsley for "London," Johnson's First Imitation of Juvenal, was *fifty pounds*. But Mr. Boswell says, "The fact is, that, at a future conference, Dodsley bargained for the whole property of it, for which he gave Johnson *ten guineas;* who told me, 'I might, perhaps, have accepted of less; but that Paul Whitehead had a little before got ten guineas for a Poem; and I did not like to be less than Whitehead.'"—For "The Vanity of Human Wishes," his second Imitation of Juvenal, in 1749, with all the fame which he had acquired, it is certain that he received only *fifteen guineas*.

P. xx. There were two persons of the name of *Macbean, Alexander* and *William;* they were both good scholars, and both were employed by the Booksellers; but I cannot distinguish which was the one who was honoured by Dr. Johnson's protection; nor can I discover any thing further of the history of either.

In p. xxix. I have stated, correctly, that there is no Preface to that Year's Volume; but in the first page of the Magazine for May, was introduced the following *Johnsonian* Address:

"It is with a mixture of compassion and indignation, that we condescend to continue the dispute with the Authors and Publishers of the London Magazine. To be engaged in a contest with such Antagonists, as it is no honour to overcome, is very disgusting; and what honour can be gained by writing against those who cannot read? There may, indeed, be some use in this mock controversy. We may, perhaps, be better prepared for a defence, if some abler Adversary should at any time attack us; as the Roman soldiers in time of peace used to preserve their dexterity by discharging their javelins at a post.

"Yet, perhaps, the deplorable stupidity of the Writers by whom it is our fate to be opposed, is so far from making the controversy more easy to be carried on in a proper manner, that it often produces difficulties and perplexities. To treat weakness and folly with severity and roughness, would be thought insolent and cruel; to use softer language and argument without satire, might probably encourage them to be less diffident of themselves, and consequently more troublesome to the world.

"We are, indeed, for the most part inclined to lenity, and wish to still their clamours by gentle means; but, since they seem absolutely insensible of our forbearance, we shall for once have recourse to severity, and prevail upon ourselves, in opposition to our natural tenderness, to punish them by re-publishing their own papers, without any alteration, except marking a few pretty words in *Italicks*.

"The following Postscript was drawn up by the Secretary of their Political Club, the greatest Genius in the whole Society, and a kind of Giant among Pigmies. We should think it, in general, by no means pardonable to make so despicable a Scribbler the object of ridicule ; but hope a little merriment may be decently indulged, when he ventures to assume an air of superiority and contempt ; when he runs away with triumph and exultation, and hides his head with the arrogance of a conqueror.

"' *An Extraordinary Postscript in the last*
London Magazine [1739], *p.* 117.

"' I find by some Advertisements lately *published* in the News Papers, that Mr. *Urban* has been pleased to *publish* some Criticisms upon the Accounts I have sent you of the Debates in the Political Club. For this Reason I must desire you will acquaint the Publick, that I *never read* any Thing he *publishes ;* nor *ever* hear of any Thing he *publishes,* in the whole Circle of my Acquaintance ; which makes me conclude, that his Monthly Bundle of *Galimatias* is neither purchased nor *read* by any Man of common Sense in the Kingdom : Therefore, I shall not give myself the Trouble to *read,* and much less to answer any Criticisms he may, in order to fill up, find necessary to *publish ;* for, if they are *read* by any Man of common Understanding, which I can hardly believe possible, he will easily discover the Falshood or Absurdity of the Criticism ; and as Fools generally favour one another, I know it is impossible to persuade them that their Brother is in a Mistake.——'

" *N. B.* This *Postscript* is published by the *Secretary,* to confute *P. 2*'s Criticism in the *Gentleman's Magazine* [1739], p. 92, and to justify what himself had asserted in the *London Magazine* of *February,* p. 62, that D is *not* sounded in COLD and BOLD."

P. xlix. Two little *Jeux d'esprits* of Mr. Edward Cave are printed in Vol. LXIV. pp. 41. 303.

P. lii. The Rev. Moses Browne died Sept. 13, 1787. See Vol. LVII. p. 840 ; and an inscription to his memory, p. 932.

The present Editor cannot conclude this desultory Preface without returning the most grateful acknowledgments to his numerous and learned Correspondents for favours which are equally the support and honour of the GENTLEMAN'S MAGAZINE : amongst whom are some of the brightest Ornaments of the Episcopal and Judicial Benches ; of the Colleges of Physicians and Surgeons ; of all the Universities ; and of almost every Scientific Society in the Empire.

March 12, 1821. J. N.

Date Due

			UML 735